GRAY WOLF

EMIL LENGYEL is the author of *Turkey* and several other books about the Middle East, the latest of which is *The Changing Middle East*. He was a correspondent of "The New York Times" for many years. Currently he is professor of History at Fairleigh Dickinson University.

GRAY WOLF

THE LIFE OF
KEMAL ATATURK

by

H. C. ARMSTRONG

With an Introduction and an Epilogue by

EMIL LENGYEL

CAPRICORN BOOKS
NEW YORK

I wish to thank innumerable friends and ac-
quaintances who have placed their personal
knowledge at my disposal, but who must remain unnamed, and also:

The Times
The Royal Institute of International Affairs
The Oriental School of Languages
The Royal Central Asian Society

for placing much material in my hands and
treating me with unfailing kindness.

H. C. A.

AUTHOR'S NOTE

I. SPELLING OF NAMES

WHEN Turkish was written with Arabic letters each European writer transcribed names as he saw fit. The result was as chaotic as the Tower of Babel. Rauf might be Raouf or Rouf. Khalif, Calif or Caliph. Hourchid, Hurshid or Hoursheid or Khurshid or Hoorsheed.

In 1928 Mustafa Kemal introduced the Latin Script. He ordered that certain of the Latin letters be given artificial sounds to correspond with the sounds of Turkish and Arabic.

These have to be learned before the words can be pronounced. They have been adjusted several times since 1928, and will require more adjustment in the future.

Thus Jemal, which might have been Djemal, has become Cemal. Abdul Hamid has become Abdulhamit or Aptulhamit.

I have ignored the new Turkish alphabet. Outside Turkey it is not known. I have retained the names as best known to English-speaking readers, but in their simplest form.

Thus *Rauf* instead of Raouf or Rouf, and *Jemal* instead of Cemal or Djemal.

II. PLACE-NAMES

THE Turks have of late changed the names of many places. Thus they have changed Angora to Ankara and Smyrna to Izmir.

I have retained the form best known to English-speaking readers—i.e. *Angora* and *Smyrna,* etc.

I HAVE been repeatedly asked whether the conversations quoted verbatim in *Gray Wolf* are actual or fictional.

Every quotation and conversation quoted verbatim in my *Gray Wolf*—with the exception of two which are of very minor importance and for which the evidence is less assured—has been supplied by Mustafa Kemal or obtained from documentary or verbal sources which have been severely tested and carefully weighed before their veracity and value have been accepted.

Some latitude must naturally be allowed in the wording as nearly all are translations.

INTRODUCTION

═══

IN the thirteenth century after Christ there came the Great Drought. From the Wall of China throughout all Central Asia the land was cracked and parched for want of rain, and the tribes were on the move searching for new pastures for their flocks. Among them were the Osmanli Turks, whose chief, Sulyman Shah, carried on his banner the head of the Gray Wolf.

They were cruel and primitive, these Osmanli Turks, animal-strong with slit eyes in flat Mongol faces. They were as brutal and relentless as the gray wolves which hunted over the wide steppes of the fierce countries of Central Asia. Yet they were disciplined, by the dangers and risks of their nomad life, to rigid obedience under their leaders.

For centuries they had pitched their black horse-hair tents in the Plains of Sungaria on the edge of the Gobi Desert. Forced by lack of water and grass, Sulyman Shah led out his people and made westward. Finding the hordes of Tartars to his north and pressing in behind him, he turned south, and so came, through Armenia into Asia Minor, into Modern History.

Sulyman died and Ertoghrul reigned in his stead, and after him came Emir Othman and Sultan Orchan, and from father to son ten generations of sultans followed each other. Often brutal and vicious, often unjust and bestial, they were rulers, leaders of men, and generals.

They found in front of them a world of dying empires, the decayed Seljuk, the worn-out Arab Empire of Baghdad and of the Caliphs, and the corrupted Byzantine. These they smashed and conquered.

Within three hundred years of the death of Sulyman Shah, his tenth descendant, Sultan Sulyman the Magnificent, the Law Giver, ruled with justice and strength an immense empire which stretched from Albania on the Adriatic coast to the Persian frontier, from Egypt to the Caucasus. Hungary and the Crimea were his vassals. The sovereigns of Europe came with presents asking his help in their quarrels. His armies stood across the road to the East. His fleet sailed supreme in all the Mediterranean. North Africa acknowledged his suzerainty. Constantinople was his. He made one great bid for World domination. In 1580 he hammered on the gates of Vienna and seized Christendom by the throat.

He failed, and after him came corruption. His heir was Selim *the Sot*. It was said that the royal blood changed and that Selim was a bastard by an Armenian servant. After him, with but one exception, came twenty-seven sultans each more degenerate than the last. The palace harem, the pimps and eunuchs took control. Without leaders the Turks went the way of all flesh. The steel fiber went out of them. Their energy, hardiness and vitality disappeared. They became corrupt in blood and morals. Their subject people revolted against them. Greece, Serbia, Bulgaria declared their independence.

Within three hundred years of the greatness of Sulyman the Magnificent the Ottoman Empire lay bankrupt, decrepit and rotting.

Convinced that it must break up, the Christian Powers pressed in eager to grab and annex where they dared. Russia seized the Crimea and the Caucasus, and laid claims to Constantinople and the road through the Dardanelles into the Mediterranean. France laid hands on Syria and Tunis. England occupied Egypt and Cyprus. The new and expanding Germany championed the Sultan, Abdul Hamid, against the rest of Europe, planning to annex as soon as the other rivals had been beaten off. All the nations claimed special rights and economic privileges.

As greedy for their meal as vultures, the Christian Powers sat waiting for the end. Afraid of each other, preparing for the stu-

pendous catastrophe of the World War, they watched each other jealously. No one Power dared rush in. And so the dying Ottoman Empire lived on, while the Red Sultan, Abdul Hamid, from his palace on the Bosphorus, cunningly played the nations one against the other.

In 1877 Russia decided to make an end of all this, declared war and advanced to within ten miles of Constantinople. Led by Disraeli at the Congress of Berlin, the rest of Europe warned her back: the integrity of the Ottoman Empire must be maintained.

Four years later there was born in the town of Salonika at the head of the Aegean Sea, of a Turk called Ali Riza and of Zubeida his wife, a boy whom they named Mustafa.

FOREWORD

by Emil Lengyel

From Basra in the sunrise land to Biskra in the *Maghrib,* Farthest West, the land had lain in the grip of the doldrums. Today the area is called the Middle East but then it was the Ottoman Empire. Its inhabitants were of many stocks—Arabs, Greeks, Armenians, Kurds and Jews—but the Turks formed the empire's dominating group. Their ancestors had erupted from the depths of Central Asia centuries before, sweeping westward with the irresistible energy of an elemental force. They established themselves along the world's great waterway, the Dardanelles, took Constantinople, which became the capital of an empire that made its bid to rule the world.

It was over a fear-scourged globe that the Ottoman Turks rampaged, surging westward along Europe's great continental highway, the Danube. They reached Vienna, a highly strategic point of Europe where the east-west transversal route was bisected by the north-south Amber Road, linking the Mediterranean with the Baltic Sea. Wherever they moved, the Turks' name was abomination. "From the Osmanlis' wrath," the West prayed on its knees, "deliver us, oh merciful God!"

The sovereign of the Ottoman Empire was the Sultan, Allah's shadow on the earth. He was also the *Padishah*—Master King. Finally, he carried the title of *Caliph,* successor of the Prophet Mohammed and head of the state religion, Islam. Thus he combined in his person both earthly and celestial powers. The Ottoman Empire was pivoted on him and his family—not on the community of its people, the nation. However, when the age of nationalism dawned, the Ottoman Empire became an anachronism, and the dynasties began to produce sterile blossoms. The people of the empire became fatalistic and ascribed all of their misery to fate. The apathetic masses were tormented by three fatal conditions, disease, ignorance, and poverty. As the country degenerated, its neighbors began to claw at it, especially the gigantic country to the North—Russia. Her only strategic maritime route to warm water and greatness, the Straits of Marmora and the Dardanelles, were in Turkish hands. Conflicts between the Ottoman and Czarist empires became chronic—one major war in each generation. These wars wore down the Turk—the "sick man" of the world.

Why not the dead man, surrounded by greedy heirs? Because these legatees were too corroded by jealousy of each other and fearful that their neighbor might get a larger slice of the carcass than they to finish off the ailing giant. Thus they kept one another in balance, and the Ottoman Empire survived.

Then, early in the twentieth century, the Great War, which later generations were to call the First World War, erupted. The Turks thought that this time they could redeem themselves. They had thrown in their lot with a youthful, virile, aggressive nation of superb military skill, the German Reich. Now the Turks fought the hated Russians as well as the British and the French. In spite of their military excellence, the Germans lost the war and the Ottoman Empire went down to defeat with them.

The final hour had struck and the sick man was dying. In one of the suburbs of Paris—Sèvres—the Ottoman empire was dismembered. Its largest chunks were handed over to the British and the French. Other valuable possessions were assigned to the Italians and Greeks. Wrested from faltering Turkish hands, glorious Constantinople and the great maritime highway of the world, the Straits, were internationalized. The parts of the former Ottoman empire inhabited by Arabs were placed under great-power tutelage. Other former Turkish possessions inhabited by non-Turkish people, Armenia and Kurdistan, were to gain freedom.

Under the Sèvres arrangement the Turks were cut off not only from the Straits but also from the Mediterranean and the Aegean. They were allowed to retain a small territory in the dour Anatolian highlands, numbed by winter frost and parched by summer heat. Without arms and legs, how long could the amputated country last? It was on the way to becoming an "un-country."

What was the Turks' reaction to these cataclysmic events? What was man in the eyes of Allah—the God of their Muslim creed? Nothing but a speck of dust was man. Life was but a fleeting moment, while the grave was the threshold of blissful eternity. Let Allah's will be done.

That was not, however, the view of the "Gray Wolf." He had been named Mustafa—Elect of God. In the Cadet School of Salonika, where he had been a student, his mathematics teacher had given him the name of *Kemal*—Perfection—to distinguish him from less brilliant Mustafas.

Years had passed, fraught with danger for the Turks, and the epoch of great wars begin. Mustafa Kemal had become a soldier of renown, a great leader of men. In the years of Turkey's cosmic darkness, which began in 1919, he attempted the impossible, the revival of a moribund country. He wanted no more than a nation inhabited by Turks, not the other nationalities of the former Ottoman empire. Thus began the age of *devrim,* revolution, revolution and, above all, resurrection.

Could the land of disease, ignorance and poverty win out against western nations bursting with health, knowledge and affluence? Yes, it could. Mustafa Kemal won, and the miracle did occur. His grateful countrymen conferred on him the epithet of *Gazi*—Conqueror. Then he set himself the task of removing the accumulated rubbish of the Ottoman Empire, laying the foundations of the new republic by following the proved methods of the West. Now his countrymen called him *Büyük Önder*—Great Leader.

It was a part of the process of westernization to adopt family names, and his people besought him to accept the designation of *Ataturk*—Father of the Turks. He burned himself out before reaching even three scores of years and his body was lowered into the grave; but he did not die. His people conferred immortality on him by calling him *Ebedi Sef*—Eternal Chief.

With his aid the apathetic Turks had shaken off their torpor and helped their man of destiny to fulfill his mission. They followed the Elect of God, the Man of Perfection, the Conqueror, the Great Leader, the Father of the Turks, the Eternal Leader. How was he able to perform this near-miracle?

The great transformation effected by Ataturk is best revealed by the comparison of the mottoes of the Ottoman empire and the Turkish republic of his creation. In the Ottoman Empire people said, "It is fate." Kemal's republic seldom heard lethargic mottoes of fatalism. Asked how they were, its people answered: *Calişirez*—We work.

Not since the days of Baghdad's Caliph, Haroun al-Rashid—Aaron the Upright—has a career so dazzled the Levant as that of the Father of the Turks. While his performance was prodigious enough, it was further encrusted with legends. Not merely a super-man was he, but also a

mythical figure. In real life, a man of many human failings, in the legends he was uncontaminated by vice.

So brightly blazed his name that petitioners besieged him by requests from all over the Middle East to lead reform movements, but his invariable reply was: "I am a Turk and Turkey is my country."

Not only in the Middle East but also in the new countries of Africa north and south of the Sahara Kemal Ataturk's imitators have arisen. He was still alive when he had his first disciple, a King of the Kings, the potentate of Persia, Shahinshah Reza Khan Pahlevi, who commanded his subjects to turn their eyes westward. Let the West fertilize the tired Persian soil with new industries, modern dwellings, he ordered, and let his people wear Occidental clothes. However, the King of Kings lacked the stature of Ataturk and his massive reform movement sputtered to a halt.

Persia's neighbor to the East, Afghanistan, also was inspired by Ataturk. King Aman Ullah, a sovereign with modern ideas, attempted to give his people a western orientation so as to be worthy of becoming the Afghans' father. However, he too, lacked the skill to lead and his people to follow, so that exile became his fate.

The new countries of the Arab world—Egypt, Syria, Lebanon, Jordan and others, also raised their eyes, scanning the western horizon. Spectacular trails of new leaders crisscrossed their skies. "Is he our Ataturk?" their people asked. Particularly great was the throng of potential Ataturks in Syria, which is in the coreland of the Middle East. At mid-century several "men of destiny" arose—Husni es-Zain, Adib Shishakli and others, but all of them were doomed to fail.

Then came the "Servant of the Victorious One," Gamel Abdul Nasser, in the Land of the Nile. Millions hailed him as the "Ataturk of the Arabs" and he proposed a massive movement of reform. He created the United Arab Republic by merging Syria with Egypt. Many Arabs saw this as the onset of greater things to come. Will he be the Arabs' "Eternal Chief?" History will provide the answer.

On the long northern shore of Africa, in lands inhabited by Muslims farther West, the same question has been heard: "Is the man our Ataturk?" Habib Bourguiba, the western-minded president of one of the new Muslim countries facing the Mediterranean, Tunisia, has drawn up a Kemalist program. The very name of his Neo-Destour—Constitution—Party smacks of the ideology of the West. Still farther West, where the waters of the Mediterranean and the Atlantic mix, in Morocco, another country newly independent, an attempt is being made at present to introduce Kemal's reformist policies. Close attention is being paid to Kemal's nation-building program south of the great African desert, and especially in the new countries of Senegal and Mali.

The very name of Mustafa Kemal has become proverbial. That name has been imbedded not only in Turkish but also in the Arabic tongue. Nor is this the extent of the fame of the Father of the Turks. The French, who have had their contacts with the civilization of the West through their North African holdings, have immortalized the late Mustafa Kemal in their dictionary. When speaking about the "labors of Hercules" in the Middle East they say: *C'est un travail d'Ataturk.*

It has become now possible to survey Mustafa Kemal's work in its historical perspective, and to compare it with other great reform movements in other epochs and in other parts of the world. The famed historian of our age, Arnold Toynbee, has undertaken to compare the record of Ataturk with those of Russia's Peter the Great and Japan's Meiji Restoration.

Russia's reforming Czar, too, attempted to turn his

people's eyes to the West by launching a movement of monumental transformation. However, neither he nor his successors could complete it. Yet, Russia has great advantages over Turkey to carry out massive reform movements. Her center of population is in Europe, the home of western civilization. Turkey is in the East. Russia can afford to experiment because she is richer in natural resources. The Russian peasant's pre-revolutionary apathy was less deeply rooted than the all-pervasive Turkish fatalism.

What about the Meiji Restoration of the sixties of the nineteenth century in Japan? It had changed a static feudal system into a dynamic industrial economy. However, the differences between Turkey and Japan were great. Japan was not a decadent country when the great restoration movement began. The Ottoman Empire, on the other hand, was gripped by decay. A maritime nation, Japan was fully exposed to western trends. The Anatolian highlands of Turkey, on the other hand, are not laced into the web of the western World. The achievement of Kemal's Turkey was more impressive than that of Russia or Japan.

* * * * *

H. C. Armstrong's narrative of the life of the "Gray Wolf" stopped with 1932. However, Ataturk lived another six years. The reader will find the sequel in this book, after Chapter LXXV. These last few years of the life of the Turkish president represented Turkey's epoch of consolidation. Ataturk was fading out of sight because of physical ailments and other reasons; nevertheless, he kept the threads of government in his own hands almost to the end. The last chapters of this book provide highlighted accounts of the foreign policy, economics and private life of Ataturk.

Ataturk continued to be the head of the country, even though his body was in the grave. New parties, new ideologies arose dispensing new solutions. Irrespective of their programs, however, all parties claimed to be the custodians of Ataturk's legacy.

Kemal's place has been determined by history. Not only was he the Father of the Turks but also the inspiration of basic reforms in many parts of the rest of the world. His achievements have provided the yardstick by which other records have been measured. He is the symbol of new Turkey, but he is also the image of the dynamism of the self-made western-minded man of the East.

GRAY WOLF

GRAY WOLF

PART ONE

I

ALI RIZA and Zubeida lived the threadbare life of the Ottoman Turk, poverty-stricken yet dignified.

Their house was in the Turkish quarter of Salonika, half-way up the hill, under the walls of the old fort, below which lay the squalid little commercial town, full of Jews, and the port to which came the export trade of the Balkans.

Ali Riza was an insignificant little man, without any deep beliefs or outstanding character. When a boy he had come down from the Albanian mountains on the Servian frontier and found work as a clerk in the offices of the Ottoman Debt Administration in the port of Salonika. Like a thousand other Turkish Government clerks he did his routine work without enthusiasm or particular ability. His pay was insufficient, and often so many months in arrears, that in order to keep his family and make both ends meet, he was forced to supplement it by private trading in his spare time.

The street in which they lived was a narrow alley-way of cobbles roofed over with twisting vines. The house was a broken-down affair with the upper story projecting at an angle over the street. All the houses in the Turkish quarter were blind and silent, the doors always shut and the windows carefully latticed. There was no movement or life. Sometimes some children played gravely in the street, or a few men lounged and dawdled drinking coffee, smoking

3

and talking before the café. Otherwise there was a sleepy silence. Occasionally a hodja passed on his way to the mosque, or a woman dressed in shapeless black clothes would come out of a house, close the door carefully behind her, draw her black cloak across her face as a veil leaving only one eye uncovered, and pass on her way to the fountain like a black ghost in the sunlight.

Each house was bolted and barred against its neighbors. In these—and they were little more than hovels—the women lived the shut-away life of a bygone and dead age, when there were harems and eunuch-guarded favorites, and rich pashas with splendid palaces.

Zubeida was shut away like the rest. Though nearly thirty when Mustafa was born, she had been veiled since she was seven. She rarely went out, and then only with an escort. Except for her family and a few women in the neighboring houses she spoke to no one. She was quite uneducated, could neither read nor write, and was ignorant of all the ordinary affairs of the outside world.

Yet she ruled the family. She was a masterful woman with a domineering manner and, when roused, a raging temper. She was of good peasant stock. Her father had been a small farmer in southern Albania and her mother a Macedonian. Tall and powerfully built, with blue eyes and flaxen hair, she had the vitality of robust health. She lived close to the good earth from which she had sprung and had the qualities of the peasant. She was profoundly religious, patriotic and conservative. She had a shrewd brain and judgment for the primitive realities of life.

Like every Turkish woman, her whole life was concentrated on her man-child—an elder son had died at birth and there was a daughter, Makboula by name. She spoilt Mustafa without restraint, but he responded very little. He was a silent, reserved boy, weak and bony, with pale blue eyes and sandy hair. He rarely showed any affection, accepted his mother's petting as a matter of course, disobeyed her orders and fiercely resented any punishment. He was abnormally self-sufficient, rarely made friends with other children, but played solemnly by himself.

Ali Riza had given up his post in the Ottoman Debt and started trading in timber. He wanted Mustafa to be a merchant. Zubeida wanted him to be a priest. They sent him first to the mosque school to learn his pot-hooks and to intone passages of the Koran, and then to the school of one Chemsi Effendi where he made good progress.

Suddenly Ali Riza died. There was no money in the wood business. The family were penniless. Zubeida shut up the house and claimed shelter with her brother, who farmed some land at Lazasan, a village outside Salonika.

There Mustafa was put to clean stables, feed the cattle, scare crows and tend the sheep. He seemed to like the life. The rough work and the open air suited him, making him tough, wiry and healthy, but as he grew older he became even more reserved, solitary and independent.

After two years, when Mustafa was eleven, Zubeida persuaded a sister to pay for his schooling. During these months when he had been working in the fields the boy had become wild and untamed: she had lost all control of him; he would not listen to her; she did not wish him to grow into a shepherd or common farm laborer.

Mustafa went back to a school in Salonika. There he was forever in hot water. After his open, free life he kicked against the discipline. He was truculent with his masters. With the other boys he was self-opinionated and boastful,

5

so that he became unpopular. He refused to join in their games; if they interfered with him he fought them.

One day he was involved in a general scrimmage. A master dragged him out, and, while he kicked and fought, gave him a sound thrashing. Blind with anger, Mustafa ran away and refused to go back to school.

II

ONCE more Zubeida had Mustafa on her hands. Her sister would waste no more money in sending him to another school and he refused obstinately to go back to the same one. When Zubeida tried to reason with him he became mulish. When she stormed at him he stormed back at her.

His uncle suggested making a soldier of him: he was a difficult boy and would never settle down to a trade: they had better send him to the Military Cadet School in Salonika: it was subsidized by the Sultan and would cost them nothing: if the boy showed he had brains he would become an officer: if not he would become a private. Anyway his future would be fixed.

Zubeida would not hear of it; but Mustafa had made up his own mind. His uncle's suggestion appealed to him. Ahmed, the son of their next door neighbor, had just become a cadet and swaggered about showing off in a uniform. Mustafa did not wish to be a priest. As to being a shop-man, that was work for Greeks, Armenians, Christians, Jews and such-like cattle, not for a Turk. He wanted to be a soldier: to be an officer, wear a uniform and give orders to men.

Without telling anyone else, he persuaded an old retired officer, who had been one of his father's friends, to stand sponsor for him with the College authorities. He sat for the examination and passed in as a cadet before his mother could stop him.

6

At the Cadet School he found his feet. He was successful, but also unpopular. Inherently thin-skinned, he became touchy and ill-natured if criticized or spoken to roughly. He kept to himself, made no friends and yet he wished always to be noticed and to be pointed to as somebody out of the ordinary.

None of the boys dared interfere with him for he fought back at once. When they tried to get him to join in with them, or asked him what he was at, he became brusque:

"I don't mean to be like the rest of you," he said. "I mean to be somebody," and went on his own way.

He succeeded in his work, for he had an uncommon flair for mathematics and all military subjects, and he was smart on parade.

In his second year one of the masters, a Captain Mustafa, took a fancy to him, promoted him to be a pupil teacher and gave him charge of a junior class. To distinguish him from himself he gave him the second name of Kemal. From that date he was known as Mustafa Kemal.

He progressed rapidly up the College, showing great ability at examinations, and even more at teaching other boys, for he enjoyed schoolmastering and lording it over his class. He showed also a jealousy, which would grow into a spiteful dislike, of any other boy who was more successful than himself. He would play second fiddle to no one. He became churlish if anyone competed with him. He must be the outstanding figure or he would not be in the picture at all.

The friendship and protection of Captain Mustafa did him no good. The friendship was unhealthy. He developed overrapidly. Before he was fourteen he had passed the boy stage: the gropings after sex: the petty dirtiness: and he had started an affair with a neighbor's daughter. While the other boys were playing games or ragging each other he was off

7

on his own, dressed up in his best clothes, swaggering down the streets, making sheep's-eyes at the women behind the latticed windows, or ogling the cheap women in the harbor.

At seventeen he passed out well from the Cadet School and was sent to the Senior Military School at Monastir.

PART TWO

===

III

MONASTIR was full of the sound and dust of marching columns and the rumble of guns. Greece had seized Crete. Turkey had declared war and troops were hurrying to the battle-front.

It was a time of trouble and strife, of wars and the rumor of wars. The Ottoman Empire was in its last agonies. The Christian Powers, with their claws set into its writhing carcass, and snarling at each other, were each getting ready to tear out a rich morsel.

It was torn also by discontent. Centered round the Sultan, its organization was the same as it had been in the great days of the Osmanlis in the sixteenth century, but it had grown effete, decrepit and corrupt. Everywhere there was poverty and inefficiency, and with them discontent. All the young men cried out for reform.

The Sultan, Abdul Hamid the Red Fox, was as afraid of his own subjects as of the foreigners. He repressed every new idea. He refused all reforms. He covered the whole Empire with a network of spies, so that wherever three men talked together there was a fourth eavesdropping and reporting to the secret police. He allowed no liberty or personal security. He filled the prisons with Turks and massacred the Christians.

The land was full of the spirit of revolt and revolution, and especially in the Balkans round Monastir, where the "fire of sedition" always glowed hot, ready to burst into flame. New ideas were abroad.

With the passionate earnestness of youth Mustafa Kemal absorbed them all. Like every Albanian and Macedonian, his instinct was to resist all authority. At heart he was a revolutionary. He pictured himself leading revolt, overthrowing the despot, saving and cleansing the country. In these pictures he saw himself always the center, the leader, the ruler obeyed and respected by all.

On his holidays he went back to Salonika, but kept out of his mother's house as much as possible. She had remarried with a well-to-do merchant from Rhodes. Mustafa Kemal had told her brutally that he disapproved. They had quarreled. After that he refused to acknowledge or speak to his step-father.

When in Salonika he spent much of his time with some Dominican monks who taught him French. He had made friends with a pleasant shy youth a little older than himself called Fethi, a Macedonian from Orchrida. Fethi knew French well. Together they devoured all the revolutionary literature they could get: Voltaire, Rousseau, all the French writers, and the political economy of Hobbes and John Stuart Mills. These were forbidden books. To be caught with them meant imprisonment. The danger made the reading all the sweeter.

Mustafa Kemal practiced oratory and harangued the other cadets: Turkey, their Turkey, must be saved from the claws of the foreigner and from the corruption of the Sultan. On freedom and liberty he wrote articles and treatises, and fiery rich-worded poetry.

At work he was as successful in Monastir as he had been in the Cadet School in Salonika. He was reported on as "a brilliant, difficult youth with whom it is impossible to be intimate." He was specially selected for the General Staff College—the Harbia—in Constantinople, gazetted as a sub-lieutenant and sent there.

IV

MUSTAFA KEMAL was twenty, wiry in build, with a tough constitution and unlimited vitality.

He had no experience of life. Salonika had been a mean little port; Lazaran a country village; Monastir a dull provincial town. He had none of his mother's deep beliefs or principles to keep him steady.

At once he plunged wildly into the unclean life of the great metropolis of Constantinople. Night after night he gambled and drank in the cafés and restaurants. With women he was not fastidious. A figure, a face in profile, a laugh, could set him on fire and reaching out to get the woman, whatever she was. Sometimes it would be with the Greek and Armenian harlots in the bawdy-houses in the garbage-stinking streets by Galata Bridge, where came the pimps and the homosexualists to cater for all the vices; then for a week or two a Levantine lady in her house in Pangaldi; or some Turkish girl who came veiled and by back-ways in fear of the police to some *maison de rendez-vous* in Pera or Stambul.

He fell in love with none of them. He was never sentimental or romantic. Without a pang of conscience he passed rapidly from one to the next. He satisfied his appetite and was gone. He was completely Oriental in his mentality: women had no place in his life except to satisfy his sex. He plunged deep down into the lecherous life of the city.

Suddenly he reacted from all this rioting and concentrated on his work with the same energy.

11

His success depended on himself. In Turkey each man must rise from the bottom by his own ability. There was no ruling class; no schools specially reserved for the rich and well-born; no preference given to sons because their fathers had succeeded or been born in the purple. That Mustafa Kemal was peasant-born would not clog his rise if he had the character and the brains.

Mustafa Kemal passed all his examinations brilliantly. He was picked for the special General Staff Course. This also he passed with brilliance and was gazetted out in January, 1905, with accelerated promotion to captain.

With his work he mixed politics. In Monastir he had been a senior boy among boys. At the Staff College he was surrounded by young officers who were specially picked men of the same age and caliber as himself.

He found them all revolutionaries. Every young officer worth his salt was in revolt against the soul-destroying despotism of the Sultan and the interference of foreign nations. They were the heirs to the Ottoman Empire and their heritage was being destroyed.

The college tutors and many of the senior officers were in sympathy with them, but though they shut their eyes to what their juniors did, they dared not come out into the open nor give them a lead.

There was already in the College a revolutionary society known as the *Vatan,* or Fatherland, which held secret debates and published a broadsheet in script which was passed from hand to hand. It attacked all the established facts of Turkish life. It was bitterly hostile to the old régime, the Sultan's inefficient officials, his tyranny and his suppression of all liberal ideas. It hated the priests. It cursed the clammy hand of Islam, which stopped all progress; the mosques and dervish monasteries which bled the people; the legal system, based on the Koran, which carried out the fantastic, anti-quated laws.

Its members bound themselves by oaths to break the Sultan's despotism and replace it by the constitutional government of a popular parliament, to release the people from the priests and the women from the veil and the harem; Turkey was being throttled by the Sultan and his spies; unless the blood of new ideas was let into its veins, Turkey would die.

Mustafa Kemal joined the *Vatan*. For the broadsheet he wrote vehement articles and boiling poetry. He spoke at the debates with exceptional bitterness.

Of the workings of the society the Commandant of the College was well aware, but he looked the other way. The Sultan's spies also knew of its existence and reported to the Palace. The Sultan was disturbed. It might be only a society of undeveloped youths, but these youths would be the future staff officers and generals of the army. He ordered Ismail Haki Pasha, the Director-General of Military Training, to see that the *Vatan* came to an end. Ismail Haki roundly cursed the Commandant of the College, who took care that no more meetings were held inside the College.

The cadets carried on the *Vatan* outside. They ceased to be a debating society and became one of the innumerable secret organizations with which Constantinople was honey-combed.

After Mustafa Kemal had finished his examinations he had some weeks on his hands before he was appointed to a post. He was better off than the average officer, for his mother could now afford to send him a regular allowance. He took over the running of the *Vatan*. He rented a room in a back street as an office and a place where the broadsheet could be written up. He arranged the meetings in private houses and the back rooms of cafés where the members came by stealth, watching over their shoulders to see that they were not followed.

The secrecy and the danger exhilarated him. He began to learn the technique of revolutionary organization, the methods of forming cells, of testing the loyalty of new members, the use of grips, codes, passwords, signs and counter-signs and oaths.

All the time the police watched the members to catch them red-handed. This was not difficult, for they were be-ginners and had more enthusiasm than knowledge. An agent-provocateur worked his way into the confidence of the society. At a time fixed by this man, when all the members were assembled to swear in a new recruit, the police rushed the house and arrested them.

With the other members of the *Vatan*, Mustafa Kemal was shut up in the Red Prison of Stambul. His case was looked on as serious. The police had plenty of evidence against him. He was isolated from the others and placed in solitary confinement. The future looked black. If the Sultan thought he was dangerous, he might just disappear, or be imprisoned for years, or exiled. Many men before him had disappeared from the Red Prison without a trace.

Zubeida, with his sister, came from Salonika to see him. They were refused permission, but were able to send him in some money.

Week after week he was shut up in a narrow cell which was dirty and verminous. The only light and air came from a small barred window far up in a wall. The confinement bit into his soul and made him savage.

One day, without warning, he was taken across the War Office Square behind the prison to the office of Ismail Haki Pasha. Well-turned-out, despite his weeks in the dirty prison,

Mustafa Kemal stood to attention between the two military police.

The Pasha sat watching him. He was a pasha of the old régime, bearded, his clothes loose and gawdy, his manner slow and dignified. He was one of the Sultan's men.

"You have shown," he said at last, "great capabilities. You have, if you wish it, a future before you in the service of His Majesty. On the other hand, you have disgraced yourself and your uniform. You have lived with the most disreputable companions, gambling, drinking, and in lechery in the loosest houses. Worse than that, you have been disloyal. You have mixed up in politics and the subversive propaganda of traitors against your Sovereign. You have encouraged your companions to do the same.

"His Majesty has, however, decided to show clemency. You are young and foolish. You are probably more headstrong and wild than actually bad.

"You will be posted to a cavalry regiment in Damascus. Your future will depend on what reports are received of you. But you must stop all this nonsense and foolishness, and confine yourself to your military duties. Take care; you will not get a second chance."

The same night Mustafa Kemal was placed by the police on a sailing-vessel for Syria. He was not allowed to see his mother or his friends.

After eighty days of rough voyage he landed at Beyrouth, and taking horse over the Lebanon mountains joined his regiment in Damascus.

He found the regiment packed up ready to march out against the Druses, who lived in the great mountains to the south of Damascus and who were always in revolt.

The expedition gave Mustafa Kemal his first experience of active service, but it was unsatisfactory work for a regular soldier. The country was all barren mountains of rocks, cut by deep ravines and without water or roads. The Druses were fierce, untamed hillmen who knew every inch of the ground.

Day after day the Turkish troops toiled along the steep tracks, but they could never get to close quarters or catch the enemy. The Druses never stood for a battle: as soon as they were threatened they moved rapidly and scattered and then sniped continuously night and day from the crags.

The most that the Turks could do was to teach the Druses a lesson by burning their empty villages—laying waste their few poor fields. That done they returned to Damascus for the winter.

V

As soon as they returned Mustafa Kemal set to work to organize a branch of the *Vatan*. The weeks in the prison cell and the threats of Haki Pasha had neither broken his spirit nor frightened him. Fundamentally he was a revolutionary with no respect for God, man or institution. Nothing was established; nothing sacred to him. He was still aflame with the enthusiasm of youth, but he had developed a steady caution and a power of cold calculation. He had given up poetry, writing and literature. He had decided that action and literature could not go together: literature weakened the will and the power of decision, introduced wrong interests, produced the wrong mentality for action. He put it behind him, but he concentrated on the practical details and the concrete organization of revolution.

He found the ground ready for the seed. As in Constantinople, all the young officers were discontented, and the senior officers sympathetic. Among them he discovered an old companion from the Military School, a Mufid Lutfi, to help him. The organization grew rapidly in numbers and spread throughout all the garrisons of Syria. Mustafa Kemal began to become a person of importance, but very soon he realized that he was only in a backwater. He had worked out the possibility of a revolt from Damascus: it was out of the question: the officers of the small Turkish garrison were ready: but the local people were hostile.

Friends had sent him word that the center of trouble was in the Balkans, and advised him to work for a transfer to Salonika.

He determined to get to Salonika with or without permission and see for himself. At the seaport of Jaffa on the Syrian coast a certain Ahmed Bey was the Commandant. Ahmed was a member of the *Vatan,* and ready to help. Mustafa Kemal arranged with Ahmed to cover up his tracks.

Asking for a few days' leave he went to Jaffa. There he faked false papers, adopted an assumed name, and dressed as a merchant took passage on a sailing-ship for Egypt. From there he crossed to Athens and then to Salonika. Everywhere he found the same discontent, secret societies and the beginnings of revolution.

In Salonika he went to ground in his mother's house and for a while lay low. His idea had been right. Salonika was the center. The most important of the junior officers were collecting there. Something big was being prepared. Through his mother and sister he got into touch with some of his companions from the Staff College and applied for a transfer.

Before he could do anything more, the Sultan's spies had recognized him. Orders came from Constantinople for his immediate arrest. Jemil, the adjutant to the Commandant of the Police, had been a member of the *Vatan* in Constantinople. He sent Mustafa Kemal a warning; the orders to arrest could be side-tracked for two days, but no more; he must get out.

Mustafa Kemal made a run for it over the frontier into Greece, and then by ship back to Jaffa, but orders for his arrest had reached Jaffa before him. The secret police had marked him down as dangerous. This time they would see he got no clemency. There would be no second chance for Mustafa Kemal in the Red Prison.

Ahmed Bey, whose duty it was to carry out the orders, met him on the ship. He brought uniform and Mustafa Kemal's papers. Then he smuggled him off the ship, out of the town, and sent him post-haste down south to Gaza. On that frontier there was trouble, and Mufid Lutfi was in command of an area. The confusion and disorder in the Ottoman Empire made a ruse of this sort possible.

Then Ahmed Bey wrote back to Constantinople: he needed further instructions; there must be some error; Mustafa Kemal had been in Gaza all the time; he had never left Syria.

It was weeks before he got a reply, and then Mufid Lutfi confirmed the fact that Mustafa Kemal had been with him all the time. By procrastination the two pigeon-holed the orders.

For a year Mustafa Kemal lay very low. He knew that if the Sultan's police got him this time he would see the light of day no more. He concentrated on his work. His seniors reported that he was an excellent officer and devoted to duty. The authorities in Constantinople came to the conclusion that the Salonika spies had made a mistake and that this young officer had been cured of his folly and was sound.

But Mustafa Kemal was as determined as ever to get to Salonika. He would not be left away in Syria when big events were being prepared at home. He knew members of the *Vatan* on all the staffs, from the War Office downwards. He pulled every string he could. Eventually he received orders for his transfer to Salonika, and he hurried post-haste to the center of revolt.

VI

MUSTAFA KEMAL was posted to the staff of the 3rd Army. His duties kept him partly in Salonika and partly traveling along the railway, inspecting.

When in Salonika he lived with his mother and sister. Zubeida was now well off; her second husband had died leaving her a big, rambling house in the center of the town and some money.

Mustafa Kemal found in the garrison many of the men he had known at the Staff College. With these he tried to create a new branch of the *Vatan,* but he made no progress. They listened to him without arguing or disagreeing with him. They appeared to be suspicious of him. Sometimes when he came on a group of them talking they would stop as if he was a spy or an agent. That they were at something he was sure, but they shut him out.

At last one of them told him, under the pledge of secrecy and behind locked doors. There was already in Salonika a large revolutionary organization; it was called the "Union and Progress." In the town were many Jews; most of these were Italian subjects and members of the Italian Masonic Lodges. As Italian subjects they were protected, by the capitulations and treaties, from arrest by the Sultan: their houses could not be searched by the police, and they could only be tried in their own consular courts.

A group of officers, many of whom Mustafa Kemal knew, including Fethi the Macedonian, had become Freemasons. Behind the protection, and using all the routine of the Masonic Lodges they had formed the "Union and Progress." They could meet in safety and plan in the houses of the Jews. They received ample funds. They could keep in touch with the important political refugees whom the Sultan had expelled and who lived in other countries.

The Committee of the Union and Progress had been watching Mustafa Kemal and testing him out. Now they invited him to join.

Mustafa Kemal was initiated as a brother of the Vedata Lodge. He found himself in an atmosphere which he disliked. The lodge was part of an international Nihilist organization. It was full of men without nationalities who talked of the evils of Russia, where Jews were oppressed, and the joys of Vienna, where they were allowed to make money. They were furtive, unhealthy men, full of secrets and cryptic talk. Mustafa Kemal was conscious that he was caught into the threads of international finance and international subversive and subterranean organizations, but without knowing exactly what they were.

He cared nothing for the international aims and troubles of Jews. He cared less for the Masonic Ritual and spoke of it with contempt. He was a Turk, proud of being a Turk, and only interested in saving Turkey from the incompetence and despotism of the Sultan and the grasping hands of the foreigners.

Moreover, he was a late-comer. Those who controlled the "Union and Progress" hid themselves behind the veils of the complicated ritual of the masonic degrees. He was only a junior brother and expected to carry out orders, whereas it was his nature that he must himself control or he would take no part at all. So far from obeying placidly, he was always sharply critical. His criticisms were trenchant and without respect of person. If opposed, he became truculent. He considered the organization of the Union and Progress casual and inefficient: too much talk and too little action. From the white-hot, molten enthusiast of the Staff College in Constantinople he was hardening down into cold steel. He wanted facts, not theories. He wanted action planned out with care. There was too much undigested theorizing in the Union and Progress to suit him.

He had no respect for the leaders. He quarreled with them all: Enver, a slap-dash fellow; Jemal, a round-shouldered swarthy, twist-minded oriental; Javid, the Jew of Salonika, a Deunme, a Jew turned Moslem; Niazi, the Albanian, a wild, unbalanced Garibaldi of a man; Talat, a post-office clerk, a lumbering great bear. These were the leaders.

Mustafa Kemal treated them all with condescension. He spoke to them as if they were boys in a class and he their teacher. On one occasion some of them in the Café Gnogno were talking of Jemal as a patriot. Mustafa Kemal interrupted them with a sneer and a homily on true greatness. Next morning, meeting Jemal in the train as they went to their offices together, he told him what he thought of him as a popularity seeker, and repeated *ad nauseam* his homily on greatness, which was full of platitudes.

His brother-officers disliked him as a self-opinionated, sneering fellow. His criticisms were always salty and bitter, with no humor to sweeten them. The Jews mistrusted him. He was never initiated into the higher degrees of the Freemasons' Craft. He was kept out of the inner circle of the Committee.

At home he was equally difficult; Zubeida was the only person whose open criticism he would accept; but even with her, if she touched his pride, he became frigid and reserved.

He would allow no one, not even Zubeida, to interfere

with his actions. On one occasion he had brought several of his fellow-conspirators to the house. The servants overheard their conversation and told Zubeida. She crept up to Mustafa Kemal's room and listened at the keyhole.

When they were gone she objected strongly. Mustafa Kemal tried to reason with her, but the two could not agree at all. She belonged to the older generation with clear-cut beliefs and steadfast loyalties; he to the younger generation which believed in little and respected nothing. Both grew irritated. Eventually Zubeida agreed to help her son: he was the head of the house, knew the world, and perhaps he might have some right on his side. In reality she was sure he was wrong, but was afraid he would leave home. Against her own judgment she helped him, but, woman-like, she continually complained, warning him that it was folly to plot against both the Sultan and Religion.

This disagreement decided Mustafa Kemal. The restraints of home life galled him. The domestic ties, the chatter of relatives, the everlasting prying of the women, the inevitable repressions irritated him. He had none of the give-and-take necessary: he must take all and give nothing; he would not allow even the smallest restriction on his liberty. Whatever the cost, he would always be master of himself. He took a room and left home. He visited his mother often, and now that he was not cheek-by-jowl with her he was more inclined to listen to her.

During the daytime he worked with exceptional energy at his military duties. Most of the evenings he spent in the cafés, where he ate, or met the other conspirators in the back room of the Café Gnogno, or in some private house with the doors locked and the shutters closed against the peering eyes of the police and their spies. There, drinking and smoking by the light of a candle or an oil lamp, they sat far into the night, talking and planning for the coming revolution.

22

Mustafa Kemal attended the meetings, and remained in the organizations, but, as time went on, bit by bit he took a less active part. The leaders still would not let him into their inner circle. He would not be a subordinate. He must control or he would do nothing.

He became more solitary and taciturn than ever.

VII

SUDDENLY and without warning the revolution for which they were working burst round them. Niazi, as impetuous and wild as ever, without prearranged plans had collected a few men, marched out of Resne into the mountains of South Macedonia and defied the Government. Enver at once published a proclamation of revolution and did the same in Eastern Macedonia. Nothing was prepared or organized. The Union and Progress itself had not more than three hundred active members. The feeling of the troops was not known.

Mustafa Kemal sat quiet, carrying on at his military duties. He was no foolish gambler to go plunging into a wild, unprepared adventure like this. If he acted it would be on a carefully considered scheme with some reasonable chance of success.

But the "wild adventure" succeeded. The history of the next few months was like a fantastic dream and as confused. A few hundred rebels were out in the hills. Troops sent against them joined them: for years the soldiers had been neglected and unpaid. Regiment after regiment, led by their officers, refused to act. Special troops sent over from the Interior of Turkey did the same. To the amazement of all, and not the least of the Committee itself, like leaves before the wind the power of the Sultan was gone.

With a quick decision the Old Fox in Stambul side-stepped: declared a constitutional government, blamed his advisers for all the misrule of the past, abolished espionage and welcomed the revolutionaries. Niazi and Enver marched back in triumph. Enthusiastic crowds of Christians and Turks, believing that the millennium had come, greeted them in Salonika.

Mustafa Kemal, with other members of the Committee who had taken no active part, met him. The new Constitution was proclaimed by Enver from the balcony of the Olympus-Palace Hotel in the main square of Salonika. In the group of officers behind him stood Mustafa Kemal unnoticed and unknown, except to a few as one of the minor and insignificant members of the Committee.

At once, from every foreign country, came hurrying back the politicians whom Abdul Hamid had for twenty years exiled: princes, ex-grand viziers, ministers of all grades. They elbowed the young officers on one side, took control of the Committee of Union and Progress and hurried to Constantinople to scramble and intrigue for power. Niazi went back to Albania and was murdered. Enver was posted as military attaché to Berlin. Mustafa Kemal was sent on a mission to North Africa to report on the garrisons in Tripoli.

Confusion was piled on confusion. Everything went wrong. Austria annexed Bosnia and Hertzegovina; Greece seized Crete; Bulgaria, backed by Russia, declared herself independent. Inside came reaction. There were revolts in Albania and Arabia. Christians and Moslems flew at each other.

In the middle of all this confusion the supporters of the old Sultan got to work. They bought over the soldiers in Constantinople, and sent out the priests and hodjas to warn the people that the new rulers with their newfangled ideas from Paris were without religion: they were Jews and Free-masons, not Turks and Moslems; they intended to destroy Islam and the Caliphate.

Roused to religious frenzy, the troops in Constantinople mutinied, killed or locked up their officers and, proclaiming their loyalty to the Religion of Islam, to the Sultan and to the Caliph of the Faithful, seized Constantinople and chased out the Committee.

The Committee appealed to the army in Macedonia for help: if they failed, Abdul Hamid and his cronies, with all their iniquities, would again be in power. The Officer Commanding in Macedonia was Mahmud Shevket Pasha, an Arab who had been a favorite of Abdul Hamid: a tall, gaunt man, cadaverous as a eunuch in looks; as a staff officer brilliant; as a commander halting in decision.

He hesitated what to do. On his staff were several of the Committee, including Mustafa Kemal who had just come back from Tripoli. Half against his own will they jockeyed Mahmud Shevket into action. He marched the Macedonian 2nd and 3rd Armies to Constantinople. The advance-guard consisted of the 1st Composite Division. In this Enver, who had hurried back from Berlin, commanded a cavalry detachment, and Mustafa Kemal was chief of the staff.

They smashed the counter-revolution, deposed and locked up Abdul Hamid in the Villa Allatini in Salonika with Fethi the Macedonian to act as his jailer, placed his decrepit cousin on the throne and restored the Committee to power.

Among the Committee, Enver caught the public eye. He became the popular hero. He had raised the standard of revolt in Macedonia and now he was leading the advance guard to complete that work.

There was about Enver a brilliance, a verve, a sparkling audacity, a flair for publicity, which made him stand out,

25

while Mustafa Kemal, dour, sardonic and cautious, went unnoticed.

He was unnoticed by the crowd and unwanted by the leaders. The Committee had marked him down as a capable but unpleasant fellow who criticized every one and would obey no one: a conceited, disgruntled man whom no one liked and who played a lone hand, without friends. They pushed him into the background and sent him back to soldiering.

VIII

MUSTAFA KEMAL went back to soldiering with energy. He was by instinct a soldier. He worked hard, organized staff rides and lectures, studied military history—Moltke and the campaigns of Napoleon. It was a time of new enthusiasms and quick promotion. Before he was thirty he was chief of staff to the 3rd Army in Macedonia.

In 1910 he was attached to the staff of General Ali Riza on a mission to France. He went first to Paris for a few days and then to the annual maneuvers in Picardy. Ali Riza reported that he had shown marked ability and judgment, and was a "go-ahead and clear-sighted officer." On his return he was put in charge of the officers' school in Salonika.

He reorganized the school with great efficiency, but he was dissatisfied and disgruntled. Though by instinct a soldier, Mustafa Kemal was forever hankering after politics; and in politics there was no place for him.

The revolution had improved nothing. Enver, Talat and Jemal, the men he had known on the Committee in Salonika, were now the rulers. Javid, the renegade Jew, was Minister of Finance. He despised them all. They were puny little men, unfit to rule.

He made no secret of his views. He preached them both

in the school and in public. The Great Powers, he said, were greedier than ever: Germany had her fingers on the throat of Turkey; her financiers were buying up concessions and rights; they already controlled the Baghdad railway; Javid had played the traitor and sold that to them; the best German diplomats were at work in Constantinople; Turkey was being sold to the foreigners, and especially to the Germans; the Turks must rule themselves without outside help or interference; inside Turkey everything was as bad as before: pay, organization and general conditions were as bad as under Abdul Hamid; poverty was general; everywhere, and especially in the army, there was discontent: something must be done and done at once.

Mustafa Kemal was now a senior officer. He was on the General Staff. His reputation for efficiency was growing. In the garrison were many officers discontented and prepared for trouble. They began to listen to him, look up to him and group round him.

His manner changed. To be the center, to be listened to and respected, braced him. He was as decisive and trenchant as ever, but he grew more expansive and even genial with those who followed him. He was becoming a person of importance and the leader of a movement.

This was reported to Mahmud Shevket Pasha, who was now Minister of War in Constantinople. He knew his man and the danger of trouble from Salonika and the Balkans. He must move Mustafa Kemal. He posted him as the Officer Commanding the 38th Infantry Regiment in Salonika; but this made no difference, for Mustafa Kemal did his military work above reproach, and even more officers began to stand in with him.

He began to plan a more definite line of action, aiming at a *coup d'état* and to organize for this. Once more his

27

evenings were spent in secret meetings behind locked doors, but now he was the controlling mind and his opponents were the old revolutionaries of the Committee who had become the rulers. His policy was for an efficient home government and the expulsion of the foreigners: "Turkey for the Turks!" was his war-cry.

The Government agents reported that he was dangerous. The Committee demanded his punishment. Mahmud Shevket Pasha sent for him, taxed him with inciting the troops to mutiny against the Government. Not being satisfied with Mustafa Kemal's replies, and yet not having enough evidence to arrest him, he relieved him from command of his regiment, recalled him to Constantinople and placed him in the War Office.

It was difficult to know how to handle him. Warnings and threats were useless, for Mustafa Kemal was quite fearless. There was nothing that could be made into a charge against him, for he was very circumspect.

In the War Office at least he was away from the Balkan storm-center and his friends, and he could be watched.

In Constantinople there was still confusion: the politicians were still scrambling and intriguing for power; ministries were in and out of office weekly; still there was no one man big enough to control. It had been possible for Mahmud Shevket Pasha, but at the decisive moment he had withdrawn.

There was a party, led by Jemal of the Committee, who were bitterly opposed to the Germans. They disliked the German instructors in the army. They hated von Wanghenheim, the German Ambassador and the friend of Enver, a massive, brutal Prussian of a man, coarse and defiant, yet cunning and subtle, an engine of energy who worked effectively and ruthlessly to make Turkey an instrument of Germany.

Mustafa Kemal found the politicians of this party friendly. He cultivated their acquaintance. He drank and gambled with them and talked with them by the hour, but he never got very far. He spent much of his time wandering on the edge of politics. He was always under the impression that very shortly they would recognize his value and invite him into their inner councils where he would become the dominating figure.

But he had neither the mentality nor the experience for politics. Like soldiers in all countries, he sneered at politics and yet wished to take a hand in them.

The politicians found him touchy and difficult, an explosive, churlish fellow. He bored them incessantly, for either he would out-talk them with a torrent of words or he would sit stubbornly and ill-naturedly silent.

He had nothing to offer them. In Salonika he might have a following. In Constantinople he was almost unknown. He did not fit anywhere into the picture.

They kept in touch with him, and encouraged him a little. He was by all reports an exceptional staff officer. He was certainly not the usual type of Turkish officer. He looked and behaved like a German with his clipped Prussian way of speaking, his blue eyes and his fixed stare. He might be useful one day against Enver and von Wanghenheim's Germans.

So Mustafa Kemal, as proud as Lucifer, went from door to door, almost cap in hand, to visit the second-class politicians. He was kept waiting in ante-rooms, sitting among the riff-raff, flicking his long riding-boots and growing more and more irritated. He despised these politicians, these rat-men, yet he wanted to be in with them. If some one had attacked him, he would have been happy. Hatred always

29

braced him. The casual indifference mixed with patronage stung his pride, yet left him helpless.

In this aimless quest he began to eat his heart out. As an antidote he drank heavily and savagely.

At that moment—in October, 1911—Italy, without warning, landed an expeditionary force in Tripoli in North Africa, seized the town and part of the coast.

PART THREE

IX

MUSTAFA KEMAL pushed politics aside. There was man's work to be done. He must get to North Africa to fight the Italians.

Except by the long land route through Syria and Egypt, Turkey was cut off from North Africa. The Italians had control of the sea and had closed the Dardanelles. The Turkish Navy consisted of two battleships and some cruisers. Their boilers were rusty; their crews had disappeared, and they lay stuck in the mud up the Golden Horn. It was impossible to send troops. Officers, who wished to go, must get to Africa as best they could. Every young officer was planning to go. Enver had gone at once. Fethi, who was military attaché in Paris, had made a run for it in a French fishing smack from Marseilles and landed in Tunis.

With two friends Mustafa Kemal took the land route. They traveled across Asia Minor and down by Syria and Palestine, using the railway where it existed, but doing the rest on horseback or with carriage. Arriving in Alexandria, they found that the English had declared Egypt neutral and closed the frontier.

Mustafa Kemal foamed at the mouth with rage: Egypt was Turkish territory; the English had no right there, and yet they had the audacity to close the frontier and forbid

Turkish officers and troops to go to the assistance of Turks in adjoining Turkish territory: it was an outrage.

Still there was nothing to be done. They must get on. The three friends separated, each to make his own way as best he could.

Mustafa Kemal dressed himself as an Arab and took the light railway that ran westwards. At the frontier he was stopped. He knew only a smattering of Arabic and, with his blue eyes and light hair, he did not look an Arab. The officer on the frontier post was an Egyptian. He had received a description of Mustafa Kemal with orders from the English commandant in Alexandria to send him back.

The Egyptian was a Moslem and he hated the English and the Italians, equally with all Christians. All his sympathies were with the Turks. He could not, however, completely ignore his orders. Making sure that Mustafa Kemal was a Turk, he arrested another passenger with blue eyes and sent Mustafa Kemal on with a blessing.

Mustafa Kemal made for Turkish headquarters, which were at Ain-al-Mansour, fifteen miles inland from the port of Derna.

He was welcomed. There was a shortage of officers and, moreover, he knew the country and the people from his tour of the previous year.

He was promoted to the rank of major and given command of the section facing Derna. His headquarters were in Ain-al-Mansour. In Ain-al-Mansour also was Enver, in command of the whole front.

The Italians, covered by their fleet, had seized the coast towns, but they could advance no farther inland. The Turks faced them. Behind the Turks was all North Africa up in arms. The *Jehad,* the Holy War, had been proclaimed. The priests had roused the people. From all Libya, from far down in the Sahara Desert and the oasis of Kufrah, the tribesmen had come swarming up to help the Turks, their brother Moslems, to fight the Christian invaders. Burning with religious fanaticism, they came pouring in to see Enver.

Enver was the center of attraction. He had come as the representative of the Caliph of all the Faithful, from the Imperial Sultan in Stambul. The Sheik of the Senussi called him "brother" and sent his warriors. The distant Touregs and Fessanis sent their volunteers.

And Enver knew how to handle them. He pitched a great tent with carpets spread on the floor and hung with draperies. Here he received in state, talked with the sheiks and listened to the wild tribesmen as they squatted round. He organized their straggling hordes into groups of forty tents, with a woman to each tent to cook and look after the men. To each group he gave three Turkish officers. He paid the tribesmen well, fed them and sent gifts to the widows of those who were killed. With untiring patience, with tenacity and immense energy, he inspired them to fight, and so pinned the Italians down to the shore.

Mustafa Kemal was constantly in touch with Enver. He was a year older than Enver, but his subordinate in rank.

The two men failed to agree. They were always at loggerheads. Both had in them the quarrelsome Albanian blood: both were proud, touchy and strong-willed; neither would stand opposition or criticism, and both were mentally and physically fearless and said openly what they thought. Otherwise they had nothing in common.

Enver was always inspired by great ideas, by far-flung schemes. The big idea absorbed him. He cared nothing for details, facts or figures.

Mustafa Kemal was cautious. He was suspicious of

33

brilliancy. Big vague ideas did not rouse him. His objectives were limited, and undertaken only after long and careful consideration and calculation. He wanted exact facts and figures. He had no sympathy with and no ability at handling Arabs or any foreigners. He was a Turk, and proud of being a Turk; he despised the rest of the world.

Since the first days in Salonika he had disliked Enver. Now he developed a contempt for him, and he did not hesitate to show it. His contempt was envenomed by jealousy. Mustafa Kemal was convinced that he was the better man and the better soldier, and yet, though he was older than Enver, he was always trailing behind him. It was Enver who was in command always, and Mustafa Kemal his subordinate.

To Enver living like a great chieftain, holding court in his fine tent, buoyed up with enthusiasm, gallant, open-handed and brilliant, Mustafa Kemal, with his gray face, his sardonic manner, his cynical remarks, was a death's head at the feast. He took the heart out of the tribesmen. He criticized every plan. He sneered at every scheme: he was always carping and critical, but never quite to the point of being insubordinate.

As time went on their relationship became more and more difficult. The fighting was a wearisome series of raids and sniping in a barren country of rocks in intense heat, and would have frayed the strongest temper. They quarreled openly. Fethi, amiable and popular with all, tried to patch up the breach between them, and failed.

Mustafa Kemal stayed in his own camp. He lived simply, in a small tent, and as hard as his men. He refused to go to the entertainments or to be part of Enver's court.

After a year of fighting there was little result. The Italians had landed more troops, dug themselves in on the shore, but could get no farther. The Turks and Arabs could not dislodge them.

Suddenly, and again without warning, in October, 1912, Montenegro declared war. All the Christian Balkan States, for the first and only time in their history, combined and attacked Turkey. In haste the Turkish Government made peace with Italy and sent urgent orders to Tripoli: the Turkish troops were to be withdrawn to Egypt and the country declared independent: all available officers were to make their way home as quickly as possible.

The enemy were at the gates. Turkey herself was in danger of complete annihilation.

X

As soon as he could hand over his command Mustafa Kemal hurried home. Thinking it to be the quickest way he crossed France, but finding the direct route closed to him he detoured through Austria and Rumania and down by the Black Sea. He was held up repeatedly so that he reached Constantinople only in the first week in December.

He found all in confusion. The Turkish armies had been smashed on all fronts. The Servians had advanced unchecked from the north; the Greeks had struck from the south and taken Salonika, with twenty-five thousand prisoners; the Bulgarians had made straight for Constantinople and were hammering on the fortified lines at Tchaldja, only fifteen miles away from the city. Except for these few miles round the capital and the great fortress of Adrianople, which lay isolated and besieged by the Bulgarians, the Turks had been swept out of Europe.

In all this disaster there had been only one bright spot. Rauf, a young naval commander, had taken out the old

35

cruiser, the "Hamidiye," and slipped through the blockade at the mouth of the Dardanelles. Chased by enemy ships, he had twisted and run up and down the Aegean Sea, now appearing suddenly to bombard a port or sink a transport. He had become a national hero, but his exploits had no effect on the general defeat.

Constantinople was crowded with wounded: hospitals, churches, mosques, private houses, were full of them. The country round was a rabble of refugee camps. The food organization had broken down. Thousands were dying of cholera and typhus; thousands more of hunger and cold. The politicians still quarreled for power, so that there was no stable government able to control or direct.

Mustafa Kemal searched anxiously for news of his family. He found many refugees from Salonika. They told him that the town had been taken by treachery: that the Greeks had murdered all Turkish civilians they could lay hands on; and that there had been much looting in the country around. At last he found his mother and sister, Makboula, in one of the refugee camps.

Arranging a room, he moved them into Constantinople. Zubeida was over sixty. She had grown heavy with the years and was getting blind. In the flight from Salonika she and Makboula had suffered severely from hunger and cold. The old woman had aged rapidly. She was overjoyed at seeing her son. She passively allowed him to move her to Constantinople, but she would not be comforted. All day long she sat cross-legged on a mattress in the room, swaying herself backwards and forwards and calling on Allah: Salonika was in the hands of the accursed Greeks; her relatives had been murdered; her house was gone; all she owned was lost: she was ruined.

As soon as he had made arrangements for them Mustafa

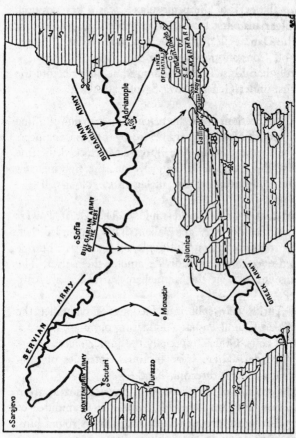

Map showing the lines of Advance of the Balkan Allies in the 1st Balkan War, 1912-13.

NOTE.—Between lines marked AA and BB was Turkey-in-Europe in 1911. Out of all this the Turks were expelled in the 1st Balkan War: only the small area behind CC to Constantinople remains to them.

Kemal reported himself at the War Office. He was posted to the Gallipoli peninsula as Chief of the Staff to a division which was holding the line of fortification in front of Bulair across the neck of the peninsula. It was a key position. If the Bulgarians burst through there they would have control of the Dardanelles, open the road into Asiatic Turkey and cut off Constantinople.

Hardly had Mustafa Kemal arrived at Bulair before the Bulgarians, under General Sava Savoff, attacked.

The fortifications were the patched-up remains of a line that had been built fifty years before by English engineers during the Crimean War. The Bulgarians attacked the line repeatedly: the Turks held doggedly on; the fighting was fierce and only stopped by an armistice along all the fronts.

After that events moved rapidly. The Great Powers called a peace conference. The Balkan States demanded that, with the exception of Constantinople, all Turkey in Europe be handed over to them to divide among themselves. The Bulgarians insisted on the immediate surrender of Adrianople.

The Turks were split into factions. Some under the Grand Vizier, Kiamil Pasha, a doddering old man, were for peace at all costs. Others, especially the junior officers, were for no surrender. There were mutinies, intrigues of politicians, chaos and no directing hand.

In the middle of this confusion Enver returned from Tripoli. He wasted no time. He called the Committee of Union and Progress, grouped the young officers round him, and, marching down to the Sublime Porte, broke in on a Cabinet meeting. He shot dead Nazim, Minister of War, who tried to stop him, chased out Kiamil Pasha and the other ministers with his revolver, and, with Talat and

Jemal of the Committee and Mahmud Shevket as Grand Vizier, took control.

He allowed no weakening. A section of politicians opposed him: he hanged them. He crushed the mutinies, and categorically refused the peace terms of the Balkan States.

But it was essential that he should save Adrianople from the besieging Bulgarians. He planned a wide turning movement. It was a fine scheme after his own heart: he would float the fleet out of the Golden Horn; under its guns the 10th Army Corps should land a little north of Bulair at Shah Kuy; the Bulair troops should attack the Bulgarians and the Shah Kuy troops would catch the enemy on the flank; the two columns would then combine and march northwards by the most direct route on to Adrianople. This would outflank the enemy and force them to retire from before the Tchaldja lines and save Adrianople.

At a staff conference on one of the battleships, Mustafa Kemal was present. He was trenchant in his criticism: reconnaissance showed that the hills above Shah Kuy were held by the Bulgarians and a landing was dangerous: the Bulair troops could not drive back the Bulgarians, and if they did the enemy had the interior lines and could mass superior numbers against them: the scheme sounded all right, but the details had not been properly worked out: they were unworkable.

Enver was annoyed. He was the master. He told Mustafa Kemal to talk less and do what he was told.

The scheme was carried out as planned. Two divisions of the Bulair troops attacked at dawn on February 8th. Mustafa Kemal was with them. They advanced a few miles and were halted by a thick blanket of fog. The Bulgarians crept round the left flank and opened fire. One division broke and ran; the other, of which Mustafa Kemal was

Chief of Staff, fought its way back with a loss of fifty per cent of its effectives. The 10th Army Corps started to land at Shah Kuy, was caught by the Bulgarians, and forced to re-embark with a loss of six thousand men.

The scheme was a complete failure. A month later Adrianople fell, and the Government under Enver was forced to sign the same terms of peace as those proposed by Kiamil Pasha and the government which it had ejected.

Mustafa Kemal returned to Constantinople. Turkey lay beaten, licking her wounds. Her enemies were haggling over the division of the country she had ceded. Suddenly they quarreled. Bulgaria attacked Servia and Greece but was beaten back inside her frontier. The late allies, forgetting the Turks, flew savagely at each other's throats.

Enver seized his opportunity. With a fine audacity, and without any declaration of war, he marched all available troops out at once, swept aside the few Bulgarians left, and made straight for Adrianople. At the head of the cavalry of the advance-guard, with bands playing and flags flying and the Turkish population strewing the road before him with olive branches, Enver rode into Adrianople as the "Victor."

On the staff of one of the columns, growling to himself with annoyance at the display Enver was making, unnoticed and little known, was Mustafa Kemal.

XI

ONCE more Mustafa Kemal was back in Constantinople living with his mother and sister, and unemployed. After the capture of Adrianople he had been promoted to lieutenant-colonel.

Dissatisfied, yet without clear aims, again he was hobnobbing with the second-class politicians whom he despised. But times were different. The new government was strong and resolute. Talat, Enver and Jemal—Mahmud Shevket had been murdered—had formed a Triumvirate and were ruling firmly. The old gangs and cliques had been broken up.

The politicians wanted Mustafa Kemal less than ever. He had fallen out of the picture altogether. His old asso-

Zubeida: Mustafa Kemal's mother.

ciates of the Committee in Salonika had left him far behind. Talat and Jemal were cabinet ministers. Enver had become an international personage. He was Minister of War. He had married a princess and lived in splendor in a palace on the Bosphorus. He had great plans: to knit all Moslems together under the Sultan-Caliph; to unite all Turkish-speaking peoples round Turkey and so to revive the glories of the Ottoman Empire: the Germans looked to him as their ally.

41

Mustafa Kemal was no more than a junior staff officer with a permanent grouse and an unpleasant manner. An awkward acquaintance, for he was disliked by the Triumvirate and the whole Committee of Union and Progress.

He had quarreled with Enver. Jemal alone had a good word for him, and that because they had a common dislike for the Germans.

To carry out his great plans Enver decided that the army must be reorganized first. He invited the Prussian, General Liman von Sanders, to carry out this work.

At the news Mustafa Kemal growled in impotent fury. He plagued all the politicians. He button-holed and harangued his brother-officers in public and private, trying to persuade them to combine in protest.

"It is madness to allow the Germans," he said, "to control the army, the basis of our power to live. We Turks should handle our own affairs. It is a national insult to call in this Prussian."

He saw Jemal and argued with him. When Enver refused to see him, he wrote him a bitter letter.

The Triumvirate found him a nuisance. He was not dangerous: no one would listen to or help him; no one would have much to do with him.

Still he was a nuisance. He would be best out of the way.

Fethi had gone to Sofia as minister: he and Mustafa Kemal had always been friends: Mustafa Kemal should go to Sofia as well. He was appointed military attaché and ordered to report at once to Fethi.

Mustafa Kemal accepted Sofia as banishment. He was cut off from the life in Constantinople; the post of military attaché gave little real work for a professional soldier. Whatever there was to do, he did well. He made friends with

Kitcheff, the Bulgarian Commander-in-Chief, and his General Staff, attended functions and maneuvers and reported his observations to Fethi.

It was characteristic of him that his best friend was Sava Savoff, the general who had driven back his division before Bulair. Rival brother-officers and politicians he hated; a brave enemy he respected. Sava Savoff had shown exceptional bravery before Bulair. Mustafa Kemal sought him out and made a close friend of him.

But he had little work to do, and that not much to his liking. He was not a man who could sit doing nothing. Whether it was work or amusement he must be at something, and at it full blast. If there was little work he would concentrate on enjoyment. The position of military attaché gave him the privileges and immunities of a diplomat with the opportunities for gallantry of a soldier. He took full advantage of both.

He learnt ball-room dancing, methodically with a teacher, and then danced whenever possible, but always as if he was on parade. He frequented the drawing-rooms and tried to become the society gallant, making love to the ladies of Sofia, but they found him excessively gauche. He was a smartly turned-out and well-set-up Turkish officer and that was all. They had no liking for Turks, at any time, and Mustafa Kemal was neither good-looking nor attractive. His manners were crude. Either he stalked stiffly about with his face set and gray, or he talked abruptly. He had no small talk, no easy gallantry or ready flattery. He understood nothing of the pleasant play of light flirtation. He bluntly demanded that each lady should bed with him; if she refused he ceased to be interested, but, as bluntly, asked another. For a short time he was half in love with a fluffy-haired pretty girl, the daughter of General Kovatchev, but she gave him the cold shoulder.

43

Very soon the ladies found him an uncouth fellow, the traditional Tartar in contrast to Fethi, the suave, polite, easygoing Turk. They laughed at his dancing and his attempts to learn the drawing-room manner. They found him a prodigious bore and forgot him.

And Mustafa Kemal, touchy and sensitive, became more lofty and aloof than ever. He began to hate the society women with their soft ways and their chatter, who would not make love wholeheartedly and yet teased and tormented his desire, who sneered at him, and who would not make a hero of him.

With men—and especially men who were deferential —and with the loose women of the capital, Mustafa Kemal was far more at ease. With these, in the cafés and the brothels, he drank and reveled night after night far into the dawn. He gambled and diced for hours against any one who would sit against him. He heaped up all the indulgences and glutted himself with them. He tried all the vices. He paid the penalty in sex disease and damaged health. In the reaction he lost all belief in women and for the time being became enamored of his own sex.

Meanwhile as time crept on there came the World War. Across the frontier in Servia the Archduke had been murdered. All the great nations were at war. Turkey had joined Germany, but Bulgaria had remained neutral and Sofia was an empty backwater.

In Sofia Mustafa Kemal was eating out his heart. Like many Turks he believed that Turkey would have been wise to have stayed neutral, sitting on the fence until she saw which side would win, and then making her terms.

But the decision had been made and Turkey was in. Like every other regular officer Mustafa Kemal believed the war would be over in a few weeks. Those weeks were slipping by. He raged with impatience. All the opportunities for which he had trained and worked were escaping him. He wired to Enver asking him for a command and received a polite but definite order to stay where he was, as he was needed there. He wired again and got no reply. He wrote and sent messages to his friends, but with no result, and Fethi could not help him.

The weeks grew into months. It was already February, 1915. Mustafa Kemal decided to go without leave and enlist, rather than be left out. He had packed his bag and made his plans when there came an order recalling him to Constantinople.

XII

ENVER was away. He had gone to the Caucasus to lead an army against the Russians. Haki Pasha the Lame, the Quartermaster-General, was in charge. He cared nothing for Enver's private dislikes. He needed officers—the best, and at once. The English had twice tried to force their way up the Dardanelles with battleships. All the information showed that they were concentrating a great army in Egypt to attack Gallipoli. At top speed Liman von Sanders was organizing a new army to resist this attack.

Haki Pasha knew Mustafa Kemal's record—a capable officer if kept away from politics. He recalled him by telegram and recommended him to Linman von Sanders, who gave him command of the troops in the southern half of the Gallipoli peninsula.

Von Sanders had a low opinion of the ordinary Turkish officer, but he very soon appreciated that Mustafa Kemal was out of the ordinary. Undoubtedly he was difficult, he did not mince his words, was brusque and harsh in expressing his opinion. On one occasion he told the German that

45

Bulgaria was right to stay neutral, as the final success of Germany was by no means sure; and on another that the German headquarters staff were criminally slack. But he knew his work as a soldier. He was clear-headed and sure in his decisions. His opinions were always backed by solid facts.

He disagreed frequently and fiercely with von Sanders, for both men were as proud as Lucifer. Nevertheless von Sanders understood his man, for Mustafa Kemal had the outlook and manners of a Prussian. He was hard, tactless, haughty; but above all he was a first-class fighting soldier.

"A splendid officer . . . a leader," said von Sanders, and trusted him.

And Mustafa Kemal, despite his dislike of foreigners and especially of the interfering Germans brought in by Enver, respected von Sanders. He recognized that the German was a brave and skillful soldier.

"Liman von Sanders," he said in an unusually generous moment, for he rarely spoke well of any one, "is all that a superior officer ought to be. We disagree often, but, once he has given his orders, he leaves me free to carry them out as I think fit."

From every agent in Cairo and Athens came the news that the English were about to attack. Eighty thousand men were ready in Egypt; a great fleet was standing by.

Von Sanders had a difficult problem. The coast-line of the Gallipoli peninsula was fifty-two miles long. The country was mountainous, and several of the mountains dominated the whole position. The English with their fleet could land their eighty thousand men anywhere they wished along that fifty-two miles of coast, rush one of the mountains, force him out of the whole position and open the road to Constantinople.

46

He had sixty thousand men. He placed them in three groups of twenty thousand each along the peninsula. He must sit and wait, for no one could tell when or where the English would come. Whichever group was attacked would have to hold out against superior numbers for two or three days until reinforcements could be got to them.

Enver, back from Russia, had sent orders to supersede Mustafa Kemal at once. Von Sanders, forced to obey the order, expressed his regret openly and gave Mustafa Kemal command of the 19th Division, which was in reserve at Maidos. At the same time he gave him orders to be cautious in employing his troops until it was clear which was the English main attack.

Angry at Enver's orders, Mustafa Kemal nonetheless realized that Liman von Sanders trusted him. In command of troops with a superior who trusted and relied on him and whom he respected, Mustafa Kemal became a different person. He ceased to be the restless grouser. He flung himslf into his work. All the ability and force latent in him developed out. His division consisted of one good Turkish and two poor Arab regiments. Within a few weeks he had knocked them into a first-class force. He studied the country and prepared for all eventualities.

On Sunday, the 25th April, came the English attack. A soft mist lay over the sea. Out of it slid a great wave of steel ships—battleships, destroyers and transports. One section struck at the north of the peninsula at Bulair. It was a feint, but it deceived von Sanders. Another made to the south.

The main attack came at the center. It consisted of Australians. Its object was to land in the low ground at Gaba Tepe and drive straight across by the valley to Maidos,

47

and then turn and take the ridge of hills known as the Chonuk Bair, which stood close above Mustafa Kemal's camp and which were one of the keys to the whole position.

A strong current swept the landing ships too far to the

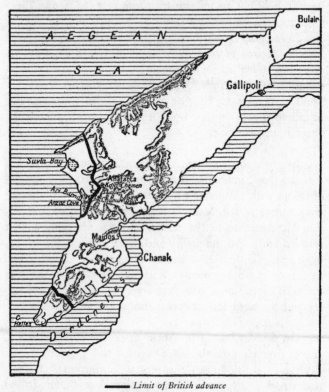

——— *Limit of British advance*

Map of the Gallipoli Campaign, 1915.

north and the Australians landed in error at Ari Burnu, and finding themselves in the foot-hills made straight up the steep hills for the crest of the Chonuk Bair.

Mustafa Kemal knew nothing of this. He had ordered

his best regiment, the 57th, to parade at 5:30 A.M. to carry out an ordinary practice maneuver up one slope of the Chonuk Bair. As he was moving up the hillside he saw a line of Turks, skirmishers, coming over the hill-top.

"What are you doing?" he shouted.

"The English have landed. We are the advanced pickets along the shore. We have been forced to retire."

"Where have they landed?"

"At Ari Burnu."

"Fix bayonets and turn about," he ordered.

A few minutes later came word from the 9th Division on his right, confirming the news and asking for a battalion to cover their left flank.

Mustafa Kemal calculated quickly. Von Sanders, he knew, believed that the attack would be at the north end near Bulair. But Chonuk Bair was the real key to the whole position. As more news came in it was clear that a large force was landing in front of him and that Chonuk Bair was their objective. In a flash, and by instinct, he realized that he must save Chonuk Bair, and at once. He could not wait for orders; minutes counted. *"Vitesse, vitesse, toujours vitesse,"* was a maxim of Napoleon's which he often quoted.

"Have we blank or ball cartridge?" he asked.

"Ball," replied a staff major.

"Then advance at once and as quickly as possible on to Chonuk Bair."

He had only a small scale-map handy. It did not even show Ari Burnu on it. With this in one hand, a compass in the other and a gendarme to guide him, he hurried ahead with two hundred men. The ground was steep, covered with bowlders and broken into ravines. The men could not keep up with him. When he reached the top there were only a few left. Directly below him, half-way up the last slope not four hundred yards away, he saw the head of the Australian column advancing.

The regimental commander was some way behind him, urging his men on over the rough country. Mustafa Kemal called the most senior near him:

"Collect all the men you can, get forward and attack the enemy," he ordered, pointing.

As the units of the 57th Regiment arrived out of wind and exhausted by the climb, he re-formed them himself and pushed them forward. A battery of guns arrived. He helped to wheel the first gun into position. Continually under fire, he was a raging madman of energy. On his own responsibility and without orders he called up his second regiment and threw it into the fight. He found that not enough. He called up the third and last, and threw it in also.

He had ignored his orders to be cautious. On his own responsibility he had thrown into direct action the whole of the army reserves; not a man remained in reserve. He was convinced that he was facing the main attack. If he was wrong and the main attack was elsewhere, his error would be disastrous. But he made no error. His instinct was right. He did not doubt his instinct.

All that day the battle surged up and down. The Australians were two-thirds of the way up the mountain. They could get no farther. The Turks were rapidly getting worn out; the 57th Regiment was decimated; the two Arab regiments were in confusion and ready to break; but the Australians were worn out too. Five hundred men on either side would have decided the battle.

When night fell the ridge was still in the hands of the Turks, and the Australians clinging to the hillside a little below them.

But Mustafa Kemal did not wait. Placing his headquarters behind an outcrop of stone a few yards behind the crest, all that night and next day he worked feverishly organizing attack after attack to push the Australians back down to the sea before they could establish themselves. As each attack failed he prepared another. He was constantly in the line encouraging the men, personally arranging that they should get rest and hot food, and inspiring them with his driving energy. But though he had stopped the Australians he could not push them back down the hills into the sea.

The crest-line of the Chonuk Bair was the key to the Dardanelles, and the Dardanelles to Constantinople. If the Dardanelles and Constantinople fell, Turkey would be cut off from Germany and forced to make peace. Greece, Rumania and Bulgaria would probably join the English. The moral effect would be world-wide. The road to Russia would be open and she would get arms and food.

Between the attacking Australians and these tremendous possibilities was Mustafa Kemal, gray-faced, determined, and holding the tired Turks in position on the narrow crest of the Chonuk Bair by his dominating personality alone.

XIII

UNABLE to force each other back, the Australians and Turks began to dig themselves in: the Australians determined to hold what they had got until they could push forward; the Turks equally determined to stop them and drive them down back into the sea.

The next few weeks were filled with the strain and drudgery of trench-warfare, the digging of trenches; the sapping and tunneling; the weary hours of sentry duty with every faculty on edge watching for danger; the constant cramped discomfort; the everlasting head-bursting crack of the snipers' bullets; the crash of bursting shells which ripped the nerves; the terror of mending barbed wire in the dark in No Man's Land between the lines; the agony of waiting grouped together in a sap-head to dash out to attack; the even greater agony of waiting for the sudden terrifying attack of the enemy with bayonets and hand-grenades; the killing in narrow trenches and underground with cold steel, savage, tormented bodies and shattering bombs.

And with all there came a parching summer. Water was short. The sun burnt down on the rocky, barren hills, turning them to red-hot dust. Between the lines the bodies of the dead rotted and great blue flies filled the air, myriads of flies which crept foully on all food, and with them came dysentery and enteritis and lice by the million. The power of resistance on both sides came near to the breaking-point.

Through it all Mustafa Kemal never relaxed. He was braced up and happy. He was in his element—fighting. He slept little; he did not seem to need sleep. He drove his staff relentlessly, even furiously, but he remained cool. He made his decisions with mathematical care and gave his orders decisively.

Herr Kannengeiser, the German general who commanded the 9th Division on his right, was struck by his ability. Mustafa Kemal is "clear-thinking and active," he said. "He decides everything for himself. He knows exactly what he wants."

He was constantly in the line talking with the company officers and the men, and so getting first-hand information. Often he was up in the sap-heads, or even in the danger zone beyond with the advanced snipers, studying the ground. During an armistice in May he worked as a sergeant in one of the burial-parties so as to be able to spy out the Australian trenches himself. He organized constant local attacks; at

52

the hour of the attack he was there to urge the men forward; sometimes he led the way himself. Not for one day did he relax or let his troops slacken in morale.

Again and again he was under fire. He never spared himself; he shared the dangers of the troops, and yet, while men all round him were killed, he was never touched. He acted with a studied recklessness which inspired his men.

On one occasion he was sitting outside a new trench. An English battery opened fire on it. As the guns found the range the shells fell closer and closer; it was a mathematical certainty that he must be hit. His staff begged him to take cover.

"No," he said, "to take cover now would be a bad example to my men." Lighting a cigarette he smoked it steadily, talking calmly and unconcernedly, while the men from the safety of the trench below looked up fascinated, watching him. The enemy guns switched on to another target. Though covered with the dust of the shell-bursts, Mustafa Kemal was not touched.

On another occasion, when traveling back to Gallipoli, an English hydroplane swept down at his car. The bombs broke up the road before and behind the car; one smashed the wind-screen and killed the chauffeur, but Mustafa Kemal was unhurt.

At times he would pick up a rifle and, half exposed above a trench, take careful and deliberate aim at some point on the Australian trenches. In exposed places he would move slowly so as to encourage his men, and even at close range the enemy snipers failed to hit him.

He was convinced, absolutely and completely sure, that no bullet could hit him. It made him utterly fearless.

In June he discovered a weak point in the enemy's line. If he burst through them he could turn all the Australian trenches and force them to retreat down the hill. He prepared an attack for the 28th of June. It was to be led by a newly-arrived and crack regiment, the 18th, backed by the whole of his division.

On the 26th, Enver, now Minister of War and Vice-Commander-in-Chief, paid a visit to the Gallipoli front. As soon as he heard of the proposed attack he vetoed it.

Mustafa Kemal during the Gallipoli campaign.

He considered it unsound. Mustafa Kemal, he said, should have got the sanction of high authority; he was far too ready to squander men in useless attacks; Mustafa Kemal had reported a capture of two machine-guns; he did not believe the report; he wanted to see the machine-guns and the prisoners first.

Mustafa Kemal flew into a rage. Enver again! Enver the useless little dandy who had scrambled up to power through cheap politics! Enver interfering and spoiling everything! He sent in his resignation.

Liman von Sanders persuaded him to withdraw it. The German could not afford to lose his best divisional commander. He sympathized with Mustafa Kemal. Like Mustafa Kemal, he was a professional soldier and had a profound contempt for Enver with his brilliant incompetence. He too disliked Enver's interference.

Enver withdrew his veto. The attack was launched. It was a complete failure. The 18th Regiment was wiped out. The preparations had been neglected and the staff work was bad.

Mustafa Kemal blamed the interference of Enver. Enver visited the 19th Division, congratulated the men on their bravery, but made it clear that he blamed Mustafa Kemal.

Again Mustafa Kemal resigned. Again Liman von Sanders tried to persuade him to withdraw, but found him obstinate. He told Kiazim, his chief of staff, to reason with Mustafa Kemal. Kiazim called up Mustafa Kemal on the telephone.

"How are you getting on? What do you make of the situation? What do you want?" asked Kiazim pleasantly.

"I've told you from day to day, but without success, what I think of the situation and what I think ought to be done," replied Mustafa Kemal brusquely. "Now there is only one thing left to do."

"And what is that?" asked Kiazim nettled.

"Place all the troops you have under my orders."

"Is that all?" said Kiazim driven to sarcasm. "But will they not be too many for you?"

"Too few!" said Mustafa Kemal, and shut off the telephone.

Eventually von Sanders persuaded Mustafa Kemal to stay, for Enver had gone back to Constantinople.

XIV

By late July it was clear that the English were preparing another big attack. Many transports with fresh regiments and a new type of motor-lighter for landing troops had been seen by agents in Egypt and the Greek islands.

From every possible source the Turks sent reinforcements to the peninsula, but, as in April, Liman von Sanders could not tell the time or place at which the attack would come. He must keep his troops mobile. He could not prepare positions.

The attack was delivered on the night of the 6th August. Its objective was the crest of the mountain known as the Hoja Chemen. This was a peak to the north of Chonuk Bair and connected to it by a saddle. It was beyond the right flank of the trenches held by Mustafa Kemal. Its lower slopes were covered by piquets, but its crest was not held. If the English gained the crest they would enfilade the Chonuk Bair, outflank all the Turkish defenses and command the whole peninsula.

The English planned for one column to burst out from the left of the Australian line straight at Hoja Chemen, another of twenty-five thousand to be landed five miles up the coast in Suvla Bay, drive inland, connect up with the column attacking Hoja Chemen, and the whole to sweep forward, grip the neck of the peninsula and so open the Dardanelles and the road to Constantinople.

For a week before, with great secrecy, each night on the beaches below the Australian lines in front of Mustafa

Kemal, fresh troops had been landed and cunningly concealed in dugouts in the gullies.

The night of the 6th was without moon. In the thick darkness a column of sixteen thousand men moved out from behind the Australians, followed the beach for a mile and then turned inland by three dry watercourses straight at the crest of Hoja Chemen. They were timed to reach the top by dawn.

Directly von Sanders received the news he ordered Kannengeiser, with the 9th Division, which was away on the right of Mustafa Kemal's division, to meet the attack on the Hoja Chemen.

Hurrying across the rough country, Kennengeiser reached the crest of the mountain at 4:30 A.M. In the faint light, three hundred yards below, he saw the head of the enemy column advancing slowly and laboriously up the steep hillside. He had with him only twenty men. He ordered them to open fire. The English, expecting to find organized resistance, lay down. They were worn out: the Turkish piquets had put up a stout resistance to them: in the darkness they had stumbled and slipped and fallen climbing the watercourses, which had been very steep, full of sharp rocks, scrub and loose shale: the night was intensely hot and there was no water: they were glad to rest.

They rested all that day while the Turks—Kannengeiser had been badly wounded—brought up reinforcements and dug themselves in. From the left Mustafa Kemal sent every man he could spare.

Meanwhile the column at Suvla had landed with little opposition and squatted down, also to rest.

Liman von Sanders saw the line of the enemy's attack and his danger. From Maidos he hurried his two reserve regiments up to Hoja Chemen. From Bulair and the Asiatic side he called up every man to face the English at Suvla, where at the moment he had there only fifteen hundred men of a gendarme battalion.

All through the 7th of August the English lay quietly resting before Suvla when they could have walked forward without effort, brushed the few Turks aside and won the whole battle.

On the slopes of the Hoja Chemen at dawn on the 8th the English attacked. Their center was aimed at the saddle, with one wing attacking Hoja Chemen and the other at Mustafa Kemal's trenches at Chonuk Bair. The fighting was fierce. The New Zealanders got a footing on the crest of Chonuk Bair. Mustafa Kemal flew at them with a counter-attack and was driven back. His staff was in a panic: they talked of retreat, the position lost, defeat.

Mustafa Kemal remained cool. Unruffled, he walked about under fire. His manner, his steady courage and his determination inspired those round him. He was a rock of strength. His men held on. The English could get no farther either on to the saddle or the Hoja Chemen, but they still held the piece of the Chonuk Bair.

Late that evening von Sanders sent for Mustafa Kemal. He found the German behind the village of Anafarta. He was in a towering rage: the troops he had ordered up from Bulair had not arrived: Fevzi, their commander, was a dilatory incompetent; he had dismissed him: the Suvla front was absolutely undefended; he had been out there himself that day and found only one battalion of gendarmes—and that worn out: there was nothing to prevent the English walking straight through and cutting off the peninsula: he had telephoned and telegraphed and sent messages all day to bring up some troops, but without result: there were signs that the English at Suvla were going to advance; they would probably attack within the next few hours: why they had not done so before God only knew! The position was critical.

"I have decided to group all the troops on this front into one, and I wish you to take command," he said.

Mustafa Kemal did not hesitate or ask questions. Responsibility and big odds against him roused the best in him. He took over quietly, made his plans deliberately and then raced into his work with tremendous energy.

Luck, as ever, was with him. The troops from Bulair were already arriving. They had come thirty miles at a good pace. It was time and space which had beaten Fevzi. No man could have got those troops up quicker, but Mustafa Kemal reaped the benefit.

As they came in, Mustafa Kemal gave them the minimum of rest and then formed them for the attack. The attack was the only hope of stopping the English; there was no time to prepare defense positions.

That night the English also were preparing. The English Commander-in-Chief, Sir Ian Hamilton, had arrived and ordered an immediate advance. It was timed for dawn of the 9th.

The two attacks were launched simultaneously. They fought each other to a standstill, but the Turks held their ground. The English could not advance. The position before Suvla was saved.

Meanwhile the battle for the Crests of Chonuk Bair and Hoja Chemen had been fought up and down, now one side getting the advantage and now the other. The Turks had forced the English some way down the Hoja Chemen; a column of Indians and English had rushed the saddle with the bayonet and were chasing the Turks down the farther slope, when, in error, the big guns of the English fleet opened fire on them, inflicted heavy losses and forced their

59

own men to retreat. The New Zealanders had extended their hold on the corner of Chonuk Bair. From there they could enfilade the Turkish lines. All counter-attacks had failed to shift them.

Once more the staff of the Turkish 19th Division was in despair. They telephoned to Mustafa Kemal; their men were tired out; they could not get them to attack any more; the terrific artillery fire of the enemy had disheartened them; there were signs of panic.

"Don't worry," called back Mustafa Kemal over the telephone, his voice, cool and quiet, giving them courage. "Just hold on for twenty-four hours while I settle things here in front of Anafarta. I will be back with you shortly, and then I will put everything right."

At 8 P.M. Mustafa Kemal was back on the Chonuk Bair. He went out personally to reconnoiter. Twice the snipers got on to him. His staff begged him to take care, but he walked close up to the New Zealand position in the gloaming, studied the ground carefully and returned at a walk and without taking cover. He saw that unless the New Zealanders were forced off the Chonuk Bair the battle was lost.

All that night he prepared. Von Sanders had sent him the 8th Division from the Asiatic side. He had increased the 19th Division by three battalions. He crowded the men into the trenches as close as they would go: close contact gave them courage. He walked among them, laughing, good-natured, encouraging. He was again happy; he was fighting.

"Don't rush it, my sons," he said. "Don't be in a hurry. We will choose exactly the right minute, then I shall go out in front. When you see me raise my hand, look to it that you have your bayonets sharp and fixed, and come out after me."

He galvanized the simple Turkish soldier with a new courage. They were ready to follow him to hell.

Opposite, in the enemy's position, two raw battalions of the new army, the 6th North Lancashires and the 5th Wiltshires, were taking over from the worn-out but veteran New Zealanders.

Before dawn every Turkish gun possible opened and concentrated fire on the enemy's position. At 3 A.M. Mustafa Kemal stepped out of the trenches and walked forward. The English opened fire. A bullet smashed his watch, but he was untouched. Had he been wounded then there would have been no attack. His men would have refused to move.

The artillery fire stopped. For a minute Mustafa Kemal stood alone, the dominating leader. Then he raised one hand and walked forward. With a wild yelling the Turkish infantry swarmed out after him, wave after wave of howling men, a sea of bayonets, irresistible. They swept over the two English battalions. The North Lancashires broke and ran; the Wiltshires were bayoneted to a man. Down over the sea edge of the slope swept the Turks. The English battle fleet opened fire on them. The monster shells tore great holes through the packed ranks. They retreated back and dug in, but they had cleared the Crest of Chonuk Bair. The position was saved.

For the next three months Mustafa Kemal, now promoted to Pasha, commanded the Anafarta front. The fighting was mainly trench-warfare.

Twice more only the English attacked from Suvla. Each time the battle was fierce, and the losses very heavy. On both occasions Mustafa Kemal was forced to throw in his last reserves, even down to the cavalry dismounted and the gendarmes. On both occasions it was the last handful of men and Mustafa Kemal's driving personality which gave the Turks the victory and saved the peninsula and Constantinople.

In December, 1915, the English gave up the contest and evacuated. The Turkish armies were reduced down to a skeleton force for patrolling duties, and Mustafa Kemal returned to Constantinople.

XV

MUSTAFA KEMAL came back to Constantinople filled with a great sense of his own importance. He was now somebody to be reckoned with. The newspapers had called him "The Savior of the Dardanelles and of the Capital." He had a military reputation. He would not be ignored as before. He would make the politicians listen to him. He would impose his views on these rat-men. He would take a hand in ruling. He still professed to despise politicians, but politics still drew him irresistibly.

He had preached consistently that the Turks should control Turkey; that the Germans, if employed at all, should be only employed as servants; that Enver with his incompetence was a national danger and would ruin the country.

He found public opinion swinging to his views. The enthusiasm for the war was dying. The Germans were exceedingly unpopular. There were repeated incidents and quarrels between Turks and Germans. Turkey had become merely a part of the German machine. It was the general opinion that whoever won it was Turkey who would pay the bill. There had been one wild plot to kidnap all the German officers and deport them.

Enver, with the help of the Germans, had made himself dictator. He too had become very unpopular. He was at loggerheads with his own supporters and party in the Committee of Union and Progress. There were many intrigues against him. He was in constant danger of assassination. He never went out without a strong escort or driven at top speed in one of his cars.

Mustafa Kemal made no secret of his views. Jemal, his friend, was away in Syria, so he went to see Talat, now Grand Vizier. Talat received him genially, listened to him attentively when he put forward his qualifications to be made Minister of War, appeared to agree with him and when he was gone laughed boisterously at his astounding conceit. Some one told Mustafa Kemal that Talat had laughed at him. This touched his pride and made him furious. He never forgave Talat.

He tried Halil, the Under-Secretary of State for Foreign Affairs, who had been with him in Sofia. Halil arranged an interview with Nessim, the Foreign Minister, who was known for his dislike of the Germans.

Nessim was busy when Mustafa Kemal arrived, and kept him waiting in his ante-room while he finished some work. By the time he sent for him Mustafa Kemal was in a thoroughly bearish temper. He told the Minister bluntly that the optimistic reports issued by the General Staff were untrue; that things were bad and Turkey was riding for a fall; that Enver was incompetent, and that he, the Minister, knowing these things, must accept responsibility for the coming crash.

Nessim, piqued, replied equally bluntly that Mustafa Kemal had come to the wrong place. As an officer, if he had such views, he should go to the War Office.

Mustafa Kemal retorted that to go to the War Office was to go to the Germans; they controlled everything and they had already tried to get rid of him. And, bristling with rage, he stamped out of the office.

He found himself, as before, shouldered out. No one wanted him. He was so angular that he fitted into no picture. He was always haughty and on his dignity; he would combine with no one, he expected every one to come to him, to agree with him, to obey him absolutely. He would meet no one half-way.

Disgruntled and irritated, he lashed out with his opinions on every occasion. Constantinople was full of plots and intrigues run by little men. As the opponent of Enver and the Germans his name began to get mixed up with these. He was, however, far too shrewd and cautious to be actively involved.

One of these plots came to a head. A certain Jacob Jemal, a noisy, talkative fellow with a personal grievance, planned to kill Enver, and talked of putting Mustafa Kemal in his place. It was a cheap, irresponsible conspiracy by a few second-rate officers. Enver waited until he had enough evidence; then he hanged Jacob and his friends as a warning to others and to Mustafa Kemal. He would have hanged Mustafa Kemal also if he could have got him, but there was no evidence that he was party to the plot.

Enver found Mustafa Kemal a nuisance. He would be best out of Constantinople. He posted him to the command of the 16th Army Corps in the Caucasus, and then to the 2nd Army, with headquarters at Diarbekir and as far away as possible from Constantinople.

XVI

From Constantinople a single line of railway ran three hundred kilometers to the rail-head at Angora. From there

Mustafa Kemal traveled by horse, cart and motor-car the six hundred further kilometers to the Caucasus front.

It was a long and tedious journey. The roads were broken down; for years they had not been repaired: in many places even the foundations had disappeared.

Angora itself was a small and primitive country town high up on the bleak plateau of the Interior. Beyond it to the east lay a great mountain country of rock—bleak, barren and fierce, practically uninhabited except in a few fertile valleys. In summer the heat was intense and in winter the cold even more severe.

Mustafa Kemal found the Turkish troops completely disorganized. In the previous year Enver, with one of his grandiose schemes, had planned to sweep round the flank of the Russians, strike at their line of retreat and drive them back across the Caucasus. For this he had massed a large army at Erzerum and himself come from Constantinople to take command. In theory his plan had been excellent, but he had ignored the practical details of distance and season, so that the Turkish columns had been caught by the January blizzards high up in the mountain passes. Of the hundred thousand who set out only twelve thousand returned. In one district alone, huddled together in groups trying to find warmth, the Russian patrols found thirty thousand Turks frozen to death. These had been the soldiers of the Anatolian regiments, the flower of the Turkish Army.

Since then the Caucasus front had been neglected. Every man and gun had been needed for the Dardanelles. The Russians had advanced slowly but steadily, building roads and railways, consolidating their gains and taking over the country. They had captured Van, Bitlis and Mush, and the great fortress of Erzerum. Hitherto, however, their main efforts had been concentrated on their German front, but now they were preparing a great offensive which would push down into the heart of Turkey. The Grand Duke Nicholas, the Russian Commander-in-Chief, had himself come to supervise.

Mustafa Kemal saw that the Turkish troops under his command had little power of resistance. They were short of food, ammunition, rifles and guns. They were in rags. Their morale was bad. All their supplies were being pilfered. The army contractors were in league with the officers, thieving and growing rich on their contracts. The medical as well as the supply services had broken down. The neglected men were dying by the thousand of dysentery, typhus and starvation.

To Mustafa Kemal all this was only one more proof of the dangerous incompetence of that upstart popinjay of a fellow, Enver. Cursing Enver for having pushed on him the duty of clearing up the mess, he set to work with his driving energy.

There was no time to lose. He calculated that the Russians would attack in the late spring of 1917, and that unless something radical was done they would walk through the Turkish position without difficulty.

He telegraphed urgently to the War Office in Constantinople, describing the state of affairs and pointing out the danger of further neglect and asking for supplies, shells, medicines, and men.

When he received no reply, he telegraphed direct to Enver at the Ministry of War in terms that were both curt and offensively blunt. Still he received no reply. The Caucasus front was far away; Enver and the General Staff were busy on other schemes; they ignored Mustafa Kemal and his telegrams.

In a rage, cursing Enver and his incompetence and his

66

German assistants, Mustafa Kemal set to work to make the best of the material under his hands.

With the contractors and the thieving officers he was ruthless. One or two mistaking his character invited him to take a share in the plunder. His reply was to hang them and bastinado any he caught pilfering. He was equally ruthless with the lazy and incompetent. He re-formed the regiments, reorganized the medical and the supply services, and labored unceasingly to inspire the troops with a new spirit.

He had as his chief of the staff a Colonel Ismet, and as his second-in-command General Kiazim Kara Bekir.

Ismet was a capable and experienced staff officer; a sallow little man; neat and wiry in build, with a small head and a large hooked nose, somewhat deaf, and with the quiet, silent manner of the deaf. Steady tempered, with unlimited patience and unlimited persistency, an expert in office work, routine and the handling of details, he carried out orders with the accurate efficiency which Mustafa Kemal always demanded.

Kiazim Kara Bekir was the complete opposite, a big, heavy man with a slow brain, but loyal, industrious, capable and loved by his men.

Both men were rigidly honest, martinets in discipline, and energetic; both accepted Mustafa Kemal loyally as their chief and combined with him admirably.

Yet despite all the efforts of himself and his staff, Mustafa Kemal realized, as the spring came, that if the Russians advanced he could not hold them up.

But once again fortune saved Mustafa Kemal. The tide turned. In Russia revolution was coming. Its insidious back-drag was already destroying the Russian armies. Their discipline slackened. They began to break up with defeatism

67

and desertion. The Grand Duke Nicholas was recalled to Moscow and the spring offensive was postponed.

All through the spring and summer of 1917 the Russian armies gradually disintegrated. They crumbled to pieces, and, like dust before a wind, they were gone.

At once Mustafa Kemal advanced, but he could move only slowly, for his troops were still in poor condition and the local Christians, the Armenians and Georgians who had been organized by the Russians, fought fiercely for their homes. He recaptured Van, Bitlis and Mush, and moved towards Batum.

The danger was over in that area. The enemy were gone, but away in the south was a new danger. The English were preparing an offensive by way of Syria.

Urgent orders came from Constantinople to send every gun and man available, and posting Mustafa Kemal to the Syrian front.

Handing over his command to Kiazim Kara Bekir, with orders to clear up, deal with the Armenians and establish the frontier, Mustafa Kemal made for Constantinople, on the way to Syria.

XVII

THE new danger zones were Mesopotamia and Syria. The English, with an army from India, had captured Baghdad and were advancing on Mosul; they were preparing an army in Egypt, to attack Palestine and Syria. They must be stopped and Baghdad recaptured.

The German High Command, at Enver's urgent request, had sent General von Falkenhayn to organize a new force, the Yildirim, "the Thunderbolt," as it was to be called. Its headquarters would be Aleppo; it would be stiffened by a large number of German officers and men. Mustafa Kemal was posted to command the 7th Army.

But he was not contented. He protested vehemently at the German control. With Liman von Sanders he had got on well, but he could not hit it off at all with Falkenhayn, who had no idea at all how to handle this headstrong, insubordinate, but exceedingly capable Turk. The German, having failed in other ways, was fool enough to send Mustafa Kemal a present of a box of gold coins. For this Mustafa Kemal sent him back a formal receipt and later returned the gold and demanded his receipt back.

At the first staff meeting in Aleppo, Enver and Jemal, who was commanding the 4th Army, were present with Mustafa Kemal and Falkenhayn and a number of German staff officers.

Mustafa Kemal was critical and pugnacious. He disapproved of all Falkenhayn's plans, especially his pet ones of an attack on Baghdad and a raid on the Suez Canal. He was convinced that both would fail. The German resented his manner and his criticisms. Jemal, who was as hostile to the Germans, backed Mustafa Kemal up.

The disagreements grew so frequent and tense that Mustafa Kemal resigned his command. Enver and Falkenhayn tried to persuade him to withdraw his resignation. He refused, and even went so far as to nominate his successor and issue an order to the army. Falkenhayn wished to deal with Mustafa Kemal for insubordination, but Enver posted him back to his old command at Diarbekir. Mustafa Kemal refused to go. To save his face and to keep some sense of discipline, Enver granted Mustafa Kemal indefinite sick leave. Mustafa Kemal was without money; Jemal advanced him some ready cash on his horses, and Mustafa Kemal took the train back to Constantinople.

The quarrel between Enver and Mustafa Kemal had come very nearly to a head. Mustafa Kemal knew he was in a strong position. Enver was by no means sure of his ground. The general feeling against the Germans and himself was increasing day by day. Mustafa Kemal was now a very senior officer with a big reputation. If Enver took disciplinary action against Mustafa Kemal for insubordination —for refusing to serve under a German or carry out plans worked out by Germans—he would rouse a popular storm and make Mustafa Kemal into a national hero.

For a while in Constantinople Mustafa Kemal lived with his mother and sister at 76 rue Aqaretler in Beshiktash, the suburb on the hills behind the city, but, as before he found family life unbearable. As in Salonika, the inevitable restraints irritated and galled him. He hated having women always round him, nagging, advising, criticizing, chattering, but, even worse, looking after him, fussing round him, nosing into his affairs. He wanted women only for casual pleasure, not for permanent companions. In all things, down to the smallest details of his life, he must be free and unfettered.

He took a room in the Pera Palace Hotel, which looked out over the Golden Horn and Stambul. There he lived, morose and disgruntled, keeping much to himself. As before, however, and on all occasions, he freely and openly denounced Enver and the German control. Gradually, as the dislike of the war and the Germans increased, a number of officers and politicians who were opposed to Enver began to group round Mustafa Kemal. He was an awkward and a dangerous man to have in the capital, and unemployed. In the early spring of 1918 a state visit by the Turkish Crown Prince, Vaheddin, to Germany was arranged. Enver attached Mustafa Kemal to the mission. It seemed a good way of getting him temporarily out of the capital, and by sending him to see the German machine at work he might persuade him of the efficiency and inevitable victory of Germany.

XVIII

MUSTAFA KEMAL accepted the appointment for something better to do. He had been three months unemployed. It was torture to him to be idle. He saw no change for the time being. Constantinople was as full of intrigues and plots as ever, but they were all run by little second-rate men and of no value: he had kept clear of them. Enver with the control of the war-machines was firmly in power. There was no sign of any opening for himself. It might be of interest to see the German front and meet the German High Command.

At first he regretted his decision. Two days before the mission was due to leave Mustafa Kemal was formally presented to the Crown Prince Vaheddin in his palace.

On an uncomfortable straight-backed chair in a room hung with oriental tapestry he sat waiting, while the palace staff stood round in frock coats whispering.

Vaheddin came in. He was a weedy, lanky man with a long neck and a weak face, and dressed in ill-fitting morning-clothes. He sat down on a brocaded sofa and after accepting the salaams of his staff closed his eyes wearily. Twice he opened them with an effort and made two inane remarks and then appeared to drowse. Mustafa Kemal concluded that he was half-witted.

At the station the Prince arrived in civilian clothes and shuffled past the guard of honor with both hands to his forehead in an oriental salute. Mustafa Kemal, all his military outlook outraged, protested against this to the Master of Ceremonies and was told to mind his own business. He found that he had been reduced from temporary general-of-division to general-of-brigade and that his carriage was at the farthest end of the train and filled with baggage and paraphernalia of the rest of the staff. When he complained, he was again snubbed.

He was treated as a junior official. He was irritated to fury by being herded with all these third-rate hangers-on of the palace with their unpleasant manners—oily with superiors, bullying with inferiors. As he watched the Prince, empty-faced and stupid-eyed, standing at a window and accepting wearily the cheers of the crowds as the train drew out, he regretted that he had been fool enough to set out on such a mission. It hurt his pride. He was a Turk and haughtily proud of being a Turk. He was ashamed to see Turkey represented in Europe by a mission headed by such an imperial decrepit.

Hardly, however, had the train crossed the Turkish frontier than an orderly brought him orders that the Crown Prince wished to speak with him in his state carriage.

Mustafa Kemal went down the corridor stiff and prickly with irritation. When he entered the state carriage he was staggered to find that the shuffling dodderer he had seen in the palace was gone. In his place sat a man very much alive who was watching him with shrewd eyes.

For sixty years Vaheddin had lived in the palace under Abdul Hamid. The old Sultan had taken a liking to him and trained him up, but none the less he had watched him continuously with spies. All those years he had lived in constant danger: one slip, one sign of ambition or interest in politics or the outside world, and he would have disappeared or have been locked away. As a disguise he had developed the somnolent, weary manners of a dodderer. Under that

72

disguise he hid a shrewd brain and an ability to know what he wanted.

His one idea was to become Sultan. Enver, Talat and the Committee wished to pass him over for his nephew, Abdul Mejid. He hated Enver and Talat, but he was as cautious with them and the spies they had set round him as he had been with the old Sultan. In Constantinople he had treated Mustafa Kemal with careful neglect.

Now he greeted him warmly, apologized that he had not been able to make his acquaintance more fully before, congratulated him on all his successes as a general, and so oiled his vanity with pleasant flattery that he had Mustafa Kemal in a good temper at once.

Very quickly they became close and intimate friends, and Mustafa Kemal the confidant of the Prince. They had a common hatred of Enver and Talat, and common interests. All that journey they were constantly closeted together in intimate talk.

Mustafa Kemal saw his opportunity. The present Sultan was a sick man and could not last long. Vaheddin was weak as water. In a very short time he would undoubtedly ascend to the throne and be Sultan and Commander-in-Chief.

He must establish his influence over Vaheddin: he would then be the force behind the Throne; he would climb to the top and grasp the power he wanted: the first thing was to prove to Vaheddin that Germany could not win the war; that the German alliance was folly and that Enver and his German backers ought to be ejected.

All through the German tour Mustafa Kemal was deliberately critical. They were received by Hindenburg at headquarters. The old Field-Marshal gave them an optimistic review of the whole situation, including that on the Syrian front. Afterwards Mustafa Kemal told Vaheddin that most of it was bluff, and he knew personally that the details of the Syrian front were incorrect.

Later they visited Ludendorff, who gave them a more detailed account, especially of the preparations for the big spring offensive. Mustafa Kemal cut into their conversation.

"What is the line you expect to reach if the offensive is successful?" he asked abruptly.

The Field-Marshal, nettled at the cross-examination of this young officer, replied in general terms:

"We usually aim at a point that is decisive to us. Any further action depends on circumstances."

"There," said Mustafa Kemal to Vaheddin, who was quite ignorant of everything military, "even the Chief of the German General Staff doesn't know his objective and trusts to luck to get him through. There must be something radically wrong here."

At a dinner given by the Kaiser he drank too much champagne, and after dinner, seeing Hindenburg standing by himself, he swaggered up to him.

"Your Excellency," he said, "the facts you supplied the other day to the Prince Vaheddin about the Syrian front were quite wrong. I know, for I was there, and the Cavalry Division of which you spoke only exists on paper. Still, be that as it may, would you do me the favor of telling me confidentially what is the objective of this big offensive you are planning."

For a while Hindenburg looked down from his great height at this presumptuous young man. Quietly ignoring him and his questions he gave him a cigarette to keep him quiet.

A tour was carefully arranged for the mission to see one section of the western front. Leaving Vaheddin, Mustafa

Kemal went off on his own with a party of German officers through the trenches and climbed to an observation-post in a tree in front of the line. He came back to tell Vaheddin that however successful the Germans appeared from the arranged tour, he had satisfied himself by personal observation that they were in a bad way.

At every opportunity Mustafa Kemal encouraged Vaheddin to ask awkward questions, even of the Kaiser himself. Always his object was the same; to make Vaheddin assert himself; to prove to him that the Germans were a failure, and that he ought to eject Enver and his German assistants and take control himself, with Mustafa Kemal as his right hand.

He could never conceal his dislike of the Germans. Now and again he showed his supreme pride in being a Turk and his belief in Turkey and the Turks.

On one occasion he flew into a passion on overhearing some one make a disparaging remark about Turkey. On another, at a dinner, the Governor of Alsace criticized the Turkish handling of the Armenians. Vaheddin referred the criticism to Mustafa Kemal, who flew straight at the Governor across the table.

How dare he talk like that to the future Sultan of Turkey? What did he know about Armenians? Turkey had sacrificed her own interests in an alliance with Germany; the Armenians were plotting to destroy Turkey and he, the Governor of a German province, dared to defend the Armenians against the allies of Germany. He boiled with suppressed fury.

The Governor, staggered by the attack, apologized hastily. Not satisfied with that, Mustafa Kemal, bristling like a fighting terrier, followed up the attack.

"We have come here," he said with bitter sarcasm, "not

75

to discuss Armenians, but to get an idea of the real German situation. We have certainly been edified by what we have seen."

As the tour came to an end Mustafa Kemal pressed his point more and more. At last, one day in the Hôtel Adlon in Berlin, he asked Vaheddin in private if he might speak out quite frankly.

"I want," said Mustafa Kemal, "to propose something that, if you agree, will link my life to yours."

Vaheddin nodded to him to go on.

"Ask for the command of an army. All the German princes command armies. The Turkish Crown Prince should have a command. It is an insult that Enver has not proposed this before. Then make me your Royal Highness's Chief of the Staff."

"Command of which army," asked Vaheddin.

"Of the 5th," said Mustafa Kemal, knowing that this controlled Constantinople and the area round, and would be the decisive factor in any political crisis.

"They would refuse it to me," said Vaheddin.

"Never mind! Show them that they have a personality to deal with; that Your Royal Highness cannot be ignored," replied Mustafa Kemal.

"We will consider it," said Vaheddin, "as soon as we return to Constantinople."

Caution was the strongest characteristic of Vaheddin. After sixty years of palace life he was muscle-bound with caution. He was frightened of Mustafa Kemal, with his driving, urging personality. He might find him useful against Enver, but he was not going to place himself into the hands of such a tempest of a man. Moreover, the palace life had sucked the marrow out of Vaheddin. He was a coward.

XIX

On the journey back Mustafa Kemal began to plan for the future. The Prince listened to him attentively. But hardly had they reached Constantinople before Mustafa Kemal was taken seriously ill.

He had allowed a quack to handle the disease he had contracted in Sofia and he had not been properly cured. Since then he had taken no care of himself. On active service he had worked relentlessly, driving himself unsparingly to immense physical and mental exertion. At times he had drunk heavily and debauched wildly.

The disease now affected his kidneys. For a month he lay in bed twisted by agonizing pains. Then the doctors ordered him to Vienna and finally to Carlsbad for a cure.

With the disease came intense fits of depression of spirit, so that Mustafa Kemal went down groping into the pits of black despair. When these passed they left him without energy or interest. In July he heard that the Sultan was dead and Vaheddin had ascended the throne. Even that did not quicken him to action.

He received many letters from Constantinople advising him to return. Izzet Pasha, an opponent of the Committee of Union and Progress, had been made chief A.D.C. to the Sultan; the title of Vice-Generalissimo had been taken away from Enver; Vaheddin was showing his teeth.

Except for a letter of congratulation to the new Sultan, Mustafa Kemal was too weary to force himself to any action. More urgent letters came from his friends, and one from Izzet Pasha. With infinite effort, for he was still very ill, he dragged himself up to the decision, and returned to Constantinople. On the road he caught influenza, which, at that time, like a great plague, was raging across Europe killing men by the thousand. Still weary and ill he arrived in Constantinople late in July, 1918.

Mustafa Kemal always lived on his nerves. It was his nervous energy that was his driving force. Back again in Constantinople, among his enemies and friends, he was braced up. He grew rapidly better. His old ambitions revived and with them his vitality. He decided that he must certainly follow up the plans he had made with Vaheddin, now he was Sultan.

He was received by the new Sultan with every show of cordiality. Vaheddin even went so far as to light a cigarette for him—a mark of almost deferential courtesy in Turkish customs—which encouraged Mustafa Kemal to speak freely.

He expanded on his old scheme. Disaster, he said, was just ahead; the Sultan should take over executive control of the army; as long as Enver and his Germans were in control the Sultan was only a name, a puppet; he should dismiss Enver, send the Germans home, make Mustafa Kemal his Chief of Staff, and save Turkey from the destruction to which she was heading; he must get away from the German alliance and make a separate peace at once—before it was too late.

"Are there any other officers of the same opinions as yourself?" asked Vaheddin.

"There are many, Sire," replied Mustafa Kemal, but Vaheddin made no promise.

At a second interview Mustafa Kemal got no farther. At a third interview he pressed his views even more emphatically. He saw close in front of him the point at which he had aimed for so long; if he succeeded in persuading Vaheddin he would have reached the top; he would have the power for which he craved; he would then chase out Enver, the accursed Enver, and all his tribe.

78

As he talked he grew excited, passionate, and even challenging, trying to convince the Sultan. Vaheddin began to reply. Ignoring etiquette Mustafa Kemal continued so that he drowned the Sultan's voice. When he had finished Vaheddin said emphatically and with some show of anger:

"I have made all my arrangements with their Excellencies Enver and Talat Pashas." Then he dismissed him.

The truth was that Enver had threatened the Sultan. Vaheddin had consulted with Damad Ferid Pasha, his brother-in-law and chief adviser. He had come to the conclusion that he was not strong enough to fight Enver and the Committee of Union and Progress, and that Mustafa Kemal had no following to help him. He was far too cautious to run any risks. Mustafa Kemal must be left out.

Mustafa Kemal boiled with sullen rage for the minute: Enver had beaten him: Vaheddin had ratted, gone back on him; all his fine plans were finished; for the moment he could do nothing; but he would be even with his opponents in the end.

And Enver was taking no risks. He was determined to get Mustafa Kemal out of Constantinople as quickly as possible. Two weeks later, after the Friday ceremony of the Selamik, the Sultan sent for Mustafa Kemal. Surrounded by his staff, which included a number of German generals, he received him with great cordiality.

"This is Mustafa Kemal Pasha," he said to the Germans, "an officer of the highest ability and in whom I have the greatest confidence."

"I have nominated you, Excellency," he said, turning to Mustafa Kemal, "to a command in Syria. That front is of vital importance. I want you to go at once, and I charge you not to let that country fall into the hands of the enemy. I know you will do with distinction the work I have confided to you." And he dismissed him.

In the ante-room were a crowd of officers, including a number of Germans. As he crossed the room Mustafa Kemal met Enver. He knew who was behind the orders of the Sultan.

For a minute he stood looking at him.

"Bravo, Enver," he said at last. "I congratulate you. You have won. From what I know of the facts the army in Syria exists only in name. In sending me there you have taken a fine revenge."

The two rivals faced each other. Enver small, dapper, covered with orders, boyish-faced, laughing gayly, debonair and bold. Mustafa Kemal taller and gray, his face set and livid, morose, his eyebrows beetling out over his eyes full of sullen anger.

At that moment a German general in one corner of the room said loudly:

"There is nothing to be done with Turkish troops. They are cattle that only know how to run away. I don't envy any one commanding them."

Mustafa Kemal flashed round on the German, his eyes now blazing with fury, his whole body bristling.

"I, too, am a soldier," he said. "I have commanded in this army," and his voice rang out like a trumpet vibrating with his passionate belief in the Turks. "The Turkish soldier never runs away. He doesn't know the word for retreat. You, my General, if you have seen the backs of Turkish soldiers you must have seen them as you yourself ran. How dare you blame the Turkish soldier for your own cowardice!"

In dead silence, the whole ante-room brought up standing by the passion in his voice, Mustafa Kemal stalked across the room, past Enver and out of the palace.

XX

IT was late August before Mustafa Kemal reached the Syrian front. He reported to Liman von Sanders, who was in supreme command with his headquarters at Nazareth—Falkenhayn had gone back to Germany in the spring. Liman von Sanders was delighted to see him. Then he made a tour of the whole front.

He found the Turks dug in on a line from west to east across Palestine, from a point ten miles north of Jaffa on the seashore across the coastal plain, the hills of Judea and the river Jordan to the Hedjaz railway and the desert of Maan. This line covered all the main lines of advance which ran from south to north to Syria: the Hedjaz railway ran up from Medina through the Maan desert to the junction at Dera-a and on to Damascus. A second railway with a new gauge at Rayak went on northwards to Aleppo and through the Taurus mountains into Turkey itself.

Mustafa Kemal took over his own command the 7th Army from General Fevzi. Fevzi was a trusty old soldier who was returning to Constantinople as Chief of the General Staff. The 7th Army held the center of the Turkish line: it had two Army Corps in the trenches under Colonel Ismet and Colonel Ali Fuad. On the right was the 8th Army with the 22nd Army Corps under Colonel Refet holding the line up to the seashore. A branch railway line ran for them the junction of Dera-a westwards towards the sea behind the 7th and 8th Armies, and supplied them. On the left the 4th Army covered the Hedjaz railway.

Mustafa Kemal had found the condition of the troops in the Caucasus bad. Here it was pitiable. Many regiments had less than 10 per cent of their effectives. The men, utterly neglected, ragged, verminous, short of food and often even of water, were dying by the thousand of dysentery and starvation under the terrific blasting sun of the desert. Their morale was gone. Only by force could they be held in the trenches; parties with machine-guns on lorries continually patrolled behind the lines with orders to shoot deserters on sight; and yet there were more deserters than men in the trenches.

The English had taken up a line opposite the Turks: it was clear that they were preparing for a big attack; they were in vastly superior numbers; their troops were fresh, vigorous and full of enthusiasm; their organization, their supply and medical services were excellent; they had ample stores, ammunition, artillery together with good mechanical transport and many aëroplanes. The Turks had in all only eight aëroplanes and two anti-aircraft guns.

The Arabs of the Emir Feisal, son of King Hussein of Mecca, had joined the English. Under the Englishman, T. E. Lawrence, they were raiding in continuously from the desert, cutting the railway, the telegraph and the telephone lines, blowing up bridges, capturing convoys, threatening the communications, creating a sense of insecurity among the troops and rousing the native population to revolt.

Once again Mustafa Kemal set to work with fury, driving, urging, pulling chaos and disorder into some organization, but he was taken ill. The kidney trouble attacked him again. During the first two weeks of September, when every report showed that the English were about to attack, he was forced to lie helpless in bed in his headquarters at Nablus.

On the 17th of September an Indian sergeant, a deserter, came to the lines of the 22nd Army Corps and reported that the big attack was to be delivered along the coast on the 19th.

Refet brought the news to Mustafa Kemal. Ismet and

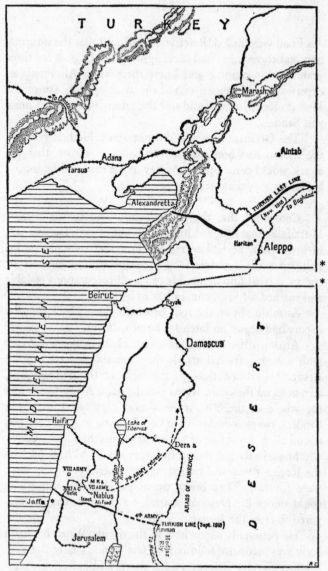

Map of Syrian Campaign, 1918.

* NOTE.—This map has been contracted as shown by the break in the printing. The area between Rayak and Aleppo, including Homs and Hama, has been omitted. *Vide* General Map, page 281.

Ali Fuad were called. Refet was convinced that the information was correct. He had been fighting the English for three years in this country and knew their ways. Ali Fuad, an experienced old soldier, was of the same opinion. Ismet and Mustafa Kemal agreed and sent the information on to Liman von Sanders.

The German, however, did not agree. He believed that the Indian had been planted on them as a ruse, that the attack would come up the railway to the east, and he moved his best troops that way.

Convinced that the Indian's information was correct, Mustafa Kemal dragged himself up out of bed. He was still in great pain, he had fever; the heat was stifling; but his will-power was stronger even than disease, and his nervous energy carried him along. He made all preparations possible and warned all his commanders to be ready.

At midnight on the 19th Ismet telephoned back that the enemy had begun an intensive bombardment.

At dawn the English attacked. Holding the 7th Army with a strong frontal attack they concentrated on the 8th Army. They burst through the right of the Turkish line, advanced up the coast, wiped out the 22nd Army Corps and the whole of the 8th Army, almost captured Liman von Sanders, swept round the Turkish flank on to their rear and cut off their direct line of retreat to the north.

Mustafa Kemal swung his army round with its back to the Jordan River and retired fighting fiercely; but his men were finished. They broke up in panic. Collecting all he could under his personal control, on the fifth day, he prepared to cross the Jordan.

He personally supervised all the details. When his main body was across he followed. A few minutes later the 11th English Cavalry Brigade raided down and cut off his rearguard, only just missing him. The 4th Turkish Army was retreating up the railway. Leading the remnants of his force, he made across the empty desert for Dera-a station.

Behind him and on his flanks came the enemy. Twice his rearguard troops were caught in defiles by machine-gunners and decimated. Close down over him swept the English aëroplanes, raking his columns with machine-gun fire, dropping bombs on his artillery and transport. On all sides were hordes of panic-stricken men making wildly for safety, abandoning arms, ammunition, guns, animals and wagons in endless confusion. On the edges were the Arab auxiliaries of Lawrence, murdering stragglers, pillaging, mutilating with all their Arab bestialities.

Through it all, keeping his small column together by his personality, giving those who were close round him courage and purpose, stalked Mustafa Kemal.

From Dera-a, without waiting, he retreated up the railway to Damascus with such speed that the English lost contact with him.

At Damascus he halted. Liman von Sanders ordered him to form a new line at Rayak. Leaving Ismet in Damascus and taking Ali Fuad, he set to work, but almost at once came news that the people of the coast towns had declared for the enemy, the English were in Beyrouth and any line on Rayak was outflanked already.

Mustafa Kemal calculated quickly. The demoralization was complete. Not merely the Turkish soldier but even officers of high rank were bolting for safety. All his attempts to stop the panic were useless. He had intercepted an army corps commander of the 4th Army on the run.

"You ought to be shot," he said facing the general, "but I will give you another chance. Place yourself under Ali Fuad at Rayak and make good."

85

The general saluted. Next morning he was gone. He had bolted again.

With such a spirit among the high command Mustafa Kemal saw that it was useless to shoot the privates or the junior officers.

He realized that he must have time to reorganize. The English were still some way away and out of touch. He must retreat at once right back the two hundred miles to Aleppo, give up all Syria, and reform on a new line in the north, covering the roads into Turkey itself.

At once he went to Liman von Sanders.

"Your plan is sound," said the German, "but I cannot give the order. I am an outsider only. I cannot take the responsibility of giving up a great slice of the Ottoman Empire to the enemy without a blow. That is a matter for you Turks, the masters of the country, to decide."

"I take full responsibility," said Mustafa Kemal, and issued orders to break off all contact with the enemy and for a general retreat to Aleppo.

He himself went ahead and prepared a new line ten miles north of Aleppo. It covered the only road by the one difficult pass through the great mountains of the Taurus into Turkey itself. Its flanks were secure. Neither deserters nor the enemy could get past unchallenged. Arabia, Palestine, Syria were Arab countries which the Turks held as conquerors and rulers only. These were lost. But here on this new line he would make his Turks, with their backs to the wall, fight to keep the enemy out of their own Turkey itself. Here they would fight to the last gasp for their mother-country.

As the broken troops arrived he re-formed them into regiments and put them into the line, inspiring them with a new spirit. He telegraphed to the Sultan, demanded that

Enver and his gang should be ejected, a new government be formed and he himself be made Minister for War.

To the telegram there came no reply, but news that Enver, Talat and Jemal had bolted up the Black Sea and a new government made with Captain Rauf and General Fevzi in the Cabinet.

From Lawrence, through the Arabs, came suggestions that Mustafa Kemal should use his influence to persuade the Turkish Government to open pourparlers for a separate peace-treaty. This he refused. He would fight. He was no craven to run like the rest as soon as threatened. He worked unceasingly to make his position impregnable.

At first the townspeople of Aleppo had been quiet. As the English advance troops came near they became hostile and truculent.

Mustafa Kemal was living in the Hôtel Baron in the center of the city. On one occasion as he drove back in his car from his office alone, except for the chauffeur, he was surrounded by a mob which howled and snarled at him like a pack of pariah dogs. He drove them off with a hunting-crop and when they followed him to the hotel bribed them with promises of money and arms.

Next morning, hearing an uproar, he went out on the balcony of his room. The streets below the hotel were full of menacing crowds. The Arabs had come raiding across the desert from the east and were in the city.

There was no time to lose. He evacuated the city and took up his headquarters at Kitma, behind the new line, and prepared to meet the coming attack.

On the 26th October the first of the English advance troops appeared, pressing forward to establish contact. Two regiments of Indian cavalry, the Jodipore and Mysore Lancers, attacked his line at the village of Hari Tan.

Mustafa Kemal went straight to the village and personally directed the fire. The Turks were recovering heart and fought well. The Indians lost heavily, fell back in confusion and sent word for reënforcements. The Turks fell back at a prepared position some ten miles farther north.

As both sides waited came news from Constantinople that the Government had signed an armistice with the English at Mudros.

Orders came for all Germans to return to Germany at once. In the local inn in the town of Adana, Mustafa Kemal took over the command of all the troops in South Turkey from Liman von Sanders.

The two men faced each other across a café table. They had carried out the formalities of handing over. Mustafa Kemal was now the host; Liman von Sanders had ceased to be his superior: he was his guest.

In this hour of complete defeat they had little to say to each other. Both were brave men, hard and experienced soldiers, both were thin-skinned and as proud as Lucifer. They had a deep respect for each other which both found hard to show.

"I have known your Excellency," said Liman von Sanders at last as he said good-by, "since you commanded at Anafarta. I pride myself that I recognized your ability from the first. We have disagreed often, yet we have become good friends. It is my one consolation that I leave my command in your capable hands."

Turkey was defeated, but Mustafa Kemal, now in sole command on this front, undaunted and pugnacious as ever, would not give way. He argued every detail of the carrying out of the terms with the enemy. He procrastinated on all occasions. When the English wished to occupy Alexandretta he denied their right, ordered the garrison to resist and threatened to attack.

When Izzet, the Grand Vizier, telegraphed first ordering and then begging him to give way he replied, "We must not cringe. If we do, we shall be annihilated."

He continued to strengthen his line. He sent officers up into the mountains behind him with arms and supplies to collect men and form irregular bands. Somehow he would stop the enemy getting into Turkey: he would prepare for the worst eventualities, a guerrilla war in the mountains if necessary.

In Constantinople a new government had been formed. Fethi, Captain Rauf, General Fevzi were all in the Cabinet. Ismet was recalled to become Under-Secretary of State for War. Mustafa Kemal was left out and ignored. At this he raged, but without effect.

Suddenly Izzet called him through on a long-distance telephone. He had quarreled with the Sultan and intended to resign. The old man, Tewfik Pasha, who was a friend of the English, was to become Grand Vizier. Izzet wished Mustafa Kemal to come back at once. He needed his help.

Handing over his command, Mustafa Kemal made for Constantinople.

PART FOUR

=

XXI

WHEN Mustafa Kemal arrived in Constantinople the Armistice was already a month old. He found the enemy in possession; English warships in the Bosphorus; English troops holding the capital, the forts in the Dardenelles and every point of vantage right across Turkey; French troops in Stambul, their Negroes and Senegalese in Galata; Italian troops in Pera and down the railways; Allied officers supervising the police, the gendarmerie, the port, the dismantling of the forts and the demobilization of the army.

The Ottoman Empire had been smashed into little pieces: Egypt, Syria, Palestine, Arabia were gone; Turkey itself was held helpless in the iron grip of the victorious and over-weening enemy; the machinery of government had broken down.

The Committee of Union and Progress were gone: Enver, Talat and Jemal had bolted to other countries; Javid and the rest were in hiding: under Tewfik, an old pasha of the reign of Abdul Hamid, known for his friendship with the English, a weak-kneed government meekly obeyed the orders of the enemy.

The show of force by the enemy did not, however, frighten Mustafa Kemal. He was ready to resist, prepared to argue and tussle each point obstinately with the enemy, but he obtained no support. The Turks of every class were worn out, utterly beaten, with no fight or resistance in them. Crushed morally and physically, they waited, without spirit or resentment, for the victorious Allies to decide their fate: they begged humbly to be allowed to exist.

Mustafa Kemal went straight to Izzet. He found him angry and depressed. Before the enemy had arrived Enver and Talat had escaped by a ship up the Black Sea; he had let them go and gladly. The Sultan had taken him to task, told him that he should have arrested and handed them over to the English, and that they must make friends with the English. Enver and Talat might be scoundrels, he said, but they were Turks; he would be no party to handing over Turks to any foreigners, even at the orders of the Sultan; he had resigned.

Mustafa Kemal argued him back into action. He agreed with his sentiments but he had no right to stand aside, to allow Tewfik and his government and the Sultan to accept defeat in this cowardly way: it meant the end of Turkey; there was no question of reviving the Empire or recovering any of the lost provinces of Arabia or Syria: the Ottoman Empire was gone; they must accept that, but it was now a question of saving Turkey herself.

They must form a strong government; Izzet must push out that old dodderer Tewfik and become Grand Vizier again; he must make him, Mustafa Kemal, his Minister of War; together they would face the enemy and with honor save what was left of Turkey.

With Izzet, Mustafa Kemal set to work to form a party. Once more he hobnobbed with the politicians. He found a dozen groups led by some minor man who hoped to climb to power: a party for an English mandate, another for an American mandate; a committee of the Friends of England, another of the Friends of France, and yet another of the

Friends of Italy; each based on the supposition that nothing could be done without outside help.

Except for a short time when he considered the idea of an American coöperation, Mustafa Kemal had no belief in any outside help: the Turks must save themselves or be destroyed.

The politicians listened to him. He was in a unique position. With Enver gone he had no rival. He was known as the only successful general in Turkey. He had driven the English back on Gallipoli and refused to let them have Alexandretta. He was believed to be a friend of the Sultan. He had consistently opposed the Germans and the Committee of Union and Progress. Above all he had not, like Enver, Talat and Jemal, bolted to save his own skin.

Day after day he worked trying to convert the politicians to his views. He spent long hours in the Parliament House arguing with them. Many appeared to agree with him. A vote of confidence in Tewfik was tabled. Before the debate Mustafa Kemal spoke in a committee room to a crowd of deputies, urging them, bullying them, to show a stiff upper lip, throw out Tewfik the Anglophile and form a strong government.

He felt sure of success. Already he saw himself Minister of War—and after that he would grasp power.

He went into the Strangers' Gallery to listen to the debate. At the voting Tewfik won by an overwhelming majority. The deputies were afraid of Mustafa Kemal and of his ideas. They were afraid of the domineering general. They suspected his ambitions. They looked on his determination to resist or be smashed in the attempt as folly.

White with anger, cursing the politicians, Mustafa Kemal went to the telephone and asked to see the Sultan— since his return he had kept away from the palace. He was told that an interview might be arranged. He was kept waiting a week.

Finally Vaheddin received him after the Friday Selamlik, the weekly function of State Prayers. He expressed pleasure at seeing him, but was not cordial. This did not deter Mustafa Kemal, who went straight to the point: His Majesty must form a strong government to face the enemy, deal with them as equals and stop the nervous, timid acceptance of total defeat; a word from His Majesty would stiffen the national courage.

"Make me Minister of War with a strong government," said Mustafa Kemal, "and I will yet save Turkey. But this Parliament must be dissolved; half the deputies are traitors, members of the Committee of Union and Progress, friends of Enver; the rest are cowards: there is no man with any backbone among them."

"You have great influence with the army," said Vaheddin, interrupting. He had grown stouter and dogmatic since he had become Sultan. "Is the army loyal to me?"

"I have only returned a short time, Sire. I do not know," said Mustafa Kemal, taken aback.

Vaheddin was sitting with his eyes closed, as if asleep—the same manner which he had adopted when he wished to disguise his real thoughts from Abdul Hamid.

"Has Your Majesty any definite proofs of disloyalty?"

"Is the army, and will the army in the future continue to be, loyal to Me?" repeated Vaheddin wearily after a pause.

"I have no reason to believe it is not and will not be loyal," said Mustafa Kemal cautiously.

"Then I look to you to use your influence to keep it loyal," said Vaheddin.

Long ago he had summed up Mustafa Kemal: an ambitious tempest of a man who might be used, but a dangerous man, for, if given power, uncontrollable. He might have been useful against Enver; now he would be useful with the army.

Under his heavy lids, with cautious eyes he watched the thin, gray-faced general in front of him, judging how far he could rely on his loyalty and support.

Next day Vaheddin dissolved the Parliament, and by making Damad Ferid, his brother-in-law and chief adviser, Grand Vizier, took control himself. His action raised a storm. He was only cursed. One paper printed extracts from his letters to Abdul Hamid. These had been found in the palace at the deposition of Abdul Hamid and showed that Vaheddin had acted as jackal and spy for the Red Sultan.

Mustafa Kemal had been given no post in the new government, but he was generally blamed for the Sultan's actions. It was generally said that he was behind the Sultan; he had tried to obtain a dissolution of Parliament by the vote of confidence in Tewfik; he had been closeted with Vaheddin for an hour in private talk; he was working for himself. Many of those who had looked to him for a lead now stood away from him. He was suspect.

And in Vaheddin's Government there was no place for him. Weak, cowardly and obstinate, Vaheddin had only one fixed idea—the Throne and Turkey were one and the same; he must insure the safety of the Throne and Himself, and so he would save Turkey; to do that he must ally with the enemy and by careful obedience obtain their good-will: the English dominated the enemy; he would stand in with the English, who had every reason to want Him, the Caliph of the Moslems, as their ally. He was convinced that all ideas of a strong government or of any form of resistance must mean quick destruction and were not to be thought of. Damad Ferid, his brother-in-law and the man he trusted most, agreed with him whole-heartedly in this policy.

XXII

FOR Mustafa Kemal there was no place. He was elbowed out on all sides. He had no following. He would not work with any one. Again he was so angular that he did not fit into any combination.

He had rented a small house in Shishli, a suburb of Constantinople. There he lived quietly, taking no part in politics or public affairs. He went often to see his mother and sister, but, as before, he refused to live with them. He kept much to himself.

He had few friends and only one intimate, a Colonel Arif.

Arif was a capable staff officer trained in Germany. He was a younger man than Mustafa Kemal. They had known each other since the days in Salonika and Monastir; they had served together in Syria, the Balkans and Gallipoli. After the Armistice they struck up a close friendship. They had common tastes; both were absorbed in all military matters; both enjoyed the same loose talk, the heavy drinking and the wild nights with women.

Mustafa Kemal's enemies said they were lovers, for Arif was the only person for whom Mustafa showed open affection, putting his arm round his shoulders and calling him endearing names. Others were convinced they were relatives, for Arif was almost a double of Mustafa Kemal. He had the same eyes, shape of head and carriage as Mustafa Kemal, the same instinct for everything military, the same cynical outlook, but he was less dour and sardonic. Moreover, he had none of Mustafa Kemal's strength of will, and he looked up to Mustafa Kemal with an almost dog-like respect and fidelity.

To Arif alone in those days Mustafa Kemal opened his

heart. To have to watch Turkey brought so low—English and French lording it in the streets of the capital, native Christians insulting Turkish women—drove him to fury. Yet he was helpless. He would have taken some action, but he had no idea what action to take. Moreover, he was being watched. The English had their agents everywhere. They were arresting any one who showed fight. He must hide his feelings and bank down the sullen fires of hatred that burned in him, or he might also be arrested.

But as the weeks went by and it came to the first months of 1919 there came a change. The grip of the enemy on the country began to slacken. Their armies were being demobilized and withdrawn. In Italy, France and England there were serious internal troubles. Throughout all the victorious countries there were the first signs of a reaction after the tremendous strain of the World War. In Paris the Allied statesmen were absorbed in dealing with Germany; they had no time for Turkey; the peace terms had not even been outlined.

"Leave Turkey alone," said Lloyd George's advisers. "She will break up automatically and we will divide up the pieces later."

In Constantinople the Allied representatives were constantly and openly quarreling, each scheming to get a favored position or some commercial advantage, and playing up to the Turks.

Here and there among the Turks came the first faint stirrings of a new hope—the belief that perhaps resistance might be possible and Turkey saved from destruction.

In Constantinople itself this was out of the question: the English, with the Sultan in alliance, had too firm and severe a grip; but away up in the mountains of the Interior, in Anatolia, something might be done.

A dozen secret organizations were formed in the Capital to steal arms and ammunition from the depôts under the enemy's control and ship them to the Interior, and to form centers where men might be collected and plans made.

Officials in high places gave help. Ismet was Under-Secretary of State for War. Fevzi was Chief of the Staff. Fethi was Minister for the Interior. Rauf, the renowned Commander of the "Hamidiye" in the Balkan War, was Minister of Marine. All were friends of Mustafa Kemal and were working secretly to the same end.

In a dozen places in the Interior a few stout-hearted men formed committees to prepare resistance. Those that Mustafa Kemal had organized in the south, before he handed over his command, began to take shape. Everywhere the old local committees of the Union and Progress were meeting again. Up in the Caucasus frontier, far away in the eastern counties, Kiazim Kara Bekir with his six undefeated divisions had begun to obstruct the Allied control officers and refuse to disband or demobilize.

But all those were as yet but the first cautious try-outs made in the expectation that the English would stamp them out at once.

The spies and agents—and there were myriads, for every Turkish Christian was looking for revenge on his Turkish neighbors, and to be paid for information—reported the danger to the English, who, however, did little except to arrest and imprison in the Bekir Aga prison a few of the men they considered dangerous. A plot to help them escape was discovered and prevented.

In that plot Mustafa Kemal had a hand, but he did not appear. Cautious and silent, he was in touch with all the new secret organizations, but he did not commit himself. He was by no means sure of their success. He was taking no unnecessary risks. On the surface he appeared to have accepted defeat and to acquiesce in the policy of the Sultan and Damad Ferid.

None the less the English suspected him. His name was put on a list of dangerous men to be arrested and deported to an internment camp in Malta.

He had left the house in Shishli and moved back to his old room in the Pera Palace Hotel, overlooking the Golden Horn. He was still ill. He was utterly depressed. Lined and gray, very short of money, somewhat shabby and down-at-heel, except for Arif without friends, suspected by Turks and English alike, he either wandered aimlessly in the streets or sat in the cafés, sullen, nerveless, without hope or plans.

PART FIVE

XXIII

SUDDENLY once more Fate gave Mustafa Kemal a full hand of cards. As Liman von Sanders had said of him, he had that essential qualification of a great commander—Luck, and again Luck. He had also the second great qualification of a great commander—the power to seize his Luck and use it.

The Sultan and the English had decided that the first movements of resistance in Anatolia must be checked at once. Some one must go as the Sultan's representative to deal with the situation on the spot, enforce the delivery of arms, the disbanding of troops and stop the meetings of the local committees of Union and Progress.

The Sultan wished to nominate Mustafa Kemal. The English military authorities objected; he was a dangerous and capable man; they remembered his attitude over Alexandretta. The English High Commissioner was of the same opinion.

Damad Ferid, the Grand Vizier, however, was prepared to vouch for him. "All the troubles in the Interior of the country are due," he said, "not to any popular sentiment but to the machinations of the accursed Committee of Union and Progress, to Enver's gang of villains. The Turks themselves want peace. Mustafa Kemal was nominally a member of the Committee; in reality he is known as its most determined opponent. He has a great reputation in the country. He is a gentleman. He can be trusted. He is clearly the man to go."

For several days the decision hung in the balance—between arrest and deportation or to go to Anatolia as the Sultan's representative. At last Damad Ferid persuaded the English. Mustafa Kemal was taken off the list for arrest. He was already A.D.C. to the Sultan. He was now appointed the Inspector-General of the Northern Area and Governor-General of the Eastern Provinces.

Though unaware of the danger he had been in, Mustafa Kemal, the minute he received the offer, saw his chance. His depression fell from him like scales; his vitality returned and with it his health. Keeping his own counsel, trusting no one but Arif with his ideas, agreeing heartily with the instructions that Damad Ferid outlined for him, he began to plan: as the Sultan's representative he would have an unquestionable standing in Anatolia among the Turks; he would pretend that he had been sent to save them from the English, he would organize resistance; he would yet save Turkey.

He was allowed to re-draft his instructions so as to give him wider powers. With Ismet and Fevzi at the War Office he arranged a secret code and agents.

After that he wasted no time. He hurried up to the house in the rue Aqaretler to say good-by to his mother. Zubeida had grown almost blind. With trembling old fingers she stroked his face, kissed him, crying a little as she always did when he left her, and let him go with a blessing. Even to Zubeida he did not this time confide his plans and hopes.

The same evening he took passage on a tramp steamer and sailed up the Bosphorus for the Black Sea coast, taking with him Arif and Colonel Refet, who had been nominated to Sivas to command the 3rd Army Corps.

Rauf came to see them off and brought the news that the Allied conference in Paris had sent Greek troops to occupy the town of Smyrna. It was clear that the enemy had condemned Turkey to death. Resistance, not parleying with the enemy, was the only hope.

At midnight the same night the Grand Vizier asked urgently to see a representative of the English High Commissioner at once. He explained that the Sultan had changed his mind: new information had come in showing that Mustafa Kemal intended to raise trouble in the Interior: he must be stopped at all costs.

Refet.

Orders were issued to intercept and bring him back, but the organization of the Occupation by the Allies was already complicated and worm-eaten with international jealousies: the English, French and Italians all had a hand in the controlling of passenger ships: the duties of the army and navy were not clearly defined. The orders were first hung up and eventually pigeon-holed. Mustafa Kemal had got away only by a few hours.

On that journey Mustafa Kemal let himself go. He talked unceasingly: his ideas, his ambitions, his plans, poured out of him. Refet listened.

He was the complete opposite to Mustafa Kemal. He was a swaggering gallant cavalry officer. He radiated good nature and humor. He had a great reputation for bravery: he had led the Macedonian gendarmerie in the Salonika revolution, and he had defended Gaza in a long siege against the English. Small and dapper, always well-dressed, his riding-boots of best patent-leather, his uniform well-cut, he was usually talking like an excited boy with his head moving, his hands waving, and his eyes full of laughter.

Now for once he sat listening. He realized Mustafa Kemal's outstanding abilities, his qualifications as a leader in a desperate venture. He was fully in agreement with his determination to organize resistance to the foreigner, but as he listened he realized that behind all was Mustafa Kemal's absorbing egoism and his determination to hold power at all costs. He decided to stand by Mustafa Kemal, but always he would watch him.

After a rough journey, on the 19th of May, 1919, they landed in a heavy storm at the Black Sea port of Samsun.

XXIV

SAMSUN was held by English troops. An English intelligence officer pried into all that Mustafa Kemal did. The local Greeks and Armenians reported his every move, his interveiws, even his telephone calls. The Turks were half afraid to talk with him.

Making an excuse he moved his headquarters to Kavsa, and then to Amassia—a town farther inland and on the main road junction between the east and west of Turkey.

Here at last he was free of the accursed English. He opened his shoulders with a sigh of relief and put out both hands to take a grip.

For six months he had sat in Constantinople boiling with rage, forced to remain passive and to hold himself in while the city writhed under the heel of the victorious Allies. For six months he had been forced to watch the politicians and officials, led by the Sultan and Damad Ferid, cringe and crawl before the English. His high pride as a Turk had been torn down to the quick. Grinding his teeth, storing up the bile of a great hatred, he had sat powerless.

Now he could act. From the drab months of sour inaction he reacted with tremendous energy. Resistance to the enemy and the accursed English! He must organize resistance. The first thing was to establish his standing with the army. From Amassia he telephoned and telegraphed out for reports from all over the country.

The position was simple: Turkey lay prostrate in defeat; she had no active power of military resistance. There were four army corps in Anatolia and one in Europe on the other side of Constantinople. Of these, four were mere skeletons: the headquarters staff remained, but the men had been disbanded and the arms had been collected in depots and were being handed over to the English. Only in the east the army corps at Diarbekir under Kiazim Kara Bekir still existed. But in front of Smyrna the mountains were full of guerrilla bands sworn to resist the invading Greeks. Rauf had resigned his post as Minister of Marine and was organizing these bands.

Mustafa Kemal realized that he must get the backing of the army corps commanders. He called Refet back from Sivas. In Angora with the 20th Army Corps was Ali Fuad. He invited Ali Fuad to meet him in Amassia. Ali Fuad came bringing with him Rauf.

The meeting was secret. Arif kept notes of what was said. Mustafa Kemal put forward his views. All agreed that resistance was their only hope. They sketched out a joint plan of action. In front of Smyrna they must raise more irregular bands to harry and hold up the Greeks. Covered by these they must, on the old army framework, build up a new national army. All through the country they must create local centers for enlisting men and collecting arms. They would find it difficult. They must be cautious, or the English would crush them at the beginning. From the Sultan and the Central Government they would get no help. The people throughout the country were tired out and would not rouse easily.

All the scattered organizations for resistance must be concentrated under one control: Ali Fuad was to command all in the west; Kiazim Kara Bekir all in the east; Mustafa Kemal to be at the center.

"Further," said Mustafa Kemal, "as the Sultan and the Central Government are in enemy hands, we must set up some temporary government here in Anatolia."

As soon as Mustafa Kemal touched politics the others hesitated and began to doubt him. They knew his revolutionary outlook. Rauf was against anything which could hurt the Sultan-Caliph or the Central Government in Constantinople. Ali Fuad was shrewd and cautious and not prepared to accept Mustafa Kemal as his senior at once. Refet suspected Mustafa Kemal. He remembered that flood of talk on the ship in which Mustafa Kemal had revealed his ambitions, his revolutionary ideas, his complete lack of respect for all traditional loyalties.

Mustafa Kemal used all his persuasive power to win them over. It was vital that he should have their support. Rauf and Ali Fuad agreed. Refet still hesitated; he saw no use in creating a separate government in Anatolia. At last, against his better judgment, he agreed.

They decided that a congress of delegates to represent all Turkey be called to Sivas as quickly as possible. From Diarbekir Kiazim Kara Bekir, from Adrianople Jaffar Tayar, and from Konia the general in command telegraphed that they agreed with these decisions. Mustafa Kemal had won the first round of the fight. He had the army leaders with him.

At once he set out to raise the country. He toured the villages, harangued the officials, collected up the officers who had become unemployed as the army was disbanded. Always and everywhere he preached resistance to the accursed English. The enemy had decided to destroy Turkey, their Turkey, to break it up; they were planning to make a Greek State round Samsun; all the villages round were full of the agents of the Greek patriarch; the Sultan, their Padishah, was helpless—a captive in English hands; the Sultan had sent him, Mustafa Kemal, to save them: but they, the Turks, must save themselves; no good sitting down and hoping for outside help; arm, volunteer for the new national army, resist; so only could they save themselves from destruction and protect their wives and homes from dishonor.

In each village he appointed representatives to form a committee and become a center of resistance.

It was heavy work. The people were worn out, utterly crushed. They had given up all hope; the idea of any resistance, or even protest, was gone. They had sunk into a dull lethargy after years of decimating wars and continuous defeat. All they wanted was peace and time to live their quiet lives and harvest their fields.

But as they listened to Mustafa Kemal they woke slowly. News was coming in from Smyrna that the Greeks were burning the villages and massacring Turks. Mustafa Kemal fanned on the poor dull embers of anger and they came to life. A flame of hatred ran through the villages stinging the people into a new energy. The officers, to a man, came in. Mustafa Kemal worked on their enthusiasm and sent them out to rouse more villages.

Leaving Amassia he made eastwards to Erzerum. Here his work was easier. In the Caucasus, out of the country evacuated by the Russians after their Revolution, the English had created an Armenian Republic with a frontier joining that of Turkey. They had promised the new republic that when peace was imposed on Turkey the Eastern Provinces of Turkey round Erzerum should be made part of the Armenian Republic.

To the local Turks this meant annihilation. They swore to fight or be wiped out before they would be ruled by Armenians. Moreover Kiazim Kara Bekir and his regular troops were handy and gave them confidence; and the English were far away.

They listened eagerly to Mustafa Kemal. Everywhere he went he electrified the people to hope and action. The men came crowding back to the colors, a ragged riff-raff of good and bad alike. One corporal in a village outside Angora collected three hundred men, drilled them and marched them in to the commander at Angora. In many places the depots under English and French guards were raided and the arms carried away and stored in the mountains, ready for use.

From Erzerum, in the name of the Sultan, Mustafa Kemal sent out orders to the military commanders to delay the handing over of arms to the English and to call back the men to the colors. He instructed the civil authorities to form local committees in the towns and villages for enlisting volunteers, to hold meetings of protest against the occupation of Smyrna, to divert the taxes and make forced collections from the well-to-do merchants.

News of these activities went quickly to Constantinople. The English threatened reprisals. The Sultan flew into a rage: resistance was folly; it was useless and would merely force the Allies to smash Turkey completely; he had sent Mustafa Kemal to the Interior to stop resistance, and now Mustafa Kemal was even using His name to encourage resistance. He had suspected as much. He ordered Mustafa Kemal to be recalled to report.

As soon as he got the orders Mustafa Kemal went to the telegraph office and sent a long, urgent and personal telegram to the Sultan, begging him as the Padishah, the Sovereign and the Leader of his people, to come out and lead them against the foreign enemy. All through that night he waited by the machine for the reply.

At dawn came a peremptory order for his return. He refused categorically.

"I shall stay in Anatolia," he telegraphed, "until the nation has won its independence."

The Sultan dismissed him from his command and notified all civil and military authorities to refuse to accept his orders. Mustafa Kemal resigned his commission in the army.

He called his supporters and the army commanders.

"We are at the parting of the ways," he said. "If we go forward we do so relying on ourselves alone. The Central Government will be against us. It may mean civil war. We shall have to face great risks and make great sacrifices. Once started no one must desert, no one look back or regret.

"You must decide, and you must choose a leader. For success one thing is vital—you must have one man at the head, one man to lead this movement, and one man only.

"If you choose me, you will have to share my fate. I am now a mere civilian. I shall certainly be declared a rebel. One condition I make, and that is that my orders are implicitly obeyed as if I were still your military commander."

One and all they decided to continue. They chose Mustafa Kemal as their leader and accepted his condition, making a condition also that he should do nothing which might injure the Sultan.

This he accepted.

"The Sultan is in the hands of the enemy and guided by bad advisers," he said. "We must resist His Majesty's advisers and the foreigners."

Promises were, for Mustafa Kemal, always a means to an end and lightly used.

He had thrown down the gantlet to the foreign enemy and the Sultan.

XXV

ALREADY Mustafa Kemal had sent out invitations for the Congress.

"The country is threatened," he had telegraphed to all districts. "The Central Government is no longer capable of carrying out its functions. The independence of our land can only be preserved by the will and energy of the nation. It has been resolved to hold a Congress in Sivas to discuss ways and means. Each district may send three delegates. Act with all secrecy."

His own position was, however, undefined. Until that Congress sat he had no official position: he was a civilian without powers. The massed weight of tradition and of the legal Government was against him. In many towns the civil authorities refused to accept his orders. He had with him, however, the army commanders, the officers generally and all the new and growing centers which were organizing resistance.

But he must have some sort of official standing. In consultation with Kiazim Kara Bekir he called the military leaders and the delegates of the neighboring districts to a conference in Erzerum.

He had a difficult task. Many of those who came were opposed to his ideas, opposed also to his assumption of authority. They were split up by a hundred little jealousies. With steady patience, sitting among them as an equal, Mustafa Kemal began to persuade them to his views; bit by bit he began to establish his personal leadership, but always he met doubt and suspicion.

In the middle of the discussions came orders from the Central Government in Constantinople instructing Kiazim Kara Bekir to arrest Mustafa Kemal and close the conference, and pack the delegates off to their homes.

The future lay in the hands of Kiazim Kara Bekir. The only regular force in Turkey was under his command. After Mustafa Kemal in 1917 had handed over to him the command of the Caucasus Army he had advanced, chasing the demoralized Russians in front of him right up the Caucasus. He had been uniformly successful when every other Turkish army was being defeated.

Heavy-built, slow in mind and action, kindly yet a hard disciplinarian, just and honest, a man of his word, very conservative by instinct and a lover of tradition, he was the old type of Turkish general and popular with his troops. He might if he wished take the lead, but he had no such ambition.

He hesitated. He had already given his word to Mustafa Kemal to stand with him and Rauf. His loyalty to the Sultan and the Central Government urged him to carry out the orders for arrest. He made no secret of the orders he had received nor of his dilemma.

It was now a tussle between two personalities: Kiazim, solid and honest; Mustafa Kemal subtle and overwhelming in one. Into persuading Kiazim, Mustafa Kemal threw his whole soul—he argued and cajoled as he had never done before. If he failed now, he was beaten. Whatever happened he was resolved never to be arrested and handed back to the Sultan and the English to be shut away in Malta in a prison cell, and perhaps hanged. The memory of the days in the Red Prison came back to him, nauseating him. Better be dead than that. He had arranged with Arif that if he failed with Kiazim, they would make a run for it; and if cornered, they would fight until killed. They must never be captured.

With all the subtlety in his character he argued with Kiazim, using the other's point of view. They must all be loyal, he said, but their loyalty was to Turkey; the Sultan and the Central Government were captives in the hands of the foreign enemy, hence the power had passed back to the people; all power was with the people, and the people must save themselves; the orders from Constantinople were in fact not from the Sultan but from the English and not legal; the only legal power was vested in the conference of representatives now sitting, and would be vested in the Congress at Sivas as soon as it sat.

He led slow-witted Kiazim through a maze of philosophical political discussion. Then he appealed to him as a comrade, and then reminded him of his promise of support.

Kiazim Kara Bekir made up his mind slowly, but once it was done he would not change or go back. He decided to stand with Mustafa Kemal, Rauf and the People.

The conference, following his lead and roused to anger by the orders of the Central Government against themselves, voted solidly "to organize resistance to the occupation and interference of the foreigner; to form a provisional government to carry on the affairs of state, if the Central Government be unable or unwilling."

They elected an executive committee to carry on and to place their views before the coming Congress at Sivas. They made Mustafa Kemal chairman with Rauf to help him. They also elected Mustafa Kemal delegate for Erzerum.

Mustafa Kemal had won the second big round of the fight. He had a recognized position, with Kiazim Kara Bekir and his troops behind him.

XXVI

To the Congress at Sivas the delegates came from all Turkey. They came secretly, in disguise, by paths over the mountains and under cover of night. The Central Government had ordered the police to intercept them. Mustafa Kemal himself only escaped arrest by a few hours. In Erzerum and Sivas, where there were regular troops, he was safe, but a party of gendarmes waited on the road to intercept him. He was warned in time, detoured into the mountains and got safely to Sivas.

The delegates had no clear aims. They had endless discussions without result. Many of them considered armed resistance to the English impossible. Very few were prepared to oppose the Central Government or to risk civil war.

Mustafa Kemal worked among them continuously with a patience that was not part of his character. When he wished he could be magnetically pleasant and companionable. He knew that all depended on his success here. He would sit among the delegates, argue and talk with them by the hour; now with subtle arguments, now with sweeping enthusiasm that carried them with him, wearing opposition down with a torrent of words. To save Turkey was his mission, and his belief in that mission gave him eloquence.

Gradually, as in Erzerum, he established his personal leadership. One by one the opposition came to his views; but still the majority distrusted him. Even Rauf and Kiazim Kara Bekir, considering that he was taking too much on himself, tried to persuade him not to stand for the chairmanship of the Congress.

It made no difference. Surely and relentlessly he won his way. Clear-headed, he knew what he wanted and he made straight for it. Even those who distrusted him fell under his spell. His personality dominated the Congress.

And again his enemies in Stambul helped him. In the middle of the session an order from the Central Government in Constantinople to Ali Ghalib, the Governor of Malatia, was intercepted. Malatia was a district to the south of Sivas in the country of the Kurds. The order instructed Ali Ghalib to raise a levy of Kurdish tribesmen, raid Sivas and arrest the delegates to the Congress. The Sultan believed he could rely on the religious fanaticism and the loyalty of the Kurds.

The Congress roused itself angrily. To order Kurdish tribesmen to arrest them was the last of insults! They instructed Mustafa Kemal to send regular troops to Malatia. Mustafa Kemal mounted an infantry regiment on mules and donkeys and sent them post haste. They intercepted the Kurds, smashed them before they were ready and chased out Ali Ghalib.

Then Mustafa Kemal carried all before him. He had the power of the orator to whip a little anger into a great hatred. He seized the opportunity. The deputies answered his lead. They proclaimed the Congress as the voice of the people. They voted solidly for resistance to the foreigner.

They drafted out and passed the terms of peace for which they would fight and named it "The National Pact." They swore never to make peace until the National Pact was accepted by the enemy.

They elected an executive committee to act as a provisional government and independent of the Central Government in Stambul. Of this executive committee they made Mustafa Kemal chairman.

The correspondence with Ali Ghalib was captured, and proved without doubt that Damad Ferid, the Grand Vizier, had ordered the Kurdish raid. The Congress sent an ultimatum to Constantinople that Damad Ferid must be dismissed and elections for a Parliament held forthwith.

When no reply came, Mustafa Kemal took control. He ordered the military authorities to take over the telegraphs and cut off Constantinople from the rest of the country, to divert the revenue and all correspondence to him and to replace the civilian officials where necessary with men they could trust.

The Sultan gave way, dismissed Damad Ferid, replaced him by Ali Riza, an old man of no value, and ordered elections. The elections gave the Congress a big majority in the new Parliament.

The Congress itself moved to the town of Angora, which was more in the center of the country. Mustafa Kemal had been elected deputy for Erzerum.

To Angora came many of the newly elected deputies to the Parliament, for a preliminary discussion. At the first meeting came up the motion that the Parliament should sit in Constantinople and that the Congress should now be dissolved.

Mustafa Kemal opposed both ideas vehemently. The Congress must continue to exist, until it was seen how the

Parliament fared. As to going to Constantinople, that he considered was folly.

"You will be under the foreigner," he said. "The English are still in control. You will be interfered with, probably arrested. The Parliament should sit here in Angora, where it will be free and independent."

This time he was defeated. One and all the deputies, glad to be legally elected, relieved that they had ceased to be rebels, were determined to sit in the proper Parliament House in the Capital under the sanction of the legal sovereign, the Sultan.

Failing to get his way, Mustafa Kemal tried to coach the deputies in their duties and line of action, but they resented his interference and his assumption of superiority. The old jealousies and dislikes of him revived.

With a sneer Mustafa Kemal watched them all stream gayly off back to Constantinople, with Rauf leading the way.

He had decided not to take his seat. He would not be party to this folly. He remained in Angora almost alone. The center of action had passed from Angora to Constantinople, the leadership from Mustafa Kemal to Rauf. Everywhere among the deputies, in the country districts, in Angora, even in the army, there was a reaction to the Sultan and the Central Government, a desire to avoid quarrels between Turk and Turk, and to show a united front under the legal sovereign. It seemed as if the Sultan had won and Mustafa Kemal had lost.

But Mustafa Kemal was unmoved. He had made up his mind. He did not change, hesitate or falter. He would not be deviated. Resistance by force to the foreigner was the only hope. He knew the Sultan: Vaheddin would never have the courage to use force against the English; moreover, it would be quite impossible from Constantinople. The English were in complete control there.

He was convinced that the Parliament sitting in Constantinople must fail. So sure was he that the deputies would all come hurrying back to him that he tried to be elected President of the Chamber in their absence, so that he would be able to deal with the crisis when it arrived. He failed, but with increased energy he pressed on, preparing armed resistance, collecting men and arms, directing the drilling and organizing.

XXVII

THE deputies met joyfully in Constantinople. They sent a message of loyalty to the Sultan and set to work early in January, 1920.

But they were in no complaisant mood. They were there to defend the rights of Turkey. Led by Rauf, bluff and hearty as ever, they refused all attempts at dictation either by the Sultan or the English. The English demanded immediate obedience of all orders; they were ignored. The allied commander demanded the dismissal of the Minister for War; when the Sultan agreed the deputies protested and, as a reply, passed and published the National Pact which they had prepared at the Erzerum conference. It laid down the principles on which they would agree to peace—a Turkey free and independent within certain stated frontiers. It was a direct challenge to the victorious enemy and the Army of Occupation.

When the English did nothing, the deputies grew more stiff-necked, for everywhere events were moving in their favor. In North Syria the local Turks had attacked the French and driven them back; the French garrisons in Urfa and Aintab were besieged; the English were withdrawing in all directions, from the Caucasus and the Crimea, and from Anatolia, as they demobilized their army.

All through the country the Turks were refusing to carry out the orders of the Army of Occupation. Control officers reported that they were being ignored and sometimes insulted; arms were not being delivered, troops were being called up and drilled, the terms of the Armistice were being broken. A party of Turks had raided a dump in Gallipoli, carried off the French guard and the arms, and could not be arrested and punished.

The English decided that some drastic and exemplary action must be taken as a punishment, but as the last of the English troops were being withdrawn from the Interior of the country the only military action possible was in Constantinople itself. On the 16th March they formally occupied Constantinople, arrested some of the deputies, including Rauf and Fethi and other leading *Nationalists*—as they were now called—deported them to an internment camp in Malta, and closed the Parliament House.

All the leading Turks in Constantinople hid or escaped into Anatolia. Ismet and Fevzi from the War Office, Halideh the woman writer and Adnan, her husband, escaped at once and made for Angora.

The Sultan followed up this blow. He was determined to finish the rebels. The terms of the Armistice and the Allied Control forbade him to use regular troops. He had ordered Sulyman Shevkat Pasha, the Minister of War, to prepare an irregular force under the name of the "Caliph's Army." Now he sent it out with his blessing.

Throughout all Turkey he summoned the priests to call out the people. He sent his agents through the villages to rouse his subjects to stand by the Caliph and the Throne.

Everywhere the people replied. In scattered groups they

rose for the Sultan. From end to end Turkey was torn in the hideous nightmare of civil war. Town was divided against town, family against family, brother against brother and father against son. Revolts flared up without warning, now in one area, now in another. The Sultan's men raised them. Mustafa Kemal's men stamped them down with merciless ferocity. Turk killed Turk, stoned each other, flogged, tortured, hanged, even crucified each other in the wild hatred of brother fighting brother.

In Konia the Sultan's men tore out the toe-nails of the officers sent to them by Mustafa Kemal, and then dragged them at the tails of their horses. Mustafa Kemal's men took revenge by shooting the leading men in Konia.

The Sultan had called back Damad Ferid, ejected from his service all who sympathized with the Nationalists, issued more proclamations calling on all loyal subjects to rise to his help against the traitors of Angora, and finally, by a solemn decree, he outlawed Mustafa Kemal and those round him, excommunicated them and condemned them to death, announcing that whoever killed them would perform a sacred duty and would be rewarded in this world and the next.

The news came to Angora on a late spring evening when the cold of winter was still in the air. Mustafa Kemal was sitting in the hall of the Agricultural School, a gaunt stone building on the hills outside the town. Below it lay the remains of a model farm but all had been deserted and neglected for several years.

He was sitting by the window. Beside him were Halideh Edib with her husband, Adnan, and Ali Fuad. Ismet was leaning by a window looking out.

The sun had set and the gray light was creeping up over the great bare Anatolian plains below them. The char-

117

coal in the brazier was covered with ash, and no one moved to stir it. The corners of the hall were in gray shadow.

The others talked in low tones of the news. Now one or another would look suddenly over his shoulder as if danger stood there: the danger of a Sultan's agent, or a religious fanatic determined on sacred murder. In every shadow there lurked danger. They were outcasts condemned to death: it would be a virtuous act to kill them. The thought weighed heavily on them.

All the news was bad. The Greeks were advancing again from Smyrna, burning, murdering and taking over the country. The French too had gained some success in the south. The Sultan's agents had raised the Kurds to revolt in the east. The civil war was closing all round them. It was like a smoldering fire: without warning it would burst out in a new place—now in one area, now in another. There was a new rising at Bolu. It had spread rapidly, and the insurgents were within a few miles of Angora itself. Several times the headquarters' telegraph wires had been cut. Two officers sent to reason with the people had been stoned, dragged to prison and then sent to Constantinople to be hanged as traitors. A division which had been sent to quell the rising had dispersed. The 24th Division sent to Hendek had been ambushed and wiped out.

The Caliph's army was succeeding. It had control of Ismid. It had captured Bighar and was in front of the city of Brusa. Konia, Ada Bazar and a dozen other towns had declared for the Sultan. Among their own troops and supporters there was disaffection. The 15th Division in Samsun was disloyal. Kiazim Kara Bekir was disgruntled and the eastern counties talked of independent action. The irregular bands in the hills before Smyrna were out of hand and truculent: Edhem the Circassian, one of their leaders, was acting as if he was an independent sovereign. There was a

118

wave of defeatism. Only that day a delegation of the women of Angora had been up to the school.

"Our men were killed in the Dardanelles," they had said. "Why should we again be martyred in Angora because the English are in Constantinople? Let Constantinople look after itself. This fight is hopeless. We need peace."

Deep in a chair Mustafa Kemal sat silent, his gray cloak drawn round him, his gray astrakhan fez pushed forward on his forehead, his chin on his chest, his face gray and lined, his eyes sightless. He was a general without an army: the head of a provisional government without money, power, or any of the machinery of government. He had made fine plans to release Turkey from the foreigners and make her great and independent. She was torn with civil war, and the foreigner had her still in his grip. All for which he had worked, all his fine plans were turned to ashes. He was himself no more than a proscribed and hunted rebel with a price on his head.

Outside it was dark. Beyond the acacia trees, in the cold sky over the black shadow of the western mountains, hung low the silver crescent of a new moon. In the farm below Karabash, the great gray wolf-hound was baying to the moon.

To the sound Mustafa Kemal stirred, shook himself like a wild animal and snarled—the Gray Wolf of Angora snarled.

He stood up. He would fight. The despair fell from him. He was alive, vibrating. His spirit filled the room and electrified the others to new hope.

He called for lights to shut out the shadows, for Arif, for his staff, for some one to take down orders and some one to rekindle the dead brazier. He would fight. He would yet save Turkey and make her great and free.

PART SIX

===

XXVIII

MUSTAFA KEMAL fought with his back to the wall. He was often ill: the kidney trouble gave him acute pain at times, with frequent fevers. He lived on in constant danger of his life. The villages round Angora were one by one joining the Caliph's army. At any moment there might be a rising in Angora itself, or a sudden raid on the School, and they would all be dragged out and murdered. A sentry reported suspicious characters moving round at night. One morning the great watch-dog, Karabash, was found poisoned. Mustafa Kemal and Arif slept in their clothes: Arif slept in the evening, and kept watch while Mustafa Kemal slept in the early hours of the morning. In the courtyard below, their horses stood ready saddled, with the bridles handy and the girths only needing to be tightened, all prepared for a dash to Sivas at a minute's notice. Halideh had learnt to use a revolver; Adnan carried poison: he would rather use poison than face the death by torture that the Caliph's men gave to all those they captured.

. . . . .

Living at top pressure, never relaxed, worn, tired and ill, Mustafa Kemal worked all day and far into each night at his desk in a corner of the main hall by the yellow light of an oil lamp, discussing problems, listening to reports and giving orders. Always the dispatches were the same: town after town reported that the Caliph's army had taken possession; failure everywhere. Frequently he called for black coffee and then, lighting another of the innumerable cigarettes, he smoked furiously, until the ash-trays were piled high with stubs.

Behind Mustafa Kemal, dressed in black, with his hands behind his back, Ismet walked steadily up and down the whole night through, now looking out of the window, now going across to the desk to consult with Mustafa Kemal on some subject. He rarely sat down. In another room Fevzi was solidly at work.

Mustafa Kemal fought like some royal animal driven into a corner. He neither asked nor showed pity. He condemned to death any of the Sultan's men who fell into his hands. To an American general who asked him what he would do if the Nationalists failed he replied with a snarl:

"A nation which makes the ultimate sacrifices for life and independence does not fail. Failure means the Nation is dead."

But he knew that the nation was not dead, but alive. This faith in the nation filled him, vibrated through him, pulsed through his every word, his orders, his speeches. He roused the Nationalists to a new enthusiasm.

"Win or be wiped out in the attempt," he called to them, and they roared back their applause, girded up their loins and swept all before them.

They held up the Greek advance. They stamped out ruthlessly the disconnected risings of the Sultan's men and freed Angora of danger. They assaulted Marash, killed the French garrison and destroyed the Armenians they had enlisted. They smashed the Kurds. They swept the Italian detachments off the railway by Konia. They attacked the English garrison on the main railway junction in Eshi Shehir, chased it out and harried it back to the sea. They arrested all the Allied control officers they could lay hands on in the Interior and held them as hostages against the deputies interned in Malta.

News of the occupation of Constantinople, the arrests, the forced closing of the Parliament and that the Sultan and the Constantinople Government had been behind the English, had reached the villages. The reaction in favor of the Sultan and the Central Government disappeared; the national pride asserted itself; public opinion swung to the Nationalists; the drag of defeatism was swept away in a wave of angry enthusiasm. Every Turk realized that nothing more could be done in Constantinople as long as the English were in control. It was useless to trust in the Sultan or the Central Government. Mustafa Kemal had been right: they must save themselves and by armed resistance rescue Turkey from the foreigner.

Men and women of all types and classes came hurrying in to volunteer: peasant women to carry ammunition and arms, women of good family to nurse and make uniforms. One and all they looked to Mustafa Kemal.

Many of the Caliph's army deserted; others refused to fight and killed their leaders. From Constantinople there came deputies who had escaped arrest, staff officers, generals, ministers, civilians rich and poor, as fast as they could escape by secret ways and in disguises through the line of English pickets round the city.

Mustafa Kemal had already issued writs for a new Parliament to sit in Angora.

Those deputies who had escaped, together with the President of the Parliament, reopened in Angora the Parliament closed by force in Constantinople and confirmed the issue of the writs.

The deputies from this new election came hurrying to Angora full of fighting spirit. They named themselves the Grand National Assembly, voted themselves the legally constituted Government of Turkey and unanimously elected Mustafa Kemal as President of the Assembly.

Yesterday Mustafa Kemal had been alone and deserted; to-day he was the acknowledged leader surrounded with supporters.

As President of the Assembly he replied haughtily to a message from the President of the French Republic:

"The Grand National Assembly sitting in Angora will preside over the destiny of Turkey, as long as the capital is in the hands of the foreigner.

"It has appointed an Executive Council, which has taken in hand the government of the country.

"Constantinople, the Sultan and the Government being in the hands of the enemy, all orders from there are automatically null and void. The nation's rights have been violated.

"The Turkish nation, though calm, is determined to maintain its right as a sovereign independent State. It desires to conclude a fair and honorable peace, but it will only do so through its own accredited representatives."

These were fine defiant phrases from the newly-elected head of the temporary government of a country lately smashed to pieces in war, still torn by civil war and occupied by the enemy. Fine defiant phrases born of a great faith.

And with that faith there was in Mustafa Kemal a great pride, pride in being a Turk and in his Turkey—the pride of a ruling race with a great history behind it. It angered him, as it had done in Germany, to hear Turks slighted. When there was read to him a speech by Lord Grey which spoke of the Turks with the high indulgent patronage of a superior being, he burst out in a rage, his voice became harsh and loud with indignation.

"They, these English, shall know that we are as good as

they are! They shall treat us as equals! Never will we bow our heads to them! To our last man we will stand against them, until we break their civilization on their heads!"

XXIX

AWAY in Paris, sitting majestically round the Peace Conference table, surrounded by their staffs, reported on daily by five hundred journalists, the Allied statesmen—President Wilson, Lloyd George, Clemenceau—planned the future of the world, issued their ponderous orders as if they were gods.

They turned uneasily. Something unusual was happening in Turkey.

"What is all this?" they asked irritably. "Turkey was beaten in the World War. She was finished."

They had heard of Mustafa Kemal, a general of some importance in the Dardanelles, but an unpleasant adventurer, a rebel against the Sultan, living somewhere up in the mountains of the Interior of Turkey.

Under pressure from their advisers they prepared a peace treaty for Turkey, called in the Treaty of Sèvres and published its terms.

The publication of the terms of the Treaty of Sèvres had an instantaneous effect. They were, if accepted, the death sentence of Turkey.

Anatolia, with Smyrna cut out, was to be left to the Turks, but every detail of their lives was to be supervised. Their finances were to be strictly controlled. There were to be Commissions to disband the Turkish army and control a new volunteer force and gendarmerie, to look after the taxes, the customs, the forest guards, the police. While left nominally with sovereign rights, the Turks were to be tied hand and foot.

At once every Turk worth his salt became a Nationalist. For five hundred years they had been a ruling people; they would never be slaves. They forgot their old jealousies, closed up their ranks and fell in solidly behind Mustafa Kemal. What he had preached had come true.

At his call they set their teeth. They smashed what was left of the Caliph's army, cleared up the areas in revolt against Angora and finished off the civil war. They swore vengeance on Damad Ferid and the Sultan's advisers who would not oppose the treaty. They proclaimed Mustafa Kemal as the leader: instead of Nationalists they called themselves "Kemalists." They set out to beat the Greeks and the Allies who were behind them.

Mustafa Kemal was ready. He formed a fighting cabinet—Bekir Sami, Adnan, Fevzi, who was to organize the national defense, and especially to organize ammunition and supplies, Ismet as Chief of the Staff. Rauf, Fethi and the other leaders were locked away in the English prison in Malta.

In the south the local Turks had attacked Bozanti and forced the French to retire and to sign an armistice.

In the east Kiazim Kara Bekir had cleared the frontier of Armenians, and made all safe.

Now Mustafa Kemal gave orders to close in on Constantinople itself. Except for the Greeks before Smyrna and the Allied forces in and round Constantinople there were no enemy forces left in Turkey.

From the European side General Jaffar Tayar moved his Turkish troops forward. From the Asiatic side Ali Fuad attacked Ismid, drove in the outposts of the Sultan's supporters and came face to face with the English.

Seeing that they held only the southern shore, Ali Fuad sent his irregular cavalry round their flank straight at the Bosphorus. They raided and burnt villages only one mile away across the water from the offices of the Allied Commander-in-Chief. Constantinople, with the so-called Allied Army of Occupation, and the Allied High Commissioners representing the Great Victorious Powers were open to direct attack. The English troops before Ismid were too few to hold back the Turks.

The Allies were helpless. The Allied statesmen in Paris woke to find that they were without force to back their mighty decisions. One and all, every country of Europe was caught in the sucking backwash of a great post-war reaction. They had all demobilized their armies. Italy was twisted in a Bolshevic revolution; France had her hands full in Syria and she was terrified still of Germany; the British Empire, buffeted by great blows, was rocking to its foundations, civil war in Ireland, rebellion in Mesopotamia and India, war with Afghanistan. America refused to be involved. The Allies had not one soldier to spare to send to Turkey. They must fight or run, and they were neither willing nor able to fight.

The Allied army in Constantinople had been reduced to a few thousand men. It was as unprotected as a hedgehog with its bristles gone. The Allied Commander had made all preparations for an evacuation at the run: documents burnt, stores and ammunition destroyed, bridges mined ready to be blown up, transports standing by with steam up in the Golden Horn.

Mustafa Kemal stood triumphant. He had only to close his hands and his Turks would chase the victorious Allies "bag and baggage" out of Turkey.

He ordered up every available man. The English battle fleet opened fire on the Turks massing before Ismid. That could not check them permanently. It would only be a matter of days before they would be strong enough to push aside the weak line of defense, march on to Constantinople and cut off the Allied army.

XXX

PRESIDENT WILSON, Lloyd George and Clemenceau at the Conference Table in Paris looked round helplessly. At last they realized what was happening: the Turks, led by that rebel leader, that unpleasant adventurer, that Mustafa Kemal, were about to chase the Allies out of Turkey.

A handful of ragged Turks to chase out the Victorious Allies!

At all costs that must be stopped! Such a disaster might upset everything, rouse revolts elsewhere, interfere with all their fine plans for the readjustment of the world. At all costs it must be stopped! But how?

From the majestic setting of the Conference Table they looked round helplessly.

Beside them, quiet, plausible, always pleasant, stood Venizelos the Greek Premier. He had one central object in his life—to make Greece into an empire owning the rich sea coast of Anatolia, and with its capital in Constantinople.

He was a Cretan, and with the persistency of a Cretan he had worked for twenty years with this one object. He had created the Balkan League with Servia and Bulgaria, which had attacked Turkey in 1913; he had forced Greece to come in on the side of the victorious Allies in the World War.

His pleasant manners, his placid face, his eyeglasses, all gave him an air of childlike simplicity, but he judged and calculated shrewdly and far ahead.

In Smyrna he had concentrated a large army of the best Greek troops. From the English and the French he had bought their surplus war stores and equipped the Greeks with arms, guns, motor-lorries, the best transport and medical organization. He had sent the best officers to Smyrna and inspired the troops with his own spirit of imperial adventure.

For a reasonable reward—more territory in Asiatic and European Turkey—he offered to place the Greek army at the disposal of the Allies. He would send the Greeks forward and force the Turks to sign the peace treaty.

In haste Wilson, Lloyd George and Clemenceau accepted; they urged him to hurry his men into action and to save them from the Turks.

As Mustafa Kemal called up his men and massed them to attack Constantinople the Greeks advanced. On the 23rd June, 1920, they moved forward. On all fronts they met with easy success. In reality Mustafa Kemal had only a few regular troops; he had only had time to reorganize a few regiments and these were underfed, poorly equipped, and without artillery or transport. The rest of his force consisted of irregular bands. To the well-conditioned Greek army they could put up no resistance.

One Greek force marched into Thrace, surrounded and captured the 1st Army Corps with its commander, Jaffar Tayar, entered Adrianople and cleared all the country on the European side of Constantinople of Turkish troops.

Another force marched north from Smyrna, pushed back the Turks before Ismid and cleared all the approaches to Constantinople from the Asiatic side.

The main force advanced in two columns straight inland with the object of capturing the railway that runs from north to south across Anatolia and the main junctions of Eski Shehir and Afion. Half-way to the railway they received orders to halt and dig in: the Allies did not wish them to advance any farther. Up in the mountains, without roads to connect them, they were forced to make a new line. On this they stopped for six months and consolidated their position.

By the early autumn of 1920 the position had crystallized. In Constantinople was the Sultan and the Central Government still thundering out denunciations against the rebels, but quite powerless. There also sat the Allies with a handful of troops and almost equally powerless. Round them, protecting them, and their only protection on all sides, was a barrier of Greek troops.

Mustafa Kemal, leaving a screen of irregulars, had withdrawn all his regular troops back up into the mountains of the Interior.

PART SEVEN

===

XXXI

BEATEN and driven back ignominiously, the Turks
were sadly discouraged. From the regular units the
men began to desert. From the villages came up the old
weary cry for peace. In Angora the politicians called for the
punishment of those responsible—Ali Fuad who was in command of the western front, and Mustafa Kemal who was
responsible for all their troubles. A wave of despondency
swept back over the country. Depressed, weary and un-
nerved, the Turks called out again for peace at any price and
to stop the useless struggling against Fate.

In the face of defeat and despondency Mustafa Kemal
remained cool and steady. He was always liable to bouts
of black depression alternating with those of bounding enthusiasm, but they were not affected by outside events: they
came from within the man. He often even reacted against
events so that failure braced him up. Now it nerved him to
greater effort.

The Grand National Assembly held its meetings in one
of the class-rooms of the broken-down agricultural school.
Without hesitation Mustafa Kemal faced the noisy deputies
who were shouting for his blood.

As he stood before them he was not impressive to look
at; he would not have attracted attention in a crowd. A

medium-sized man with blue eyes and a set expression, his face gray and lined, and, in repose, dull in expression.

But as soon as he began to speak the uproar ceased. The personality of the man asserted itself. His voice in ordinary conversation somewhat hoarse and indistinct became resonant and clear, full of passion and strength, full of his belief in his mission and himself.

He reasoned with the deputies. He browbeat them. They were unreasonable he said: they could not expect the Turkish army to be ready to face the Greeks yet; the Sultan's advisers were to blame for defeat; they had allowed the old army to be disbanded and the munitions to be handed over to the enemy; they had started the civil war; the deputies must be reasonable and patient, giving him time for reorganization.

Then he woke in them their pride and gave them new hope. The issue now was clear: it was a straight fight with the Greeks: true the English were behind them, but only morally: the English would take no further active part in the fight.

"You," he cried, "you are Turks! Will you crawl to these Greeks who, yesterday, were your subjects and slaves! I cannot believe it. Combine, prepare and victory is ours."

The opposition died away. The Grand National Assembly was with him to a man.

Throughout the country he sent the same message. With untiring persistency he drove the army commanders to collect more men and arms and expand the regular army.

At those who advised him to make peace before it was too late he sneered: they were cowards.

To a representative of the French Government he was defiant:

"You may have Syria and Arabia," he said, "but keep your hands off Turkey. We claim the right of every nation, to be a free community within our national boundaries, not one inch more, but not an inch less."

With a fierce tenacity he kept his grip, goaded the Turks back to resistance when they would have sat down wearily with folded hands to await their fate.

XXXII

Now came a new danger from within. Hitherto the main fighting against the Greeks before Smyrna had been done by irregular bands, with the few regular units in reserve.

These bands had been recruited from all manners of men—villagers driven out by the Greeks, brigands, criminals, deserting soldiers, patriots. Without discipline, uniform or formation they acknowledged certain leaders. They carried on a guerrilla warfare of sudden raids and equally sudden retreats back into the mountains, which, while irritating to the enemy, could have no lasting military result.

The chief of the band-leaders was Edhem the Circassian. He had collected a large force of men with light artillery and machine-guns. This force he had named the "Green Army." He had made his headquarters in the town of Kutahia, and even published a newspaper full of articles of half-digested Bolshevism.

It was the Green Army which had faced the Greek attacks, stamped out the civil war, saved Angora from the insurgents and established the Angora Government.

From Kutahia, Edhem increased his influence out all across the country. He began to act independently of Angora, to collect taxes, to requisition supplies and horses, to issue orders to the civil authorities and punish them if these were neglected. He even condemned men to death, and, when he considered them traitors, crucified them on a hill-top outside the town. He oppressed the villagers unmercifully. When called to account by Angora, he claimed his right to independent action. He was fast becoming a brigand dictator, like some feudal baron of the Middle Ages.

As long as the irregulars were the only force in the field, there was nothing to be done, and Edhem waxed haughty and stiff-necked.

But under the skilled hands of Ismet and Fevzi the new regular army was growing fast. At every point it came into conflict with the irregulars: the officers could not agree with the band-leaders; they quarreled incessantly; the soldiers in the regular units had small pay and stern discipline; they deserted continually to the haphazard organization of Edhem where the pay was good and there was loot; when the regular officers claimed them back the band-leaders refused to give them up; the regular army leaders were determined to absorb the irregulars; the irregulars were equally determined to remain independent.

This conflict now came quickly to a head. Ali Fuad was in command of the western front. All his plans and dispositions were based on the use of irregulars. His regulars could only be used as a thin stiffening. His military outlook had become that of a guerrilla fighter, a band-leader. He even dressed like an irregular and carried a rifle slung over his shoulder. He worked hand in glove with Edhem, but Edhem was the stronger character and the real commander.

In October, on the advice of Edhem and against the advice of Ismet as Chief of the Staff, Ali Fuad made an attack on the Greeks and was severely defeated.

Mustafa Kemal decided that the time was ripe for a radical change. The irregulars must be absorbed and the regular army must take over. Using Ali Fuad's ill-timed attack as an excuse, he recalled him, replaced him with Ismet and Fevzi and Refet with the cavalry, and instructed Edhem to come under the orders of Ismet.

Edhem refused. He would not accept Ismet as his senior. He would not be interfered with. He boasted to his men that if ever he went to Angora "he would hang Mustafa Kemal before the door of the Assembly House."

Mustafa Kemal invited Edhem to Angora. He came haughtily, drove into the town in Mustafa Kemal's car—the only car in Angora—and swaggered pugnaciously into Mustafa Kemal's office.

The streets of Angora and the ante-room of the office were full of his bodyguard, wild-faced men with bandoliers and belts of ammunition slung across them, hooded caps with long tails drawn over their fezzes, and rifles carried ready in their hands. In their skin shoes they moved like soft-padded animals over the cobbles of the streets of the town.

Mustafa Kemal and Edhem faced each other. Edhem was a bony great giant. Before him Mustafa Kemal looked small and even mean, but they had much in common. Both had the same gray-white faces, the same cold, pale eyes which went gray in the sunlight, and the same fixed expression. Both were at heart rebels, brave men without scruples or pity. Both were masterful, used to obedience and determined to have power and to command.

Mustafa Kemal called for coffee and cigarettes, and with much flattery tried to persuade Edhem that it was for the good of Turkey that the regular army should take control. Edhem refused to agree. He and his men had borne the heat and the burden of the day, stood up to the Greeks, frightened the English; he would not give way to Ismet or Fevzi who had been sitting comfortably in Constantinople and came now at the eleventh hour to join up. Moreover, it was not for the good of Turkey: the guerrilla fighters were best; no regular army could be formed to stand up to the Greeks with the English behind them.

As he talked, he watched Mustafa Kemal; he was suspicious of him. Quick as a wild animal to scent danger, he wondered if he had walked into a trap. Under his hand, loose and ready for use, was his favorite revolver, embossed with silver and notched for each man he had killed. Mustafa Kemal saw the movement of the hand on the revolver and remained unmoved. These men were like two gray wolves maneuvering to attack.

"Let us take the train," said Mustafa Kemal. "Go down to Eski Shehir and talk with Ismet. We may find some arrangement that will suit us all."

He was in a difficulty. The threat of that revolver under Edhem's hand did not influence him at all, but a mission under Izzet Pasha had come from the Sultan to negotiate a truce and alliance between Constantinople and Angora so that all Turks might unite to face the Greeks. The Assembly was very sympathetic, and once more there was the beginning of a reaction to the Sultan.

Edhem, too, was popular with the deputies, many of whom supported him. They praised all he had done; they believed that guerrilla war was the only one possible. They resented the "staff officer and military government" of Mustafa Kemal. There was a stock catchword in Angora: "Mustafa Kemal will make us all button up our tunics. And we won't. We will wear Edhem's uniform." They said openly that Mustafa Kemal was determined to make himself a military dictator, and Edhem alone could prevent this.

Mustafa Kemal realized that to crush the irregulars would be unpopular. If he and Edhem went to meet Ismet at Eski Shehir, then Ismet could be shouldered with the responsibility and, moreover, Edhem would be well away from his political supporters.

135

On the journey Edhem became more suspicious. In Eski Shehir he would be surrounded by regular troops. Already he felt the steel teeth of the trap closing on him. He dropped quietly off the train and joined his men.

Now he became defiant. He would keep his power somehow. If the Angora Government did not want him, he would go elsewhere. He began negotiations with the Sultan, and then with the Greek commanders. He surrounded and disbanded the regular Turkish troops in Kutahia and sent them home. He dismissed officials sent from Angora and refused to accept any orders. Finally he proclaimed himself "Commander-in-Chief of all the Nationalist Forces" and sent to the Grand National Assembly a message:

"The country is too tired to fight.... The mission under Izzet Pasha should be given powers to negotiate peace.... I am interpreting the desire of the nation and of the soldiers."

Mustafa Kemal sent him a message in reply:

"Hitherto I have talked with you as an old comrade with a comrade. From now it is as the Chief of the State that I must deal with you."

He gave Ismet orders to smash the irregulars. Under Refet the regular army took Kutahia and drove out Edhem. All the villagers, rejoicing to be free of the nightmare in which they had lived under the rule of the bands, joined in and helped destroy the irregulars.

Edhem, swearing vengeance on Mustafa Kemal, joined the Greeks with some of his men. The Greeks, though not prepared, seeing that the Turks were quarreling among themselves, attacked. They took Afion and part of the railway in front of them. Ismet counter-attacked with his regular troops at In Eunu and drove them out again. Surprised at this new resistance the Greeks retired to their old line and sat down throughout the spring and early summer of 1921 to prepare for a big offensive.

XXXIII

At the battle of In Eunu the Kemalists had gained their first military success. Their hopes began to revive.

The news was good. Kiazim Kara Bekir had invaded Armenia, taken Kars and joined forces with the Bolshevics. Russia was sending money and arms. Russia and Turkey had a common enemy in England.

Greece was torn by fierce political quarrels which were spreading to the army. Venizelos and his friends had been ejected from Athens.

England, France and Italy wished to end the Greco-Turkish war. They had offered to mediate between Greece and Turkey; the Greeks had refused, and the Powers had declared themselves neutral. It was a straight fight between the Greeks and the Turks. France was sending secret messengers to Angora with promises of help. Italy was selling them arms. From Afghanistan and Persia had come delegates proposing alliances. In India and Egypt a great Moslem agitation had been started to help Turkey.

The Turks themselves were united. The civil war was finished. The Caliph's and the Green Armies were both gone. Except for a few old men around the Sultan in Constantinople all Turks had grouped themselves under Mustafa Kemal in Angora, to fight the invading Greeks.

Mustafa Kemal saw clearly that there was no time to lose: the Greeks were preparing a big offensive. He must create a force to meet them.

He worked at tremendous pressure. He had a power of complete concentration, an ability to absorb details at speed and reproduce them at will, and a clear judgment as to essential facts. He would work for hours at a stretch without rest or sleep until those with him were worn out, and still he was untired.

When he was not reading, dispatching or issuing orders, he was with Fevzi at work on the organization of the new army. The two men were complete opposites: Mustafa Kemal with his concentrated energy driving, urging, goading all into action, living on his nerves, now elated, now depressed; Fevzi steady and solid, rarely talking, keeping in the background, usually pessimistic, trustworthy and reliable, a steadying influence on the other.

It was poor, second-rate material they had to work on, unwilling men, returned prisoners of war, old guns and rifles, country carts, porters and village women as transport. Out of these they must create a first-class fighting force. In the face of immense difficulties, never for one minute did Mustafa Kemal relax.

He had, moreover, to meet the politicians. The deputies in their newly-elected positions were very jealous of their rights. In theory they were the rulers. Again and again Mustafa Kemal repeated to them: "The Grand National Assembly is the incarnation of the People. All authority belongs to the People and absolutely." But it seemed to them that in fact Mustafa Kemal often usurped their powers. They were suspicious of him. To meet them he had no privileged position, none of the prestige that century-old tradition and custom gives to high position in an established state. In Angora everything was new and raw. Mustafa Kemal's only power was his own ability and personality.

To get even the smallest thing he had to attend their meetings, argue with them, bully and persuade them. In public he remained patient and self-controlled; to his intimates at times he showed how the incessant petty opposition and the criticism drove him to fury.

He returned late one evening to the model farm after

a sitting of the Assembly; the deputies had been particularly difficult. His staff were collected in the hall by the fire. As soon as he came in Mustafa Kemal burst into a storm of abuse of politicians: democracy was the rule of the many-headed, the muddle-headed, the fools; the only sound form of government was the absolute rule of one man.

"What do you think?" he shouted, turning suddenly on Halideh Edib. He knew she was theoretically a democrat and opposed to all dictators.

"I am not clear what you mean, pasha," she replied.

"I will tell you what I mean," he said, his eyes turning gray with anger, his eyebrows beetling out, his jaw set, his whole attitude menacing. "I mean that I will have every one to do as I wish, carry out what I command. I will have no criticism or advice. I will have my own way. All, and you too, shall do as I wish absolutely and without question."

As long as there was work, it absorbed Mustafa Kemal's every minute; nothing could divert him. When work slackened, he grew irritable and restless and began to interfere with his subordinates.

It was then that with Arif and one or two other men he would disappear on heavy drinking bouts which, with gambling, would last whole nights; or he went a whoring with the painted women of the poor brothels of the town.

In these things Ismet and Fevzi took no part. They did not belong to this side of his life. Both were fathers of families, staid and conventional in morals. Fevzi in particular had strong, old-fashioned views; he kept his wife veiled and his women shut away; he was devout and never touched alcohol. Both he and Ismet disapproved of the orgies in which Mustafa Kemal indulged and of his companions on these orgies.

It was at this period particularly that Mustafa Kemal

showed his amazing capacity for talking. For days he would be silent, making only a few remarks in clipped, abrupt phrases. Then, without warning, he would talk with a ceaseless torrent of words for hours on end.

Sometimes it was that in his mind, like minerals in solution, hung ideas, vague and nebulous. Talk crystallized the vague ideas into solid facts. For hours he would bore his listeners with aimless labyrinthine theorizing and futile verbosity, demanding their opinions, and interrupting them as soon as they gave them. Then suddenly he would startle them by crisp decisions which showed a master-mind at work.

At other times he wished to convince opponents. He would talk unceasingly until he had battered down the opposition and left his opponents exhausted. It was quite usual for him to start such a talk at nine o'clock at night as soon as the evening meal was over. At five o'clock in the morning he would still be holding the floor, still fresh and full of argument while his opponents had collapsed into acceptance.

Now and again he talked to amuse. With one hand he played with a string of amber beads. Occasionally, very occasionally, he laughed softly, showing a mouth of gold-filled teeth. Usually in this mood he talked with a cynical half-smile on his face. With an uncanny insight into character he would pick to pieces his friends and enemies alike, strip them of all their pretences until he left them, exposing all their faults in vulgar nakedness.

No one escaped: the vanity of Refet, the cosmopolitan swash-buckler; the flabby sentimentality of Halideh Edib; the old-maidishness of Adnan; Bekir Sami who thought he was a soldier and would have been better at a clerk's desk; Kiazim Kara Bekir who wanted to play at being a big man and could only play the violin—and that badly. These were all friends who had stood by him in the stress and strain of the early days of the revolution.

He sneered at and ripped to pieces all the accepted ideals and morals: morals were a cover for hypocrites or the folly of fools; ideals were dust in the mouth.

It was brilliant, cutting satire, without any of the gentle oil of humor to soften it. It showed him without fine feelings, and with no loyalties for men, ideas or institutions. It showed him as more animal than man: the wolf, hard, without sentiment or scruples, without morals or guiding principles of conduct except his animal desires.

XXXIV

At first Mustafa Kemal had lived at the model farm with the rest of his staff. Then he took a room in the station-master's house to be near the telegraph office.

He used telegrams as other men use letters and interviews. It was quite common for him to send a three-hundred word telegram either as some protest to the Grand Vizier in Constantinople or as orders to an army corps commander in Sivas. On receipt of the answer he would send off another three-hundred word telegram.

In this house he was guarded by his special bodyguard of Lazzes, mountaineers from the south coast of the Black Sea. They were wild, black-eyed men with long mustaches, and as lithe as cats. On duty they swaggered up and down before his house. Off duty they went out over the hills looking after the sheep which Mustafa Kemal had given them.

He paid them well, gave them special privileges, dressed them in their national costume of black with long, slashed coats and high boots, much like that worn by Cossacks, and put them under the command of a well-known Lazz mountain brigand, one Osman Agha. He could count on their absolute loyalty, and they appealed to his sense of the dramatic.

None the less he lived openly and freely with little or no ceremony. When not at work indoors, it was his habit to walk about with his hands in his pockets and to talk to anyone he met, soldiers or civilians. When he went to the Assembly, he rarely sat in the President's box, but preferred to be at a desk among the deputies.

He often growled and complained at those round him, and often unjustly. He rarely, and then only grudgingly, showed his gratitude to his subordinates. He was a man to avoid, for his mood decided his outlook; he was more often ill-natured than pleasant, and, if displeased, would be harsh and merciless. He also changed very rapidly in looks. One day he would seem young and full of life, and the next ten years older, lined and tired.

Later, finding Angora uncomfortable to live in, hot and dusty in summer, wet and muddy in winter, he took a stone house at Chan Kaya, a village on a bare ridge some four miles outside Angora. Behind the house he built some shanties for Osman Agha and the Lazz guard. There he lived in all the discomforts of the bachelor soldier with a minimum of furniture and irregular meals.

His doctor repeatedly warned him that he must go slow, work and drink less, and lead a regular life with someone to look after him; he was living on his nerves: even his energy and the stout constitution inherited from clean-living parents could not stand the strain indefinitely. The old kidney trouble came back repeatedly. He suffered from malaria, which came up from the marshes round Angora.

From a break-down he was saved by Fikriye Hanum. She was a distant relative of his from Stambul who had volunteered as an army nurse and come to Angora. As soon as he saw her, Mustafa Kemal took her to his house.

She was a strange mate for this hard man with his brutal outlook and his wild orgies, for she was a delicate, fragile girl, quiet and refined, with a white, oval face and deep brown eyes with long, tremulous lashes.

But she brought him comfort. She had a garden cut in terraces round the house, planted with trees, and an old-fashioned summer-house built at one end, a *kiosque* such as the pashas of the old days used on the Bosphorus on summer evening: it had windows on all sides to look over the great yellow plains that stretched far away below.

In the central room, which was like a roofed courtyard, she had built in white marble a fountain which could play on hot summer days, when the plains were full of dust and the glare beat up bruising the eyeballs.

Mustafa Kemal had chosen as his study a room from where he could look over the plains and see in the distance Angora, crowded on a bare hillside with the ancient fortress above it.

She arranged his study with Turkish and Persian carpets. She hung on the walls the fine sword that the Sheik of the Senussi had sent him and some daggers in a pattern. She arranged his books. Already sure that he would one day rule Turkey, he was reading Moslem ecclesiastical history and studying social problems. Above his table she fixed a square of green cloth covered with cryptic signs. Unbeliever in all else Mustafa Kemal was superstitious and he believed in the virtue of these signs.

She watched over all his needs. When he was ill, she nursed him. She was his mistress and his absolute slave, for she was Turkish and oriental. With complete abandon of self she gave all, and in return asked nothing but the right to be a slave, to lie at his feet and be trampled on. Woman-like she asked for nothing, yet asked for all.

For a while Mustafa Kemal was absorbed in her. She aroused him. But very soon he tired. He went back more and more to his painted women, his drinking companions and his cards, so that Fikriye ate out her heart with gnawing jealousy. As he grew cold, she loved him the more.

XXXV

WHILE Mustafa Kemal and Fevzi worked in Angora, away at the front Ismet was straining every nerve to meet the Greeks, preparing his positions before Afion and Eski Shehir. They were massing troops, bringing up more guns and aëroplanes, continually searching out his line with raids and air reconnaissance; they were clearly better equipped and in vastly superior numbers.

In the first week in July, before he was ready, they attacked. They swept forward carrying all before them, took Kutahia and Afion and concentrated on to Eski Shehir— the railway junction and the key to all Western Anatolia.

Away up in his headquarters in the village of Karaja Bey behind Eski Shehir, Ismet was waiting. His office was a mean little room with dirty walls and a broken floor. In one corner was his camp-bed. By the window, covered by lattice work, was a chair, and a table covered with a map.

Usually Ismet was even and steady tempered with the quiet manner and the listening stillness of a deaf man. Now the strain was telling on him. His face was drawn and lined. Dressed as usual in the uniform of a private soldier, he looked shriveled up and smaller than ever. He was utterly weary, for days he had worked feverishly, but he had not Mustafa

Kemal's immense reserve of vitality, so that often as he read a report or studied a map, he fell asleep in his chair from sheer weariness.

A vital decision had to be made. The Greek columns were advancing from three sides on Eski Shehir: their object was to encircle it and the main Turkish army. All the counter-attacks which he had ordered had failed. Should he evacuate and order a general retreat or hold his ground?

He could not make up his mind. He walked up and down nervously, his hands behind his back. Now and again he called a staff officer and snapped at him angrily.

It would mean throwing away great dumps of ammunition and stores collected and brought up with herculean effort; it would also mean giving up a place of vital strategical importance, leaving the Turkish civilian population to the brutalities of the Greeks, and it would mean his acknowledging a first-class defeat.

He could not make up his mind. He was waiting for Mustafa Kemal. He had telegraphed for him to come at once from Angora. Mustafa Kemal should decide. It was true what Ismet had once said:

"Mustafa Kemal is the master. We all are only his assistants."

Mustafa Kemal wasted no time. He came post-haste. He did not hesitate or side-step the responsibility. At once he took control. He was the master-mind, the master-personality. It was as if a great weight had slipped from the shoulders of Ismet. There was a new courage in the air, for Mustafa Kemal had that power, which Ismet did not possess, of inspiring confidence and reviving courage and action in men, whether things were good or bad.

He listened to the reports, studied the map, moved the flags, calculated. His face was set; his eyes, without expression, did not show his thoughts. He was concentrated on the problem. When Liman von Sanders had left it to him at Damascus to decide on a general retreat from Syria, he had been giving up territory that was not Turkish and a population of Arabs and Syrians. If he ordered this retreat now, he gave up Turkish soil and Turkish men and women to the national enemy, who would burn, rape and destroy. But that did not complicate his decision. He saw the problem as a military one; if they stood and fought at Eski Shehir, the Turkish main army would be wiped out.

"Evacuate Eski Shehir," he said suddenly in curt Turkish phrases. "Order a general retreat. Retire back three hundred kilometers to the Sakkaria River and prepare a new position there to cover Angora. That will lengthen the enemy's line of communication, get him into many difficulties and give us the time to re-form." With a few flags he showed his decisions on a map.

At once he hurried back to Angora to meet the new crisis. He found the townspeople packing up to escape away into the mountains of the east, and the deputies again shouting for the blood of those responsible.

Once again he faced them. This time he demanded to be made Commander-in-Chief with full powers of a dictator. The Assembly hesitated, afraid of him. He refused to haggle; if he was to save Turkey, he must have absolute control. The Assembly, with certain conditions to protect their ultimate sovereignty, agreed.

At once Mustafa Kemal took full control. With tremendous energy he made all preparations to form the new line of defense and meet the advancing Greeks. A fall from his horse damaged a rib and kept him in bed two days. The old kidney trouble worried him; the heat of that July was overpowering; but nothing could stop him. Raging with energy, he drove all to work, and then himself hurried down

146

to the front which was being prepared behind the Sakkaria River.

XXXVI

THE Sakkaria River twisted through mountain country, range on range of hills broken up and thrown into confusion as the rollers of a sea are broken up and confused by a cross-current.

Into these hills, straight at the Turkish last line of defense where it straddled the road to Angora, the Greeks attacked with a heavy artillery bombardment at dawn on the 24th August, 1921.

Greeks and Turks alike fought with reckless courage, threw themselves into the storms of lead in a white madness to get at each other with cold steel. Neither had any moral superiority; both were filled with the venom of a hereditary hatred. The Turks were fighting for their homes. Half the Greek army were local Christians, Turkish subjects, condemned to death as traitors. They too were fighting for their hearths and homes, and with no hope, if defeated. A Greek regiment refused to take cover or use trenches: the divisional staff came up into the line with it, and both were wiped out by machine-gun fire. A Turkish battalion wavered: the brigade general ran forward over the open, pulled up the colonel, blew his brains out with his revolver, steadied the battalion, and was himself blown to pieces by Greek riflemen. One division lost three-quarters of its men, another was blotted right out. Seven divisional generals were killed in close fighting.

Day after day, for fourteen consecutive days, under the burning heat of the August sun, their supply services broken down so that there was little water and their ration was at last reduced to a handful of dry maize, the Greeks attacked with reckless fury, and the Turks hung grimly on.

Up in the village of Ala Geuz, behind the Turkish line, Mustafa Kemal paced restlessly up and down in his room in headquarters, his gray cloak slung round his shoulders, his face gray and drawn. He walked with a limp, for his ribs still hurt him.

He slept rarely and in his clothes; he snatched a meal now and again. He listened to the continuous stream of reports, pored over his map pinned out on a table, calculated and plotted the latest news.

At night by the light of an acetylene lamp he would review the position, moving the flags and rehearsing aloud all the possibilities; how the Greeks might attack and how he would forestall them. Now and again he would call Arif and cross-question him. Arif knew the ground in detail and many of the commanders. Leaning over Mustafa Kemal's shoulder, his face like that of a twin brother, he would say, "The village of X...? It lies ten kilometers to the north: there are two mounds on the left."

"The commandant of that regiment? Stupid, but what a soldier, and the men are veterans. No fear of artillery panic there. When they run out of ammunition they will fight with bayonets, commander and all."

Then once more Mustafa Kemal would pace up and down still working out aloud every possibility and preparing for it.

The position was critical. If he were beaten on the Sakkaria, he must retreat far away up to the mountains of the east and give up Angora. It would be an end of Turkey. This was the last ditch. Already the Greeks were feeling for a flank and might get round. Should he attack them from the rear or should he retreat? He had so few men to use. He remembered with regret the days in Gallipoli when he could order ten thousand men into action at once. Now he must count every man. He could take no risks.

Moreover, the active control of the battle had passed from him to the commanders of the battalions and companies and even of platoons. Except for the few troops he held in reserve he could not for the time being influence the result. Throughout all that broken country, in corners of valleys, on hill-tops, in mountain gorges, the units, sometimes a whole regiment, sometimes just a few men with a corporal, fought ding-dong their desperate individual battles. The decision rested with the captains, the subalterns, even the sergeants and the corporals.

And yet, even when only his last handful of reserves remained, Mustafa Kemal still dominated the battle. His personality, driving and urging, inspired the whole Turkish army to grit their teeth and hold on. Time and again a commanding hill-top was lost, defeat seemed certain, the Turkish line began to bend back, to crack, but it did not break, for always at the critical moment and at the critical point Mustafa Kemal threw in his help. He had learned each inch of the ground; he knew the value of each section of his troops and even the capabilities of each battalion commander. He held and dominated the battle from the room in Ala Geuz.

After fourteen days of continuous fighting the battle was undecided, but Mustafa Kemal realized that the critical moment was at hand. One side or the other must break. The strain was too great.

Up and down his office he limped. He was strung up with nerves. He swore and cursed at everything and everyone. He kept reviewing the position over and over again in a loud voice. Should he order the retreat before it was too late? Or should he hold on?

The night crept on. It was two o'clock. The telephone rang shrilly. An officer came in, clicked his heels, saluted:

"Fevzi Pasha wishes to speak to you, sir," he said and was gone.

In the telephone room Mustafa Kemal sat with the receiver to his ear. The Lazzes of the guard and the staff officers crowded up as close as they dared to hear, their faces white—anxious in the half-light.

"What do you say?" asked Mustafa Kemal, his voice rising. "The day is in our favor, you say. The Greeks are at the end of their strength. They are preparing for a general retreat!"

With a great chuckle he put down the receiver and limped back into his office. For a while he sat moving flags on the map, or calculating. Under the light of the lamp his face showed the strain of the last few days: his cheeks were drawn, and there were enormous dark circles round his eyes.

Then he gave his orders. "The Greek attack hesitates and will give ground. I will take the initiative. Throw in all the reserves here to the north," he said pointing, "and threaten the enemy's line of retreat along here."

Then he turned and shouted for coffee. In the reaction of the pent-up strain he again cursed and swore at everyone—the sergeant who brought the coffee, the Lazzes, his staff officers—but with a new tone in his voice.

For a week the Greeks stood, fighting fiercely but their impetus was gone.

Mustafa Kemal had gone to the front. He was in his element once more, fighting. As ever, he went among the men, living rough in the trenches, over the open, under fire, taking no precautions and yet escaping being wounded when all round him men were killed.

On the twenty-second day the Greeks re-crossed the Sakkaria River and retired steadily. As they went they systematically burned and destroyed, so that for two hundred miles behind them they left a desert.

After them came hurrying Mustafa Kemal, but he had to stop short. The Turkish army was crumpled and smashed. It had ceased to be an effective force. By superhuman effort he collected and re-formed a few regiments. Several days

Mustafa Kemal during the Sakkaria Campaign.

behind the enemy he set off in pursuit. He found the Greeks in the trenches from which they had advanced in July and which covered Eski Shehir and the railway. Taking up a line facing them, he gave orders to dig in and hold them; and himself returned to Angora.

PART EIGHT

===

XXXVII

IN Angora the people went mad with joy. They had sat listening to the sound of the guns, with their household goods packed, ready to evacuate into the mountains to the east. Now they were safe. They fêted Mustafa Kemal. They gave him the title of *Gazi,* "The Destroyer of Christians," the highest honor for a Moslem. They acknowledged him as master.

Foreign countries joined in the applause. From Russia and Afghanistan, from India and America, and even from France and Italy, came telegrams of congratulations.

But Mustafa Kemal had no delusions. He loved applause. He loved to parade in the public eye, to be the center of admiration, to be the hero. He was determined to dominate and be master, but none the less his judgment remained cool, practical, steady. He knew the real facts. The Greek advance had been stopped. The Turks had won their first real victory. Possibly the tide had turned; but Sakkaria was no decisive victory. With their backs to the wall the Turks had just escaped destruction. A little more persistency and the Greeks would have broken through. The Greek soldier had shown himself as brave and stout-hearted as the Turk. There was no question of taking the offensive now. The Turkish army was too badly mauled for that. It had been decimated. He would have to hold the Greeks while he reorganized the whole army from the bottom, the supply services, replaced the crippling casualities, found arms and guns. It would take time, weeks, perhaps months, and victory would lie as much with the grit and staying power of the civilian population as with the military organization and the decisive battle.

He set to work at once. Night and day, backed by Ismet and Fevzi, with astounding energy and skill Mustafa Kemal reorganized. He had to find arms, guns, ammunition, machines. He came to terms with France, signed a secret treaty with the French representative, Franklin-Bouillon, which released eighty thousand men from the Syrian front and gave him equipment for forty thousand more. But that was not enough. He bought arms from Italy and America with money borrowed from Moscow. Men he must have, men and more men! He called up more classes; he combed the towns and villages for men.

It was slow, dreary, uphill work. As month followed month of preparation, there came after the tremendous efforts and the outburst of joy the inevitable reaction. The people were utterly war-weary. The villagers begged again to be left in peace, to till their fields and be quiet. The Greeks were gone out of sight! Why worry any more? It was time that the war ended. They were tired.

There was opposition too. In the moment of danger before Sakkaria the politicians in the Grand National Assembly had given Mustafa Kemal the powers of dictator. Now in the hour of success they wanted their powers back. On every side there were intrigues. The officers began to form cliques and talk politics. Enver had made himself Amir of Bokhara and hoped to return to Turkey. Jemal was in Afghanistan as adviser to the Amir and also wished to return. He had written to Mustafa Kemal suggesting an alliance. In contact with them, the Committees of Union and Progress party had begun to organize underground. The army had become restless, demanded a winter offensive against the Greeks, grumbled and muttered with discontent.

The best men with the levelest judgment advised Mustafa Kemal to make peace at once on the best terms he could get, and while he had the chance.

But Mustafa Kemal would have none of it. Unafraid, convinced that he was right, he held sternly on his way. He would defeat the Greeks in battle. He never faltered. Up and down the country he worked and raged, lashing the people into energy. With the fire of his personality he burned and stung them out of their lassitude and coma. He would have nothing to do with Enver or Jemal. He stamped on politics and cliques among the officers: twenty-five he hung for an attempted *coup d'état*. He set his grip on the army; it knew its master and obeyed.

Rauf and Fethi, with the rest of deputies imprisoned in Malta, had been released by the English and returned to Angora. At first they backed Mustafa Kemal wholeheartedly, but as he became more dictatorial they became discontented. Led by Rauf, the politicians began to oppose Mustafa Kemal. They were afraid of his vindictiveness, and his ambition to be absolute. They resented his sarcastic temper and his open rudeness to them. They knew he was ruthless, and, if given the opportunity, would hang any of them. They tried to reduce his power.

He fought them back fiercely and without compromise. All the autocrat in him swelled up in anger at their interference. He was, and would remain, master.

Under the strain his nerves became ragged and his temper uncontrolled. At home he found no relief. His mother had come from Constantinople and was living with him at Chan Kaya. She was very old and very querulous. Now quite blind, all day long she squatted cross-legged in peasant fashion on a mattress in one corner. Her greatest pleasure was to be allowed to talk to the Greek prisoners, who could give her news of the village in southern Albania where she had been born. Otherwise her mind usually wandered back to Salonika and the days when Mustafa Kemal was a boy.

Fikriye still kept house for Mustafa Kemal, but she had been sickly and nerveless for some time. The doctors were afraid that her lungs were touched with consumption.

Once upon a time Fikriye might have soothed him, but now he was wearied to death of her, of her aimless flat chatter about trifles, about the servants and the meals. As a mistress she could rouse him no more. It angered him when she was weak and helpless. Often she began to complain and to cry without reason. He had no time or sentiment to waste on such things. His house at Chan Kaya was full of her everlasting tiring cough and the shrill exacting voice of his mother, for she hated Fikriye. She wanted Mustafa Kemal married, and married well. The old woman took every chance to find fault and criticize the girl, who was to her like a blister on a tender heel.

Moreover Zubeida, as imperious and haughty-tempered as himself, flamed out when he told her of opposition. Was her son not the Chosen One? Who were these pigs to oppose him? So far from soothing him she urged and incited him to strike at his opponents.

He was drinking heavily. The drink stimulated him, gave him energy, but increased his irritability. Both in private and public he was sarcastic, brutal and abrupt. He flared up at the least criticism. He cut short all attempts to reason with him. He flew into a passion at the least opposition. He would neither confide in nor coöperate with any one. When one politician gave him some harmless advice, he roughly told him to get out. When a venerable member of the Cabinet suggested that it was unseemly for Turkish ladies to dance in public, he threw a Koran at him and chased him out of his office with a stick. Yet through all he kept one clear aim—to prepare for the big military offensive, smash the Greeks and then dictate terms of peace. If that failed, then Turkey and he would be better destroyed in the attempt.

He was ready for others to try by peaceful and diplomatic means, but he had no belief in their success. He let Fethi go to Paris and London. When he failed and was even treated rudely, Mustafa Kemal smiled sardonically at the failure.

Meanwhile, relentlessly, strong as steel, he prepared, while the winter of 1921 passed into the spring of 1922 and summer was come again.

XXXVIII

At last, in late August, when the heat still lay heavy on the plains of the Anatolian plateau and the dust deep on every road and path, Mustafa Kemal decided to strike. He chose the 26th as the date.

In the first week, with Fevzi as Chief of the Staff, and Ismet in command of the field army, he took direct control of the army in the field and at once he braced the organization, so that even the privates felt his personality and knew that something was at hand. With infinite care and skill he prepared the details for secrecy and so for success. He had ordered a football competition to be organized. Now he visited the troops to see the finals played, met all the commanders there, gave his orders and returned to Angora without rousing suspicion.

A week before the date all communications between

Turkey and the outside world were cut, and the rumor spread that a revolution had broken out.

On the 24th he issued invitations to a ball for the night of the 26th, gave orders to the sentries round his house that he was busy, and that no one was to be allowed near the house until further orders. In the dead of night he moved with his staff up to headquarters behind the front line. Even Fikriye and his mother had no idea of his moves.

The Turkish storm-troops had already been secretly massed before Afion. A few mobile units were ready to feint at Eski Shehir, to draw off the Greeks to the north. The Greek commanders had no suspicions of what was coming. They were quarreling amongst themselves. Negotiations were in progress in London, and the Greek Government hoped for peace without fighting, with the help of the English. The Greek Commander-in-Chief was General Hadji-anestes. He had developed queer delusions: that he was dead, or that he was brittle and made of glass, so that one morning he refused to get out of bed for fear that his legs might break. Once a good soldier, he had become unbalanced and partially mad. He spent all his time loafing pathetically in the cafés of Smyrna out of touch with his troops. He had been given command as the result of the intrigues of the politicians who were fighting each other for power in Athens and had no time for the battle-front. Officials and officers had been changed repeatedly, and each new batch were more corrupt and inefficient than their predecessors. The administrative services had gone to pieces and the Greek soldiers in the trenches were left short of food, pay, clothes and ammunition. Out of the Greek troops, as out of the nation, the enthusiasm for the war had been sapped away.

At last Mustafa Kemal had every detail planned and ready—except one. Irreligious, scoffer at all beliefs, all gods,

Mustafa Kemal was yet doubly superstitious. He was afraid of Fate and Chance. He must have with him, as his mascot, Halideh Edib; she had meant success before. She was in Konia. He telegraphed to her to come at once. Lately she had annoyed him with her pacifist talk and her everlasting arguments about the evils of war. Yet he must have her near. Even by one small neglect or error he must not risk falling foul of the Unknown. When she arrived at headquarters he felt sure of success.

As the zero hour approached, he issued a battle-call: "Soldiers, forward! Your goal is the Mediterranean."

At four o'clock in the morning of the 26th August the Turks assaulted Dumlau Punar, the key to Afion and the Greek position. By the evening they had burst through, cut the Greek army in half and destroyed its direct communications with its rear.

XXXIX

THE Greek army broke. The officers made for safety, each to save his own skin. The Greek soldiers, starved for food and ammunition, discontented, home-sick, without heart in the fight, made off as fast as they could for Smyrna and the sea. Divisions ceased to exist; regiments split up and became a rabble of individuals. The retreat, harassed by the Turkish cavalry, became a rout and a nightmare of horror.

Back swept the undisciplined armed mobs across the barren rocky plains of the plateau, leaving behind them trenches and barbed wire lines, débris of rifles, stores, clothes, guns, ammunition dumps and tents—and everywhere the fantastic corpses of the dead staring up into the sky. Already the flies and the kites and the pariah dogs had found the

dead. Over all, over the marching columns in great clouds, over the pursuing cavalry, over the dead—thick on everything moving or still was the red choking dust under the burning sun.

Back they swept, the armed mobs, the local Christians with them, killing all the Turks they met, old men, women and children, burning the villages, sometimes to cover their retreat, more often in wanton revenge and wild, destructive hatred.

The Turkish infantry could not keep the pace. They had to advance with more caution, feeling their way, for now and again Greek units which had held together turned and fought them fiercely. Only the Turkish cavalry kept close. Now driving through the crowds, now sweeping round the flanks, they killed mercilessly, taking no prisoners, revenging the murder and burning, only stopping when fatigue brought them and their horses, sweating and blood-stained, to a standstill.

Within ten days the Greeks had covered the one hundred and ninety miles to the sea, clambered on their ships and were gone, and the Turks, victorious, stood on the shore, but with the sea between them and their enemy.

Anatolia was free of the enemy: that was a miracle, but again the Greek army had escaped.

XL

BEHIND the pursuing Turks came general headquarters, and Mustafa Kemal foreseeing, planning, urging on his men to keep contact with the enemy. Where the plateau ended, and where began the soft fertile valleys that lead down to Smyrna and the rich plain along the shore, he waited.

Before the coming of the Greek army this had been a

land of laughing streams, of trees and green grass, a land of plenty, of wine and figs and happy villages. Now it too was filled with horror; ash smears of buildings where there had been villages, bodies of children and raped women in the vineyards; Turkish women killing Greek stragglers vindictively; stench of charred flesh; stench of unburied dead in the cool orchards.

But it was not these horrors that made Mustafa Kemal wait. Greeks who came praying for protection, Turks who came with their list of wrongs, or crying for redress, alike got no sympathy from him.

When he was told that the cloud of dust behind a village was caused by Turkish women stoning to death a Turkish girl who had played harlot for the Greek troops, or that a Greek was being crucified and another being torn in pieces, he snarled with savage pleasure. But neither pity nor sentiment touched him at all. These horrors left him unmoved. They were the ordinary, inevitable incidents of war, of his trade. He was thinking not in terms of flesh and blood and pain, not in sentiments and individuals, but in facts, geographical facts, maps, hours of marching, figures of marching columns, numbers of men and guns.

Through them all he saw himself standing out supreme. His troops were now in Smyrna. The telegraph had told the world of his victory, that he had driven out the Greek Army, and thrown it back in the face of the Great Nations who had sent it. It was his hour of dramatic triumph. The Eyes of the World were focused on him. He would enter Smyrna as a Victor in Triumph. He only waited for the word that the stage was ready set for him.

At Ushak came word that the Greek Commander-in-Chief, General Tricoupis—Hadjianestes had been recalled—

with his second-in-command, Dionis, had been captured. Mustafa Kemal ordered them to be brought to his headquarters in the town hall.

He received them with all respect standing, with Ismet on one side of him and Fevzi on the other. He shook hands with them, gave them cigarettes and coffee and asked them if they had all that was necessary. That these men had ordered the massed burning and brutality did not matter; they were soldiers, they were his military opponents and must be treated with respect.

All the time he watched them with his cold, pale eyes. He wanted to know them and to understand and judge the men against whom he had been pitted.

He was disappointed. They were sickly-looking and flashily dressed. They moaned over their fate. They complained of everything. They quarreled noisily with each other.

He discussed the fighting with them. When Tricoupis explained a move, Mustafa Kemal showed how he had intended to counteract it. But the Greek generals did not seem to know their business as soldiers. He was disappointed that they had been fighting men not up to his own standard.

"Anyway," he said as they left, "war is a game of chance. You have done your best. The responsibility rests with Luck. Do not be distressed."

When they were gone, he looked at Ismet with a sneer and a shrug of his shoulders. They were poor stuff.

At length news came from Smyrna that all was ready for him. He drove the last few miles at the head of a line of cars decked with the laurel boughs of the victor. Beside all the roads were crowds cheering, weeping, praying, thanking God on their knees for this deliverance from the terror of the Greek.

At the gates of Smyrna a regiment of cavalry closed

round him with drawn swords. Slowly they rode across the city, through the narrow streets, under the booming arches of the closed bazaar, while the stallions of the escort pranced and struck sparks from the cobbles, and the men with drawn swords cheered and shouted insults at the enemy.

The enemy! Not a stone's throw away from the quay, immense, towering over all with their monster guns, yet helpless to interfere, lay at anchor the battleships of the Allies.

Past them Mustafa Kemal rode with a sneer to the house chosen for his headquarters. In their powerless might he knew the full force of his own power.

XLI

In the headquarters' offices there was already rush and bustle, staff officers hurrying in and out, orderlies, messages, telegrams coming and going. The Greeks had been chased out of Asiatic Turkey, but across the sea in Europe they were massing again to attack Constantinople. The Turkish army had to be re-formed at once and sent north to the danger-point. The devastated country, newly evacuated by the enemy, had to be taken over and administered. The representatives of the foreign powers—England, France, America and Italy—had to be dealt with. A thousand problems needed his immediate and urgent decisions.

Into this work Mustafa Kemal plunged at once; with relentless energy he worked from early dawn far into the night, issuing orders and decrees, sleeping only for a few hours in a room above the office.

It was on the third day that the orderly on duty reported that a lady wished to see the Gazi. She was a young lady;

she would give no message and she was insistent in her demand to see him. As the orderly was speaking, the lady walked in. She announced herself; her name was Latifa Hanum.

For a minute Mustafa Kemal sat still. He was angry. He was not used to any one walking into his office without permission. Then he sized her up, nodded to the orderly, and asked her to sit down. She was something different from the local ladies and the peasant women of Anatolia.

He looked her over shrewdly. After the dust and the discomforts of the last few days, she was very pleasant to look at. Except for the Turkish head-dress, which increased the rounded prettiness of her face, she wore European clothes, which were chic and elegant. She was unveiled, dark-eyed, young and fresh skinned, clearly a girl of good family, no cheap woman of the bazaar. She had a quiet air of authority, as one used to being obeyed, and she looked him straight in the eye as man to man, and not with the veiled-sex looks of the women to whom he was accustomed. It was not usual for a Turkish girl of good family to walk and talk so freely. Still she appealed to him. He was intrigued. What did she want? What could he do for her?

In the hot September morning the windows of the office were open. From outside came now and again the sounds of rifle fire, the hoarse, brutal shouts of men killing, and the screams of their victims, for in the streets and on the quays the Turks were ferreting out and killing the Greeks, as the Greeks had killed Turks in their day of power.

Mustafa Kemal listened a minute. Then he shrugged his shoulders; the Greeks had to go; there must be no more Christian traitors in Turkey; one way was as good as another; dead men were no trouble, and if the English and French and Americans could see what was happening from their battleships, well! what did it matter? He was master. They should interfere no more in Turkey.

A staff officer came in to report that fire had broken out in several places in the Christian quarters; it looked like the work of incendiaries; all the fire-brigade's water-pipes had been cut to pieces; there was much ammunition hidden under the churches; there was danger of explosion and that the fire would spread.

The staff officer was gone, and Mustafa Kemal turned back to the girl. Her request was simple. Her father was the well-known shipowner of Smyrna. She had just come back from Paris and Biarritz and had left her parents there. They had a big house and servants up on the hills at Bornovo behind Smyrna. This house and office in this town were too noisy and uncomfortable. Would he and his staff come as her guests and she would see they were well looked after?

Mustafa Kemal accepted, and moved to her house. It suited him. It was quiet. It was out of the stench and the rattle and uproar of the city. Up on the top of the Bornovo hills, surrounded by vineyards and gardens, it looked down over the great panorama of Smyrna and its harbor and the sea beyond.

His personal comforts were looked after. The house was well run and the servants and the food were good. Above all, there was the girl. She was capable, gave her orders precisely, and yet she was dainty and feminine. She attracted him. Already he desired her. Within a day or two he was in love with her, crazily, passionately in love with Latifa— Latifa, dark haired, with black, laughing eyes small and dainty, now vivacious, now with dignity of her own, tiny-limbed, and soft voiced as she talked the musical Turkish. She was to him a child in years, yet she was wise and full of knowledge.

Of late he had felt himself growing old, crusted over with the toils of the day, dusty and wrinkled with the strain of life. To steady his nerves during these last few weeks he had been drinking even more heavily than ever. Now he gave it up. He needed it no more. His youth had returned to him. Once more the blood pulsed through his veins. He was alive and vibrating.

And Latifa responded. Quite openly she adored him. He was the Hero, the Savior of her Country.

He wasted no time, made love, direct, impetuous, brutally as he understood it. She responded to his caresses, was soft, alluring, yet never gave herself, always evaded him at the end, leaving him unsatisfied, wondering how far she cared. He tried to impose his will. He played on her patriotism and hero-worship with all the guile his experiences had given him, but in vain, and because his experience was at fault.

For since he was a boy he had lived uncleanly, and when the wildness of youth had passed, he had not put uncleanness from him. He had no morals nor any belief in women or in virtue, nor had he even good taste to keep him steady in his lack of morals. In his affairs there had been no great pulse of love to give them glamour or excuse their sins. They had been crude, sweaty intrigues of the *maison de rendezvous* of bastard Levantine Constantinople, with now and again a peasant girl. He had lusted in Paris, and Sofia, and Pera with the harlots, and paid the price of disease and reaction. He had indulged in many vices, debased himself in uncleanliness, and grown coarse-fibered. He had taken his pleasure with the loose painted women, who drank with him as his boon companions in the house at Chan Kaya.

He had no delusions about women. They were to be used and enjoyed. When done with they must be pushed

165

aside, and their complaints stifled with money. Of the possibilities of Woman and Love he had a vague academic knowledge from the western books he had read. In reality he had no such conception. He was oriental right through, and moreover an oriental despot.

Now he had met something new, a girl of breeding, free, self-possessed, educated in the West, absorbed in Western ideas, capable of meeting him intellectually, of holding his interest beyond the passing of sex, capable of being a partner and a helper. And withal, soft and scented, rousing desire, exquisite and maddening. He was swept off his feet. He was on fire. For the first time he was in love.

Word came to him that Fikriye was on the way to Smyrna. The news angered him; true, once she had meant much to him; but why should she cling to him now? She must realize that he was tired of her; he knew that he hated her; she was in his way; he would allow neither Fikriye nor any one else to be in his way; if she had been ill-natured or unfaithful, it would have been easy to turn her out, but she was always faithful and pathetic; still, she must go.

She had served him well; he would see that she did not suffer; he would send her to Paris and Munich with plenty of money; she should do a cure, have a good time and be gay.

He dismissed her from his mind and hurried back to the house above Bornovo, and to Latifa. She was his. He could wait no more. All this evading was merely a woman's guile. He would take her at once, that night.

After the evening meal they stood together, Latifa and Mustafa Kemal, on the veranda of the upper room looking down. Cut into little terraced gardens, each walled up with gray stone, the hills ran steeply down below them to the sea.

Among the olive trees and the vines the camp-fires had begun to twinkle.

Below them lay the city of Smyrna. The fire in the Christian quarters had spread. It was sweeping across one end of the city, licking up the houses. In the gloaming, it glowed red-hot; now there would be a fierce explosion as some dump of ammunition blew up; now the wind would fan a wooden house into flame and it crashed in ruins. In the glare of the fire the harbor showed full of corpses bobbing in the waves, and beyond that, red also in the glare, lay the battleships of Europe.

"It is a sign," said Mustafa Kemal pointing to the fire, "a sign that Turkey is purged of the traitors, the Christians, and of the foreigners, and that Turkey is for the Turks."

From the garden came up all the soft, sweet sounds of the night, and a warm wind brought up the scent of roses and jasmine.

He drew Latifa to him, and kissed her, covered her face with kisses, half-carried her towards the inner room where his orderly had already made his bed.

For answer she drew suddenly away from him. "You do not understand," she said. "I love you, but I will not be your mistress. Marry me and I am yours."

"What is marriage?" he replied, "a few empty words said by a dirty bearded priest. Do they make so much difference? Moreover, I have sworn not to marry until my work for Turkey is done. I need you. I need you now."

"I too have sworn," she replied, "I will not give myself except in marriage. It is my condition. My oath holds as well as yours."

They stood facing each other in the dark upper room, with the great fire below reddening the windows and the ceiling—the girl haughty and imperious, the man with his fingers crooked to take her. It was long since he had been

167

so refused. Yet there was something about the girl that made him hesitate to take her by force. Despotic, self-willed, self-indulged, he was maddened to fury by her refusal. In a fury he flung himself away, and went out. In the morning his room was empty. He had gone to the army.

PART NINE

XLII

FOR weeks there came no word, though Latifa waited. She adored Mustafa Kemal. She would have given her eyes or her life to have saved him from the least trouble; but she had learned the Western outlook, for she had been educated in England and France: her man must respect what he would have. She had kept her honor to keep her man. Yet she wondered if she had been wise. Had she mishandled and lost him? As time went by and still there was no word from him she took up old interests—the study of law and French literature, and she helped refugees, of whom there were thousands round Smyrna.

And Mustafa Kemal was hard at work. He had blotted out from his mind the house on the hills at Bornovo. He was living at terrific pressure. Now he was in Brusa, now making vital decisions in Angora. Sleeping badly and drinking heavily again to steady his nerves.

A military crisis was at hand and he had to make the most important decision of his life. The Greek Army, though beaten, had slipped away at Smyrna across the sea. With fresh troops from Athens it was re-forming in Thrace, beyond Constantinople.

Mustafa Kemal had no ships. He must go after the enemy by land. He had hurried his troops northwards to get at them and smash them before they re-formed. His road lay across the Dardanelles. There, at Chanak, he had found an English Army which refused to let him pass into Europe, and stood between him and the Greeks. There was the problem: the Greek Army re-forming in Thrace; the Turkish Army hurrying up to get at the Greeks; the English Army of Occupation holding the road and standing between them.

Back in Angora, Mustafa Kemal was calculating, as he always did, weighing every possibility before he made his decision. He could not afford to wait. Time was a vital factor. He must smash the Greeks before they were re-formed and dug in.

The Greeks! He could beat them to pulp; but the English! That was a different matter.

The Turkish troops though blown up with the pride and excitement of victory were tired, in rags, short of ammunition, without big guns or the advantages of mechanical warfare.

The English troops were seasoned, their officers experienced, their positions strong and well-entrenched. Behind them lay a great armada of battleships with big guns, and aëroplanes, and behind that again all the might of the British Empire.

If the English meant to fight, the Turks would be beaten. But did they mean to fight? Were they bluffing? That was the question.

The French and Italians said they were bluffing. So did the Russians; but they were always for trouble. The English papers were howling against war and against Lloyd George. Lloyd George was determined to fight, but many said that his power was at an end and the English would not follow him.

The vital factor was the English commander, Sir Charles Harington. It was a battle of wits and character between these two. The Turk away up in the mountains of

Anatolia was absolute dictator; in his hands was a nation wild with success and fighting for its home and its existence. The Irishman in Constantinople was unsure of his ground; he was nominally in command of an Allied Army; his English troops were good enough, but the French and Italian would not stand by him, and he was not sure that England would either. He was not fighting for any great ideal; his only object was to extract himself and his army from an awkward and a false position with the least loss of men and prestige.

And the characters of the two commanders suited the rôles they had to play. The Turk was steel-willed and resolute. He knew his objective. He was determined to get it or smash Turkey and himself in the attempt. He had studied his opponent. He had read many of his telegrams to London, intercepted by the Turkish Intelligence; he had received letters from him and reports on him from Turkish observers in Constantinople. He saw that Harington was more diplomat than soldier. He could make his troops contented, but he could not stiffen them. He was a good staff-officer, clever, highly nervous and pleasant mannered, but he was no gambler, no leader in a time of crisis. He would never take the big decision with the big risk.

Mustafa Kemal made up his mind. Some of his advisers wished him to make peace at once and not risk defeat. The majority demanded fiercely that he should attack at once, brush the English aside, get at the Greeks and chase them down to Athens. Mustafa Kemal, with his cool judgment, his surer sense of true values, held his hand from the empty boastings of the one and the weakness of the other.

He decided against asking for peace. He would never get the terms he wanted. He would dictate terms, not negotiate for them. He would get at the Greeks now. He believed that Harington would at the last minute weaken, and let him pass.

He would make a "try-out." He ordered two thousand of his cavalry to advance towards the English lines. They were stopped firmly; that looked serious.

He must gamble, trust his star. He would try a trick, a *ruse de guerre,* which might work with a weak-willed opponent. He sent his infantry towards the English position with orders to advance with arms reversed, and to be friendly, and peaceful; if possible, to walk through and make the English entrenched position untenable.

The danger was great. On both sides among the troops tempers were rising. One shot, one misunderstood order, one hot-headed command, and the battle would start and Turkey be at war with England.

But no shot was fired. The English troops in the trenches were at a loss what to do: their orders were a weak compromise—to hold up the Turks, but not to fire or use force —and the Turks kept advancing and would neither stop nor fight. The position had become critical: the Turks were close up to the barbed wire; they had started to come through, when the order came to stand fast. An armistice had been arranged.

The French had sent a representative, Monsieur Franklin-Bouillon, direct to Mustafa Kemal. France was terrified that war with England might blaze up into another world catastrophe, with Bolshevic Russia joining Turkey. Franklin-Bouillon came pathetically eager to stop all chance of war: for the Allies and for England too he was prepared to promise anything: the Allies would be responsible for the evacuation of the Greek Army out of Thrace and the restitution of European Turkey to the Turks: anything that Mustafa Kemal wanted, anything to avoid even the threat of war.

And, as a favor, Mustafa Kemal agreed. In reality he had got all he wanted. This was victory. It would have cost him perhaps fifty thousand men and months of fighting to get this result, and the odds were that he would have been beaten. The English bluff had failed.

He ordered his troops to stand fast and sent Ismet to meet Harington at the village of Mudania to fix the details.

At Mudania the Allies agreed to turn the Greeks out of Thrace and themselves in due course to evacuate Constantinople and all Turkey.

Mustafa Kemal had triumphed. Sakkaria was the turning of the tide: Smyrna was a showy success: this was the real victory. It was his victory. It was his courage, determination, skill, and judgment that had made his little underfed, under-equipped, ragged army chase out the Greeks, forced the British Empire to give him his terms, and frighten all Europe.

Now he would dictate terms of peace at home and abroad.

XLIII

IN the lull his thoughts went back to Latifa and the house among the gardens in the Bornovo hills above Smyrna. Always reserved and secretive, he had told no one of his failure. His cronies in Angora and his drinking companions had dug each other in the ribs, chuckled and made their coarse jokes about it; the Gazi had been successful once more with a woman, they said.

The house at Chan Kaya was quiet. Fikriye was gone. She had cried, pleaded, clung to him, when he had told her that she must go to Munich for a cure. He had been kind to her, soothed her, given her money, but he had made her

173

go. She had sent him messages. He had not replied. He wished to close this page of his life. He did not want her back; and yet he missed her.

His mother was bedridden. He would talk to her. He wondered how the old woman would receive Latifa. She had been so very jealous of Fikriye. He found her all for solid marriage, and the making of a family.

As ever, he made up his mind slowly, weighing all possibilities, and then he acted with the speed and force of a cyclone, and without looking back or regretting. He called for his car, told no one where he was going, drove pell-mell half across Turkey to Smyrna, and up to Bornovo. Latifa was in the upper room. He ran up the stairs.

"We will marry, now at once!" he said without waiting to be announced or to explain, or any preliminaries, catching her to him. "At once, without delay, without any ceremony or invitations."

He gave orders as the despot. She had refused him before. He had failed to get his way then. She should keep her scruples, her sentiment about marriage, but he would have his way and impose his will.

For a minute the girl was taken aback at the suddenness of his arrival and the suddenness of his proposal. She must have a few hours. He agreed impatiently.

Soon after dawn he was back urging her to be ready. He hurried her out into the road, caught hold of the first bearded priest on his way to his mosque, and ordered him to marry them, there, at once, in the street, without delay, so that the formalities might be done.

Even then he told no one. He traveled with Latifa through the ruined country round Smyrna. Only when she drove beside him in state to a review did his friends and his cronies realize that the Gazi had taken a wife.

Some sneered. Some prophesied a failure. Others read into his marriage his desire to become a king or sultan and found a dynasty. But his mother and the simple peasant folk of Turkey rejoiced.

PART TEN

===

XLIV

IN the full flood-light of his great prestige, high up alone on a pinnacle of greatness, stood Mustafa Kemal, the victorious general; a dangerous place for a vain man.

The Turks had won. The enemy—the English, the French, the Italians and the Greeks—had no more fight in them. They were quarreling amongst themselves. Their alliance had turned to enmities. Above all the people of England, France, Italy and Greece did not care one jot what happened in Turkey. They were not going to waste a man or horse, or even a shilling, on fighting the Turks. They wanted peace, whatever the price.

Mustafa Kemal saw the one effective weapon in the coming peace negotiations was his little army of a hundred thousand ragged Turkish fighting men, backed by the determination of the Turks to win, or fight until destroyed.

True, there were a few enemy troops still in Constantinople, but he could afford to leave them there; though irritating, they were powerless; they were there only on sufferance; they might even be useful as hostages, for with Thrace in his hands—he had already sent Refet post haste to supervise the taking over from the Greeks—he could surround them or squeeze them out when it suited him.

Now he repeated publicly the terms on which Turkey would make peace. They were the same as those laid down in the National Pact. Turkey must be an independent sovereign State within its own frontiers, and free of all foreign interference.

A smaller man might well have increased his demands, been blown up with new ambitions, dreamt dreams of conquest, for from every Islamic country—from India, Africa, from the Malay States, Russia, Afghanistan, Persia and China, even from Christian Hungary, came addresses of congratulation, swords of honor, telegrams of praise: praise on fulsome praise, enough to turn any man's head. All across the world subject races stirred in hope. Wherever there was massed hostility to the imperial nations of the West men looked up expectant to Mustafa Kemal, believing that a champion had arisen. They saw in this Moslem general, who had defeated all the might of Europe, the spearhead of their advance towards freedom from the white man and the Christian. The Soviets were urging him on. Persia and Afghanistan were proposing offensive alliances. The Indians, the Syrians and the Egyptians wanted his help. From all sides came invitations to become the champion of the East against the West.

But, as ever, though reveling in the praise, drinking in all the flattery, strutting down the center of the stage, Mustafa Kemal remained level-headed, steady in his judgment, clear in his aims. He had no delusions. He knew exactly what the Turks could do. He was not going adventuring with dreams of empire or foreign conquest. The Ottoman Empire was dead and broken up: good riddance to it, for it had sucked the marrow out of the bones of the real Turks. For five centuries, in Irak, in Arabia and Africa, Turks had fought and died; they had been exploited shamelessly by their Sultans, and without any profit. Enough of that! He would not revive any Ottoman Empire.

To some of those who came to him he replied, "We

all wish to see our Moslem brothers live free. Beyond our wishes we can give them no help."

In the Assembly he said, "I am neither a believer in a league of all the nations of Islam, nor even in a league of the Turkish peoples. Each of us has the right to hold to his ideals, but the Government must be stable with a fixed policy, grounded on facts, and with one view and one alone —to safeguard the life and the independence of the nation within its natural frontiers. Neither sentiment nor illusion must influence our policy. Away with dreams and shadows! They have cost us dear in the past."

To the Bolshevics he was even clearer. A delegation had come from Moscow headed by the Ukranian general, Frunze. The Azerbaijan Minister gave a dinner in honor of the delegation. After the wine the general spoke at length, elaborating the Bolshevic theme of the great oppressor nations of the West and the oppressed subject races, and calling on Turkey to join in the work of deliverance.

Mustafa Kemal rose. He was brief, even curt: "There are no oppressors, nor any oppressed," he said. "There are only those who allow themselves to be oppressed. The Turks are not among these. The Turks can look after themselves; let others do the same."

He would not lead Turkey into these follies nor become the champion of the East against the West, of Islam against Christianity, of subject races against their masters.

"We have but one principle: to see all problems through Turkish eyes and to guard Turkish interests."

He would make Turkey, within its natural frontiers, into a small, compact nation and into a prosperous State.

But within these limits he would be master. He believed that he, and he alone, could create and organize this new Turkey and bring it to success and prosperity.

XLV

YET all his military success, the flattery, the cheers of the army, had not blinded Mustafa Kemal to the fact that with the exception of Ismet and Fevzi and a few close friends the generals round him, the politicians and his old enemies, did not accept him as their superior. Many of them hated him personally. None of them, now the foreign enemy was beaten, were going to allow him to remain the master. He must fight for power and they would oppose him. Twice the Assembly had called him back to Angora to discuss with him the situation and the arrangements for the coming Peace Conference. He knew that they wanted him back under their thumb. They had made him dictator temporarily to meet the military crisis. They were determined not to let the victorious general become the permanent dictator.

He was ready for them. One evening Halideh Edib in her quiet way said to him:

"After peace, Pasha, you will rest; you have struggled so hard."

"Rest, what rest?" he replied savagely. "After the Greeks we will fight each other; we will eat each other."

"Why should we?" she asked.

"What about the men who have opposed me?" he shouted. His eyes squinted and glittered sinisterly, as they did when he was angry. "I will have them lynched by the people. No! We will not rest. We will kill each other. Moreover," he continued, dropping his voice, "when this struggle is over, it will be dull. We must find some other excitement."

He sent word to Angora that he could not come back; his military duties took him to Smyrna.

Rauf, the Prime Minister, and a string of politicians

came after him. They wanted his views. What was the Government to be in new Turkey? In Angora was the provisional government with the power. In Constantinople was the Sultan-Caliph with his Grand Vizier and ministers, but it was a government only in name. General opinion favored an amalgamation with a Sultan as a constitutional sovereign and Mustafa Kemal as the first Prime Minister. What did Mustafa Kemal think of that?

But he kept his own counsel. He had no intention of becoming Prime Minister to a constitutional Sultan. His own ideas were clear and revolutionary. As soon as the foreign enemies were gone the Sultanate, the Caliphate, all the lumber of the Ottoman Empire must go after them: all the old useless pomp and the antiquated nonsense left over from the past. He would proclaim a Republic, and under this disguise he would be its absolute ruler. After that he would reform Turkey in every detail.

But for the time being he must move with caution and cover his intentions. He was not sure of the strength of the opposition. All Turks were conservative and religious. The army was loyal to him, but even the soldiers might resist an attack on the Sultan or the Caliph. Without the army he was no one.

Rauf was suspicious. He persisted in his questions; refused to be diverted into discussing the details of the coming Peace Conference. To gain time Mustafa Kemal agreed to meet him in Angora and tell him his views.

They met in Angora round a table of drinks. Refet was there as talkative as ever, chatting as usual with his hands and head as well as his tongue; Ali Fuad also, just back from a mission in Moscow, and with them Rauf. They were the same men who had sat with Mustafa Kemal in the first conference at Amassia in 1919. Then he had needed their support. All three were important men who had done big things.

Opposite them sat the Gazi, gray and sinister, conscious of his power and prestige, strong in his success, hard and strong because he had no pity or sentiment to weaken his will, no loyalties to complicate his decisions. He was strong too in a supreme belief in his own judgment, ability and star. He knew his own mind: he was prepared to prevaricate to cover his plans, but he was determined, ruthlessly and without scruple, to get his ends, however long he must wait, whatever weapons he must use and whatever the price, he was a very different man from the Mustafa Kemal who had pleaded for their support at Amassia.

Rauf and Refet knew Mustafa Kemal's ideas. They had heard all his revolutionary views. But whereas in the past these had been the theories of a man fighting with his back to the wall, now Mustafa Kemal had the power to make them into facts. Would he do it? Or, as so often, would the fiery revolutionary cool down into the staid ruler when power came to him?

They must find out; all the future depended on it. Rauf wasted no time, used no finesse, but came straight to the point.

"Some say that you intend to destroy the Sultanate and Caliphate. Is it true, Pasha?" he asked.

"I would like your opinion first as to whether it would be wise," replied Mustafa Kemal cautiously.

Between these two—both great personalities, both driven by ambitions—was beginning the inevitable rivalry now that they had no common enemy in the Greeks; the conservative against the revolutionary with no loyalties; the believer in constitutional government against the would-be dictator; the believer in tradition and steady growth against the man determined to uproot and destroy wholesale.

"My fathers and I," said Rauf, "have eaten the Sultan's salt. I do not speak of the man Vaheddin, the traitor who sits in the seat of the Sultans. He must go and be replaced. But I, and every true Turk also, am loyal to the Sultan-Caliph. We must stand by the sovereign. There must, moreover, be one in the State so high and lifted up that no

Rauf.

subject can aspire to his position." He expressed the sentiments of the whole Turkish people at that minute.

Refet agreed. Ali Fuad side-stepped, excused himself because he had only just come back from Moscow and did not know the position as yet. Mustafa Kemal prevaricated. He saw that the time was not ripe for action. He must wait.

"I do not see the need to discuss this," he said; and when Rauf pressed for something definite: "I have no intentions such as you suggest. I will in fact make a statement in the Assembly to that effect to-morrow."

The other three, satisfied, dropped the subject, and they drank pleasantly together until it was dawn. Next day Mustafa Kemal spoke in the Assembly as he had promised.

XLVI

MUSTAFA KEMAL saw that he must go slowly. The opposition was even stronger than he expected. He must wait for or he must create his opportunity. As he waited events played straight into his hands.

A week after the meeting in Refet's house, the English invited the Sultan to send a delegation to Lausanne to discuss peace terms, and requested him to repeat the invitation to the National Assembly in Angora. It was a clumsy error.

The result was electric. Except for his few personal supporters, every true Turk now hated Vaheddin. He was the traitor who had sided with the English and with the Greeks to destroy Turkey. Vaheddin and Lloyd George, they were the real national enemies! And they hated Vaheddin with double bitterness as a traitor.

As soon as the invitation was received there went up a howl of rage. In Constantinople the Sultan's men were beaten. Ali Kemal, a journalist who had backed the Sultan, was dragged out from the principal club in broad daylight, under the eyes of the Allied police, transported to Ismia and stoned to death. The Sultan's servants, his ministers, even the Grand Vizier, dared not show their faces in the streets.

In Angora the Assembly met and the deputies screamed with fury. What was this Constantinople Government? What had it done to save Turkey? What right had that antiquated old fool, Tewfik Pasha, the Grand Vizier, to sign the invitation? He and all his Cabinet were dogs, decrepits, traitors, spittle-lickers to the Toad Sultan of Stambul. There was only one government in Turkey and that was themselves, the Grand National Assembly.

Mustafa Kemal realized that, whether the time was ripe or no, he must act at once. He saw that he could persuade the deputies to drive out Vaheddin, possibly to destroy the Sultanate. He could not risk attacking the Caliphate: that would touch the religious sentiments of the whole people, down to the poorest peasants, and he was by no means sure of his ground there.

In the middle of the uproar in the House, when every deputy had shouted himself hoarse with rage, Mustafa Kemal stepped in, asked the Assembly to listen to him and proposed that the Sultanate and Caliphate be separated, the Sultanate abolished and Vaheddin expelled.

Even in its rage the Assembly realized that it was being jockeyed suddenly into a vital decision. The deputies began to cool rapidly and to debate the motion.

Mustafa Kemal had partly shown his hand. He could not afford to fail now. Backed by eighty of his personal followers he pressed for an immediate vote. The Assembly referred the motion back to the Special Committee of Law.

The Special Committee sat next day. It consisted of lawyers and priests. Hour after monotonous hour they discussed the separation of the Sultanate from the Caliphate. The chairman was a prelate, dignified in his flowing robes, and his long beard. Bearded priest followed bearded priest and prosing lawyer following prosing lawyer. Out of ancient documents they produced learned expositions of the Koran and the Sacred Law. They quoted a hundred examples from the dead histories of the Caliphs of Baghdad, and Cairo. They droned through the lagging hours, discussing each shade of meaning of the Arabic words. They split hairs on every point and broke up the simple sentences with complicated arguments, and chewed over the words with the relish of argument.

In a corner, watching, taut as a savage animal about to spring, keyed up yet silent, sat Mustafa Kemal in the gray uniform of a general.

The Committee were against him. Not one member had spoken in favor of his motion. He would lose.

But he could not afford to lose this first round. The aimless, eternal discussion of trifles angered him. His temper was rising. Was he the Conquerer, the Master, to sit all day while this pack of learned dolts played with words, looked for material to shore up the rotten structure of a dead institution?

Suddenly he lost control of himself. Shaking with anger, snarling, he leapt on to a bench and interrupted the meeting. "Gentlemen, the Ottoman Sultan took the suzerainty from the people by force," he said, "and by force the people have taken it back. The Sultanate must be separated from the Caliphate, and go. You may agree or you may not, nonetheless it will happen; only some of your heads will fall in the process."

The dictator was giving his orders. The venerable chairman rose and spoke, *"Effendiler,* gentlemen," he said, "the Gazi has explained the question before us from a different point of view from that which we had taken."

In a hurry to get out of the way of danger, the members of the Committee tumbled over each other to recommend the motion to the Assembly to be passed into law; the Sultanate should certainly be separated from the Caliphate they said; the Sultanate most certainly ought to be destroyed and Vaheddin expelled. Collecting their gowns

185

round them they hurried away to escape before the wild beast, unchained, leapt at them.

The Assembly sat at once to discuss the proposal. They began to debate. Mustafa Kemal saw that the feeling of the Chamber was against him. He must rush the vote through. He must win at all costs. He collected his personal followers round him on one side of the House and ordered an immediate vote by acclamation. Several deputies demanded a vote by name. Mustafa Kemal refused to agree. His followers were armed; some of them were capable of any action; they would shoot, if he ordered it.

"I am sure the House will be unanimous in accepting," he said with a threat in his voice, and his followers shifted their revolvers in their cases. "A show of hands will suffice."

The President with one eye on Mustafa Kemal put the motion. A few hands went up.

"Carried unanimously," said the President.

A dozen deputies leaped on to benches to protest. "It is untrue! I am against it!" Others shouted and cat-called, "Sit down! Shut up! Pigs! Swine!"; spat filth and abuse at each other.

There was pandemonium. At a nod from Mustafa Kemal, the President repeated his decision, shouting above the uproar.

"By the unanimous vote of the Grand National Assembly of Turkey the Sultanate is abolished," and closed the Assembly. Surrounded by his followers, Mustafa Kemal left the Chamber.

The rest followed quickly. Five days later Refet took over control of Constantinople by a *coup d'état*, carried out under the nose of Harington, and abolished the government of the Sultan.

For a few days the Sultan stood his ground. Then he sent a messenger to Harington. The messenger was the only man in his entourage whom Vaheddin still trusted: he was the conductor of the palace orchestra.

The conductor was old and doddering. He came to the English Army Headquarters with immense secrecy. He had nothing in writing—Vaheddin refused to write anything—and he would talk to no one but to the General Commanding-in-Chief.

At last Harington saw him. Fumbling and shivering with fright the old conductor had difficulty in explaining his message—His Imperial Master, the Sultan, craved the benign protection of the English General and of the benevolent English Government: His Imperial Master was sure that His life was in danger: His Imperial Majesty had decided to bolt, and the quicker the better.

Two days later an English ambulance car drew up at a back door of the palace. With his son, some baggage, and a eunuch carrying a bag, Vaheddin came out.

The morning was overcast and there was a slight drizzle.

An English orderly let down the wooden steps at the back of the ambulance. With an umbrella clutched in one hand the last of the Imperial Ottoman Sultans, the Emperor of All the Turks, the Grand Seigneur, the Terror of the World, tried to clamber up the wooden steps. The umbrella got stuck in the doorway, and refused to go in. The old man struggled with it feebly and began to grow peevish and irritated: he could not close it for he would get wet, and he refused to leave it behind. An English officer took the umbrella away from him, gave him a heave up and shut the door. The ambulance drove away.

From a quay a motor-boat raced out. On an English battleship the Admiral Commanding-in-Chief received the Sultan with due ceremony.

Suddenly there was an outcry: Vaheddin came hurrying back to the gangway; he was cursing the eunuch, who piped and screeched back at him like a young girl; the bag which the eunuch had been carrying was gone; where was it?

At last it was found in the launch. Vaheddin looked inside. It was all right; and with a sigh of relief he went to his state cabin; the bag contained the Imperial coffee-cups which were of gold, and any jewels that he had been able to collect.

An hour later Vaheddin sailed away out of Turkey in an English battleship—to the end a decrepit, flabby, terrified old man.

His nephew, Abdul Mejid, was created Caliph of All the Faithful in his stead, but without any temporal power or position.

XLVII

MUSTAFA KEMAL had won, but only by a narrow margin. His prestige as the victorious general, and the universal hatred of Vaheddin, had carried him through. The Sultan and the Sultanate were gone.

But he had also learned his lesson. It was clear that to retain power he would have to fight every inch. The deputies, whether soldiers or politicians, were against him. Most of them were afraid of him and distrusted him; many of them disliked him personally.

During the fight against the foreign invaders they had stood beside him. Now very few would accept him as ruler or even leader. With the Sultan driven out there was no legal ruler in the country. The form of government of New Turkey would have to be decided within the next few weeks. The people were at heart conservative. The Assembly was for some sort of constitutional monarchy. The minute he attempted to become dictator they would oppose him. The mildest of his revolutionary reforms would raise a storm.

It was his habit to prepare and make up his mind slowly and then strike only when he was sure. He had been rushed into action against the Sultan, and showed his hand before he was ready. He must sit back and think out his plans this time.

He might combine with Rauf, but that would mean at the best that he would be the nominal head of a constitutional government. He had no intention of trying that. He would be the dictator.

For the moment he had force with him, but that would not see him through. The army was loyal to him to-day, but very soon, in the hard days of peace and poverty ahead, they would forget his victories. His handful of personal supporters were always ready with their revolvers, but he could not continually overawe the Assembly and the nation with them.

He must have something more than force. He must create a political fighting machine as his weapon; such a machine was waiting ready to his hand.

The Committees for Local Resistance which he had, with Rauf and Refet, created in 1919 had grown in time into an organization which covered the whole country. It had been the backbone of the Nationalist organization which drove out the Greeks and the English and carried Turkey to victory.

The organization still remained. It was a military organization. It was still inspired by a white-hot patriotism.

As he was Commander-in-Chief, it was under his direct orders.

This organization he decided to turn into a party machine, strictly disciplined, and, under his immediate control, it should be the real ruler of Turkey. He would call it the "People's Party." Its members should have the special privileges that are the perquisites of rulers, power and patronage in their own areas. The Committee of the "People's Party" in a village should decide who should be the mayor, the azar, the muktar, the priest, the schoolmaster, policeman, postman, street-cleaner, the char-woman in the Government offices. Thus the Committees would be bound to him personally; his success or failure would react on each of them.

He made his plans and set out on a tour of the country. Everywhere he was received with acclaim: the Gazi, the Liberator of the Fatherland. The people went wild with enthusiasm at seeing their hero. He was their ideal of a ruler, a strong man, and a successful soldier; that he was brutal, and evil liver, did not change their views; that they understood.

As he toured, he gathered in the reins of the organization he had planned. At every place he stopped, he called the Committees, treated them with respect, listened to their ideas and their requests.

"Keep your organization," he explained to them. "The foreign enemy is gone, but the war is not over. The country is full of traitors. Expand your organization; stand by me; obey me. Together we can build this Turkey—your Turkey which you have won back by your blood—on to such firm foundations that it can resist the attacks of all enemies from without *and from within*. You will be the People's Party. Collect all loyal good Turks into your organization. It is you, the people, and the People's Party, who must rule our Turkey."

He avoided all mention of the revolutionary changes in his mind: that would frighten these simple, loyal, conservative village folk, especially any mention of attacks on religion. He would work up to these as time and opportunity served him.

The Committees agreed gladly. The peasants were with him to a man. They swore loyalty to him. They joined up with the People's Party—and the peasants' loyalty meant a loyal army, provided it was reasonably paid.

So having established his personal ascendancy, sensed the feeling of the people, and having braced up the organization and named his representatives, Mustafa Kemal returned to Angora to face his enemies.

XLVIII

Mustafa Kemal opened the attack by an ordinance to abolish the personal immunities from arrest of members of Assembly, and followed it up with a stricter censorship of the newspapers, and orders to the police to prevent any public speaking. The deputies threw out the ordinance angrily, but were powerless to prevent the censorship or police action. A state of war still existed, the form of government was as yet undecided and Mustafa Kemal was still the ruler. They understood the significance of his tour; they knew what he was after; they knew he would take revenge on any of them who opposed him the minute he got the chance; they realized that as yet he was not sure of his ground, nor prepared to take too drastic action, but at the same time they could not get at him to stop him.

They attacked on another line. Mustafa Kemal had

kept all the arrangements for the Peace Conference in his own hands. Despite many protests he had sent Ismet as the Turkish delegate, and had personally given him his instructions. The Cabinet and the Assembly had been ignored.

The Conference had opened in November. From the beginning it had gone badly. Lord Curzon dominated the Allied delegations. He and Ismet disagreed on every point. They irritated each other inordinately; Curzon, lofty, haughty, the great pro-consul, the great Panjandrum, coming down majestically to talk with and dictate to Turks; Ismet, perky, deaf and obtuse. Both equally obstinate, they quarreled and argued with each other week after week of that winter, while the other delegates hovered round trying to produce some agreement. In February the Conference broke up without result, and Ismet set out for Angora.

For Mustafa Kemal success at the Conference was essential. A failure would destroy the value of his military victories. He hurried down to meet Ismet at Eski Shehir, got the latest news, and the two traveled back together. At Angora, Rauf, the Prime Minister, and many of the deputies were not, as etiquette demanded, on the station to meet them.

Mustafa Kemal, in a rage, sent for Rauf and demanded an explanation. Rauf replied that he refused to meet Ismet; he, and not Ismet, was Prime Minister; Ismet had been sent to Lausanne without his being consulted. Moreover, Mustafa Kemal had no right to go and meet Ismet without consulting his ministers; his action was unconstitutional; he had prejudged the decision of the Assembly on Ismet's work. As a protest he resigned the premiership. From that time he was Ismet's enemy, and Mustafa Kemal's opponent.

The Assembly massed to the attack behind Rauf. For nine days they discussed the Peace Conference. They hinted that Mustafa Kemal had been bluffed by the English at

Mudania; he should have refused the Armistice, marched into Constantinople, taken his terms with the bayonet and if necessary marched on down to Athens. As to Ismet, little deaf Ismet, they said bluntly that he had handled the diplomacy as stupidly as they had expected he would; he ought never to have been sent to Lausanne, and especially without their approval; they had no respect for or belief in him; as a general he might be good, though he had never won a battle in his life, and he had lost Eski Shehir to the Greeks; as a diplomatist he was fatuous; he was making a mess of things. They prepared to censure him and to send some one else to resume the Conference.

By every guile and piece of influence which he possessed Mustafa Kemal worked to side-track that vote of censure. Ismet, whether wise or stupid, was his man; he would obey his orders implicitly; he must go back to Lausanne and succeed; Lausanne must be a success, and his success.

Some of the deputies he set against Rauf by telling them that he had resigned out of personal pique, because he had wished to go himself to Lausanne. To others he made promises; others he threatened; he collected his personal supporters ready.

The vote of censure was side-tracked. Ismet went back to Lausanne with his teeth set. He must succeed. Failure at Lausanne meant the end of Mustafa Kemal's prestige: failure meant the end of Mustafa Kemal and of himself.

Meanwhile night and day Mustafa Kemal worked at the organization of the People's Party. Time was short. A crisis was approaching. The Assembly had recognized their danger. With such a machine under his hands Mustafa Kemal would become absolute. Somehow they must prevent that. They sent a deputation to Mustafa Kemal requesting him to resign the presidency of the new party; he should not be head of any one of the political parties they said; as head of the State he should be neutral and above all party.

Mustafa Kemal rounded on the deputation. "I cannot agree," he said. "You speak of leadership of one of the political parties. There is only one political party in the State. Unity is essential. There can be no rival parties, no rival theories. For me it is a point of honor that I remain both leader of the *one* party, the People's Party, and Head of the State. There is no other party but the People's Party."

The reply was a challenge to the Assembly. Tempers began to rise. Mustafa Kemal's old comrades, the men who had stood beside him in the black days of the last four years, now stood away and grouped themselves against him under Rauf.

Rahmi, Adnan, the four great military pashas, Kiazim Kara Bekir, Refet, Ali Fuad and Nureddin: all the best men in Turkey were against him. He was isolated with only Ismet and Fevzi, his band of personal friends and drinking cronies, the beginnings of the newly-formed People's Party and his personal prestige with the army and the people on his side.

The Assembly grew truculent. Deputy after deputy joined Rauf. They openly criticized Mustafa Kemal. They would agree to no dictatorship, especially that of Mustafa Kemal. They knew him intimately. He was not fitted to rule; he had no right to dictatorship because he had led them to victory. A good general—yes! but no more. Not a man to be trusted either; revengeful, brutal, ill-mannered and full of fantastic revolutionary ideas. No man would be safe under such a ruler. And who was Mustafa Kemel to usurp such power? Had they not all done their share to win the victory? Had not Kiazim Kara Bekir destroyed Armenia and forced Russia to make a treaty; had not Refet and Rauf organized against the Greeks in front of Smyrna while Mustafa Kemal was still talking politics and masquerading as the Sultan's aide-de-camp well out of danger in Samsun and Sivas?

Mustafa Kemal's majority in the Assembly began to dwindle fast. Hoping that his new party would see him through before he was in an actual minority, he dissolved the Assembly and held an election.

The new House was as truculent and hostile as the old. It would not vote to his orders. When he spoke to it as a schoolmaster might speak to his awkward class, it refused to listen quietly.

Clearly there was no time to lose. His agents reported that the People's Party was rapidly getting into its stride. Fevzi assured him that the army was with him to a man; as long as the soldiers got their pay, rations and decent treatment they would not care what he did. His principal opponents, Rauf, Kiazim Kara Bekir, Ali Fuad and Nureddin, happened, for the minute, to be away out of Angora. Ismet had carried the Peace Conference through to a brilliant success: the Turks had got almost all of what they had demanded. The last of the enemy troops with Harington had evacuated Constantinople, with their tails between their legs. Once more the full glare of publicity was on Mustafa Kemal as the victorious general. It was the moment, before his opponents grew any stronger, to decide the future government of New Turkey. He would proclaim a republic and himself be elected the president and legal ruler.

But the Assembly, given a free vote, would never agree. He must jockey it into these decisions. He planned a queer little political intrigue; he would create a crisis and use it.

He lost no time. He invited the Cabinet Ministers to

dine with him in his house at Chan Kaya. They discussed at length the future government, and the unworkability of the present system, by which each minister was responsible direct to the Assembly and was under a constant fire of criticism and interference of any deputy who wished to be unpleasant.

"We must show the Assembly," said Mustafa Kemal, after they had drunk well, "that a country cannot be governed in this way. You, the Cabinet, the Ministers, you must rule. The deputies must not interfere with you as they do now."

Each and all the ministers agreed. They all resented the constant criticism and control of the deputies.

"Now I want you to resign to-morrow," he continued. "I will ask the Assembly to take over and form a government. Whatever the proposal, each of you must refuse to take office again, and each of you must make everything as difficult as possible. We will then see what a mess the Assembly will get itself into. They will soon be glad to have us all back."

Next day the Cabinet resigned and the Assembly set to work to make a new government. In the absence of Rauf and the opposition leaders the deputies could not agree between themselves. They lobbied and argued, each one voting for his own interests and friends. They discussed, harangued and quarreled until there was confusion and pandemonium, but no government.

Two days later Mustafa Kemal gave another dinner-party to a few intimate friends. Ismet, Fethi and Kemalledin were among them. He smiled as they told him of the confusion. His plans were working out. There was still no government. In the House there was nothing but intrigue and quarreling, until the deputies were nearly come to blows.

"It is time," he said suddenly, "to make an end of this. To-morrow we will proclaim the republic. It is the way out of all the difficulties.

"You, Fethi," he continued, "will to-morrow complicate the discussions in the House as far as possible; work the members up until the Assembly has tied itself into knots. You, Kemalledin, will then propose that I be called to take charge and straighten out the tangle into which the Assembly have got themselves."

After the others had gone, through the night far into the dawn, Ismet and Mustafa sat drafting the Bill which should make Turkey into a republic.

The little intrigue worked out according to plan. The Assembly came completely to a standstill. The deputies were split up into small groups, which glared at each other, shouted abuse, and prepared to go for each other's throats. They gladly voted Kemalledin's proposal to call in Mustafa Kemal and hand over to him the power to form a new Cabinet.

Mustafa Kemal was in his house at Chan Kaya. At the first request he would not come, and until the Assembly had sent him word a second time that they had failed to form a government and prayed him to take over, he did not move. Even then he came only on condition that his decisions must be accepted as final.

In an ante-room of the House he collected the friends whom he had chosen to form the new Cabinet—all his opponents were excluded—and then returned to the House and mounted the rostrum.

For a minute he looked down over the rows of deputies beneath him, his face set, sinister and gray—half sneering: an overpowering personality dominating these little men below him, these rats who had been showing their teeth at him. In the bitterness of their own disagreements they had forgotten their quarrel with him. They looked up, waiting, silent.

"You have sent for me," he said at last, "to take control at a moment of difficulty. The difficulty is of your own making. This crisis is due to no passing difficulty. It is due to a fundamental error in our form of government. The Assembly is both the legislative and the executive authority. Each one of you, each deputy," he continued, "wants to vote on every Cabinet decision, have his fingers in every government office, and his thumb on every minister. Gentlemen, no ministers can take office under such conditions. You must realize that government on these terms is impossible: it is not government, but chaos.

"We must change the system. I decide that Turkey become a Republic with a President."

The Assembly was staggered by the sudden declaration. They had handed their powers over to Mustafa Kemal to choose a Cabinet to meet a temporary crisis. He had declared a new form of government. They had agreed to accept his decision: they had no choice but to accept.

Though forty percentage of the deputies did not vote, the Bill prepared by Mustafa Kemal and Ismet making Turkey into a republic was passed, and Mustafa Kemal was elected the first President.

With that vote Mustafa Kemal became the legal autocrat. He was President of the Republic with power to appoint his Prime Minister and ministers. He was also President of the Council of Ministers, of the Assembly and of the People's Party, which very soon was to be the ruling machine of the country. He was Commander-in-Chief and held the army and the people in his hands.

The Government newspapers—the rest were silenced

by the censor—wrote glowing paragraphs of the joy with which all through Turkey the proclamation of the Republic was celebrated. In reality the Turkish peasants and townsmen cared little except that it made a topic for talk in the cafés. They lived very near the starvation line. Their interests were in the primitive hard facts of life, their fields, their animals, their little shops, the tax gatherer's dishonesties, whether their sons came back from conscription safe and sound to look after them in their old age, whether their daughters got good husbands. The complaints of their wives meant more to them than all the discussions of the Assembly in Angora. Whether Mustafa Kemal, their hero, was Sultan or President, meant nothing to them as long as they had peace, enough to eat, and somewhere to live and sleep.

XLIX

MUSTAFA KEMAL had his hands almost on the absolute power at which he aimed. In every town and village the People's Party, his political weapon, was getting a hold. The army was under his direct orders. His grip was on all the machinery of state. But his real fight was still ahead.

To his friends he had always made it clear that he would root out religion from Turkey. When he talked of religion, he became eloquent and violent. Religion was for him the cold, clogging lava that held down below its crust the flaming soul of the nation. He would tear that crust aside and release the volcanic energy of the people. It was a poison that had rotted the body politic. He would purge the State of that poison. Until religion was gone, he could not make of Turkey a vigorous modern nation.

"For five hundred years these rules and theories of an Arab sheik," he said, "and the interpretations of generations of lazy, good-for-nothing priests have decided the civil and the criminal law of Turkey.

"They had decided the form of the constitution, the details of the lives of each Turk, his food, his hours of rising and sleeping, the shape of his clothes, the routine of the midwife who produced his children, what he learnt in his schools, his customs, his thoughts, even his most intimate habits.

"Islam, this theology of an immoral Arab, is a dead thing." Possibly it might have suited tribes of nomads in the desert. It was no good for a modern progressive State. "God's revelation!" There was no God. That was one of the chains by which the priests and bad rulers bound the people down.

"A ruler who needs religion to help him rule is a weakling. No weakling should rule."

And the priests! How he hated them. The lazy, unproductive priests who ate up the sustenance of the people. He would chase them out of their mosques and monasteries to work like men.

Religion! He would tear religion from Turkey as one might tear the throttling ivy away to save a young tree.

These were his views, held with the passion and hatred of the revolutionary. How far he could carry them out, he was doubtful.

The Turks, villagers and townsmen alike, still clung to their religion. Religious and conservative, they disliked all change. If roused by the priests, they became fanatical. Religion was the woof and warp of the texture of their lives. To tear it out was to destroy the whole fabric. If their religion was touched, would they quietly acquiesce or would they resist?

Mustafa Kemal was not sure. He must move with caution. When a journalist asked him if the new Republic would have a religion, he avoided a definite reply. In his outline of the policy of his People's Party he made no mention of religion. He made no public pronouncement on the subject. He had decided that he must bide his time, hoping to wean the people from their old allegiance.

L

BUT his opponents gave him no chance to wait. Outmaneuvered and half-beaten, they dared not let him get firmly into the saddle. They were his old intimates and they knew Mustafa Kemal too well. This would be no kid-glove affair: no matter of parliamentary debates and verbal maneuvers. They knew that once he was firmly in the saddle he would hang or exile the lot of them.

Already the word had gone through the country that Mustafa Kemal intended to destroy Islam and drive out the Caliph. During the last few months, in the heat of his fight with his political opponents, he had shown his hand more than once. When Abdul Mejid was elected Caliph, Mustafa Kemal had refused to allow the full ceremony to be performed. When the Assembly began to discuss the position and the power of the new Caliph, Mustafa Kemal cut the debate short. "The Caliph," he said, "has no power or position except as a nominal figurehead."

When Abdul Mejid had written asking for an increase of his allowance, Mustafa Kemal had replied brutally: "The Caliphate, your office, is no more than an historical relic. It has no justification for existence. It is a piece of impertinence that you should dare to write to one of my secretaries."

Further, it was public knowledge that he was irreligious, broke all the rules of decency, and scoffed at sacred things. He had chased the Sheik-ul-Islam, the High Priest of Islam, out of his office and thrown the Koran after him. He had forced the women in Angora to unveil. He had encouraged them to dance body close to body with accursed foreign men and Christians. His wife went unveiled and dressed like a man, and was stirring up the women in Angora to ask for equal rights with men.

The word went round that the rulers in Angora were accursed and without religion.

In the mosques and the market-places the hojas and the dervishes preached, warning the people against the government. They denounced Mustafa Kemal and his sacrilegious acts, his sneers at sacred things. Caricatures and pamphlets were circulated broadcast from the schools and the dervish monasteries.

His opponents encouraged the agitation. They sent out agents into the city. They left Angora and grouped themselves round Abdul Mejid, the Caliph, in Constantinople. They calculated that they were on firm ground. They did not believe that Mustafa Kemal would dare to touch the Caliph.

But Abdul Mejid, the Caliph, was no schemer. He was a simple, honest, good-looking quiet gentleman, fifty years of age, who had studied painting and loved his books and his garden. He had lived simply since youth in his palace on the Bosphorus. Even dirty-tongued Stambul had not one unclean story about him.

But after the flight of Vaheddin, elected by the Assembly to be Caliph, Pope of all the faithful of Islam, the Shadow of God on earth, he took his high office as a supreme duty. He revived the traditions of the great Sultan-Caliphs. Instead of using a hackney carriage like his predecessor, he rode gallantly like Mohammed the Conqueror on a white charger across the Golden Horn to Santa Sophia to say the prayers each Friday, with an escort of hussars behind him, and the crowd cheering. When he prayed in the great mosque of Skutari, he was rowed across the Bosphorus in the imperial barge with fourteen oarsmen dressed in his splendid livery, and great crowds lined the seashore. He received visitors, ambassadors, and delegates in his palace with regal dignity, conscious that he was the religious head of one hundred million of Moslems.

Yet though Abdul Mejid had no ambition, and though he did not desire political power, nonetheless, he attracted all the discontented elements in Turkey like a magnet. All the débris of the dead Ottoman Empire, the priests, the hojas and ulemas, the palace officials out of work, the dismissed officers of the old régime, the disgruntled people of Constantinople which had now ceased to be the capital, flocked round him.

Last of all came Mustafa Kemal's political opponents, Rauf, Adnan, Refet, and Kiazim Kara Bekir. They planned to make Abdul Mejid the constitutional sovereign of Turkey, with themselves as his ministers. He would be ideal for that—wise in advice, respected, trusted, holding religious as well as civil power, and yet without sufficient character or ambition to bring him into conflict with his ministers.

And Abdul Mejid, against all his wishes and inclinations, found himself the center and weapon of the opposition to Mustafa Kemal and Angora: the quiet, cultured, well-bred gentleman against the raging wild beast of Angora.

LI

MUSTAFA KEMAL saw the danger. In the hostile city of Constantinople, where the population hated him, round the

Caliph, and led by his most capable opponents, was forming a monarchical and religious movement against him. In the country the religious agitation, also against him, was increasing; the people looked up to the Caliph as their religious head. If these two were organized and combined he would be defeated.

He was at a loss how to deal with the situation. If he acted too soon, he might light a charge that would blow him sky-high. If he waited too long, he was beaten.

As he waited wondering how to act, once more Chance came to help him, once more England supplied him with a weapon. The Agha Khan and the aged and revered Amir Ali, two Indian Moslems, decided to write a letter of protest on behalf of the Moslems of India, demanding that the dignity of the Caliph be respected. This letter was sent to the Constantinople press and published before it reached the Government in Angora.

It was Mustafa Kemal's opportunity. He unearthed the history of the Agha Khan; he was a Moslem of some importance in India; the leader of the heretical sect of the Ishmaeli; he lived in England, kept English racehorses, wore English clothes, and hobnobbed with English politicians and ambassadors; during the World War the English had increased his prestige by careful propaganda, until he was looked on as the head of the Indian Moslems; they had used him as a counterpoise to the Sultan and the Turkish propaganda in the East.

"He is," said Mustafa Kemal, "a special agent of the English."

To work up the agitation was easy. England, the crafty, subtle enemy, who had failed to destroy Turkey with the Greeks, was at her intrigues again, using the Indian Moslems and the Agha Khan to back the Caliph and split the Turks into two camps.

The Assembly flew into a blind passion. The speakers cursed the hojas, the priests, the opposition leaders, the Caliphate, the Caliph, and passed a law that all opposition to the Republic, all sympathy with the expelled Sultan, was treason and punishable by death.

When some of the deputies spoke of the diplomatic value of the Caliphate to Turkey, the House howled them down. In the silence that followed Mustafa Kemal turned to them. "Was it not," he said, "for the Caliphate, for Islam, for the priests and such-like cattle, that for centuries the Turkish peasant has fought and died in every climate?

"It is time that Turkey looks to herself, ignores Indians and Arabs, rids herself of her contacts with them, rids herself of the leadership of Islam. Turkey has enough to do to look after herself. The Caliphate has sucked us white for centuries."

He expanded his propaganda throughout the country. The editors of the Constantinople newspapers who had published the letter were tried. The description of the case was broadcast by the local Committees of the People's Party, by the Government newspapers and the Government agents. The editors, together with Abdul Mejid, were shown to be blackguards and traitors, acting as agents of the crafty unprincipled national enemy, England.

The religious agitation against Mustafa Kemal disappeared. From the country came up a growl of anger. Turkey was in danger. Mustafa Kemal must save the nation.

Still Mustafa Kemal was uncertain if he could act with safety. He must be sure of the army. Without that he was helpless. He went down to the annual maneuvers near Smyrna. For days he discussed the question with Fevzi and

205

Ismet, made discreet inquiries, tried out the feeling of junior officers and the soldiers. What would the army do if he expelled the Caliph, separated the State from religion and made Turkey a lay republic? Would the soldiers refuse to stand by him?

He could not make up his mind. Night after night he talked the whole night through, a torrent of words, trying over all possibilities, irresolute, now one mind, now of another, changing, hesitating, until a stranger would have set him down as a windbag and a weak man without courage or will.

Suddenly he decided. He would act. The army would stand by him.

As suddenly he passed from words to deeds. He was as silent now as he had been verbose before; as clear in aim as he had been undecided; as violent and strong as he had been weak. He smashed at his enemies with relentless fury. The pent-up irritations of the weeks of indecision burst out into destructive revolutionary fury.

He would intimidate his opponents first. A hostile deputy was over-voluble in the Assembly; the same night he was murdered on his way home. The Commissaire for Religion had made a speech for the Caliph. Mustafa Kemal threatened to hang him if he spoke again.

He summoned Rauf from Constantinople before the Central Committee of the People's Party and forced him to swear loyalty to the Republic and the President, on pain of expulsion from the Party and the Assembly. He sent abrupt orders to the Governor of Stambul that all the useless pomp of Abdul Mejid must stop at once; if he wished to go to prayer he must go in the old hackney carriage, the hussar escort was to be disbanded, the imperial barge put away, the Caliph's salary reduced to a minimum, and his supporters warned to leave him. There must be no Pope in Constantinople to challenge the power in Angora.

Some of the moderates begged Mustafa Kemal to become Caliph himself; a delegation from India and another from Egypt repeated the request at the same time. It was a great position; behind it was tradition, prestige and an international position. Mustafa Kemal had all the necessary attributes: he was a victorious general, the ruler of a free Moslem people, the most outstanding figure in the Moslem world. He might well have been tempted.

With a gesture of impatience he refused. Clear-headed, fixed in his aims, his greatness lay in his knowledge of the limitations of himself and his country.

"Are you," he said, frowning down on one delegation, "are you, who ask me to be Caliph, in a position to see that my orders are carried out? If not, I should be made a laughing-stock," and he turned his back on them abruptly.

To the deputies who believed that the Caliphate gave strength to Turkey he sent a reply by Ismet: "If other Moslems have helped us, or wish to help us again, it is not because we hold the Caliphate, which is a rotten dead thing, without strength. It is because we, the Turks, are strong."

In his clearness of vision lay his success. In the limitations of his aim was founded his greatness.

Now at last he was ready. The Assembly was angry; the people and the army were growling against the foreign enemy and the Caliph its ally. His opponents were frightened by his violence and muzzled by the new law of treason.

On the 3rd of March, 1924, he presented a Bill to the Assembly to secularize the whole State and expel the Caliph.

"At all costs," he said to the excited deputies, "the Republic must be maintained. It is threatened. The Ottoman Empire was a crazy structure based on broken religious foundations. The new Republic must have good foundations and a well-made, scientific structure. The Caliph and the remains of the house of Osman must go. The antiquated religious courts and codes must be replaced by modern scientific civil codes. The schools of the priests must give way to secular government schools. State and religion must be separated. The Republic must finally become a secular State."

The Bill was passed without a debate. In one hour Mustafa Kemal had ripped up all the foundations of the old State.

The same night orders were sent to the Governor of Stambul that Abdul Mejid must be gone out of Turkey before the next dawn.

With a posse of police and a military escort the Governor, at midnight, without respect or ceremony, bundled the Caliph, the Shadow of God on Earth, into a car, gave him a bag of clothes and a few pounds for his passage, and drove him across the frontier for Switzerland.

Two days later, with equally abrupt roughness, all the princes and princesses of the old régime were bundled out and pushed across the frontier.

Throughout Turkey there was no demonstration, protest or resistance. Mustafa Kemal had triumphed.

LII

Mustafa Kemal was supreme, but as his hands grasped at the power for which he had labored his grip failed. This was due partly to himself, partly to circumstances.

He was ill and tired. The kidney trouble attacked him

continuously. To dull the pain he drank heavily, which made him morose and irritable. The mental stimulus of fighting had kept him taut during the last six years. In the hour of success he went slack. Fits of depression carried him down to black depths of despair, where he lost belief in himself, his mission and his star.

"I have conquered the enemy; I have conquered the country; but can I conquer the people? That is the hardest," he said.

His private life gave him no relief. He had no one in whom he would confide, no one to whom he would open up his intimate self and so get peace of mind.

His mother was gone. For two years she had lived at Chan Kaya, and then, in the severe Angora climate, her health had begun to fail. Latifa had taken her down to Smyrna for a change of air. There she had died. Even to the end Mustafa Kemal had confided in her. He had trusted her, talked to her, listened to her sage old simple advice. She was the only person he had allowed to criticize him. He knew that she was the one person who loved him for himself. She cared nothing for his success. Had he been a cheap failure, she would have loved him equally well. He missed her.

And Latifa? For the first few months after marriage he had lived in paradise. He was madly in love with her. It delighted him to have her constantly by his side as his companion. He was happy in the ordered life of the home which she made for him.

But that passed quickly. Women were to him only for pleasure. Latifa was just one woman out of many. His love was just lust and cooled rapidly.

As it cooled he became once more the bachelor. Women could only be incidents and extras in life. He did not need them except for desire. The orderly life of the home annoyed him. A woman constantly with him began to irritate him.

"Always," he once said, "I wished to live alone: to be free, to live my own life alone."

He wanted his long nights of drinking in smoke-filled rooms with his boon-companions, and his painted women.

A man cannot escape his nature. His past will mark him as surely as the small-pox. Mustafa Kemal's tastes in friends, women and amusements were coarse—drunkards, harlots, cards and drinking.

Latifa, though in theory a modern emancipated woman with advanced free ideas, was as jealous as any harem-woman. She flared out at him because he was unfaithful, opposed his drinking and drove his friends away.

Her family had come to Angora. They demanded privileges and special rights, until they became an intolerable burden, and Mustafa Kemal in annoyance drove them harshly back to Smyrna. Latifa resented his action.

They quarreled constantly. Latifa was a politician. She had the most advanced and pronounced views on the position of woman in the State: equal rights and equal opportunities for the two sexes. As Mustafa Kemal became more dictatorial, she disagreed with him and his unconstitutional acts. She sympathized with his opponents. She took up her own line in politics and developed ambitions in opposition to his. She criticized him in public as well as in private. She interfered with his work and his duties.

As long as she kept to her women's meetings Mustafa Kemal did not mind, but he would not have her criticize or interfere with him.

Both she and Mustafa Kemal were equally imperious and domineering; both were strong-willed, hard and un-yielding. She was as quick-witted and as caustic-tongued as he was. She would not stand criticism any more than he would. There was no child to soften them and to hold them together.

Their quarrels increased. The house was filled with the uproar of the disagreements. At last Mustafa Kemal decided: Latifa must go, and at once.

Always silent and reserved in his private affairs, he

Mustafa Kemal and Latifa.

discussed it with no one. He wrote out and himself signed a deed of divorce; sent a short message to the Assembly, the newspapers and the Embassies announcing the divorce, and ordered Latifa to leave the house and Chan Kaya at once. Then he went back to the long nights in smoke-filled rooms with his drinking friends—the "desperadoes" as they were nicknamed—his painted women and the life to which he belonged.

After that he became shameless. He drank deeper than

ever. He started a number of open affairs with women, and with men. Male youth attracted him. He made advances to the wives and daughters of his supporters. Even important men sent their women-folk away from Angora out of his way. Power brought out in him the brute and the beast, the throw-back to the coarse savage Tartar—the wolf-stock of the central steppes of Asia.

He did not seem to care whom he insulted or who became his enemies. He insulted Arif in one of his wild moments, and Arif left him in anger and joined his political opponents.

A certain well-known pasha came to the Gazi's house. He complained that the Gazi was too friendly with his wife; people were talking and he would be grateful if the Gazi would not single her out so often for special attention at public functions; there was probably nothing in it, but people said unkind things.

For answer Mustafa Kemal glared at him.

"I know you," he shouted, "you have been intriguing against me. Yes! it is true. I have had your wife. I took her to punish you for your intrigues," and he shouted for the guard to chase the pasha from the house. Timurlane or one of the savage horde-leaders might have shouted like that.

And Fikriye came back—Fikriye who had lived with him for so long, until he had tired of her and sent her to Munich. Oriental and Turkish she had given him all, flung all at his feet to be trampled on as her master desired. Without Mustafa Kemal life meant nothing to her. She had stayed in Munich for two years. Now she crept back and up to Chan Kaya. She pleaded with Mustafa Kemal. He drove her harshly away. Next day she was found dead in one of the stony valleys below the house, where she had shot herself. All Turkey was sorry for her.

LIII

Mustafa Kemal's whole attitude and manner of life changed. He ceased to mix freely with the people or to stroll about as he used to do, hands in pockets, to talk with any one he met. He became reserved, secluded, and difficult to see.

There had been two attempts to murder him: one with bombs which had failed clumsily, the other with poison in his food. The poison had almost killed him, so that he came back to life only with great effort, gasping his way through an agony of pain.

He became intensely suspicious. He never went out without the Lazz guard. He had searchlights fitted up over his house and gave orders that without special permits no one should be allowed near the house. If he went from Chan Kaya to Angora, all the four miles of the road were lined with soldiers with fixed bayonets. If he visited a restaurant or even a private house, it was filled before his arrival with police agents and plain-clothes detectives with their revolvers handy. Except for members of the Government such as Ismet and a few of his main supporters and the "desperadoes," he saw practically no one.

He had always been a lone man, a solitary, playing a lone hand. He had trusted no one. He would listen to no opinions that were contrary to his own. He would insult any one who dared to disagree with him. He judged all actions by the meanest motives of self-interest. He was intensely jealous. A clever or capable man was a danger to be got rid of. He was bitterly critical of any other man's abilities. He took a savage pleasure in tearing up the characters and sneering at the actions of any one mentioned, even of those who supported him. He rarely said a kind or generous thing, and then only with a qualification that was a sneer. He confided in no one. He had no intimates. His friends were the evil little men who drank with him, pandered to his pleasures and fed his vanity. Except for Ismet to act watch-dog and bark for him, and Fevzi to keep the army loyal and a handful of third-rate deputies—the scum in the Assembly—all the men of value, the men who had stood beside him in the black days of the War for Liberation, were against him. Any of them who would have stood beside him he had driven away.

And there was a storm rising. The ground beneath Mustafa Kemal's feet was sagging. Like the faint rumble of an approaching earthquake came up the voice of the people of Turkey groaning with discontent. Ismet, Fevzi and his agents warned him of the danger.

The Turkish villagers and townsmen, solid, placid, lazy people with few needs, a simple outlook and a courteous, lovable manner, would stand many privations and hardships without complaint, but even for them there was a limit. That limit had been reached.

Turkey lay in ruins. Vast areas had been devastated in the wars. Everywhere there was poverty, and the people wanted to know why. In the wars they had been made fine promises of the golden days of prosperity ahead, as soon as they were free. They were willing enough to fight to save Turkey. They had driven out the Greeks and the foreigners, and shown England and the capitalists what they thought of them. Now they were free. Times ought to be better; but they were worse, far worse than they had been under the old régime in the days of Sultan Abdul Hamid.

In those days a man could eat well and find money for tobacco and coffee, and sweetmeats for his children, and a new dress for his wife. Of an evening he could sit contentedly under the trees in the square by the coffee-shop, and discuss the news with dignity, until it was time to go to the mosque for evening prayer. Life had been easy and pleasant and well-ordered.

To-day food was hard to get. The prices were impossible. Money was scarce, and even if there was any, there was nothing to buy, for the shops were empty not only of luxuries, but of necessities. Their children were in rags. Their women had to slave to find the meals. The taxes were heavier and the tax-gatherers more greedy. All the young men had been conscripted to the army, though the wars were over. The farms and houses had fallen down, and they could not repair. Their cattle had died for lack of fodder. Their crops had been parched by droughts, and there was no more seed-corn. Life had become a wearisome, dreary struggle to keep alive. All Turkey was in ashes, burnt villages, ruined fields and vineyards, broken roads. There was poverty and want such as no man had ever before known in the land.

In reality, after the terrific strain of the war effort, had come the inevitable drag-back; and Mustafa Kemal's opponents, the politicians and the priests, used it. They fanned the flames of discontent. They incited the anger of the people. "What was the Government doing to help?" they asked. "Building a railway to carry soldiers? Making Angora into a city? Giving themselves more pay, and living on the fat of the land and quarreling among themselves, or issuing proclamations, and passing laws to change the good and ancient customs of their fathers? What was the good of these?

"Men cannot live on old victories," they said, "or on reforms, and proclamations. They need bread, seed-corn, cattle, sheep, irrigation against the droughts, money to work their farms and fill their shops. It is this ungodly Government with its irreligious theories, its upheaving changes, that is the cause of all their want."

As the mutterings and growlings increased, Mustafa Kemal's opponents in the Assembly took heart again. It was said that the army was disaffected, that in some villages the committee of the People's Party had been broken up, that in many places the villagers had refused to pay their taxes and beaten the tax-gatherers.

For some time the politicians had lain low and walked cautiously. Now they began to be more openly critical. They attacked Ismet, who had been Prime Minister since he came back from Lausanne. As this attack met with no reprisals they tabled a motion of censure on the whole work of the Government. The debate developed into a virulent attack on Ismet, and so of his master, Mustafa Kemal. "The economics and the finances of the country are in criminal confusion," said speaker after speaker. "It is the fault of Ismet."

The Turkish lira was falling; credit was disappearing. There was no capital left in Turkey. Ismet would allow none in. The foreign financiers were the only people who had any, and Ismet refused to negotiate with them, and drove them away with curses. No one would lend Turkey money, as long as Ismet was in power. The great port of Smyrna had been in ruins for two years and nothing done to rebuild it. Constantinople was being deliberately bankrupted, because it had opposed Angora; that was folly. The new commercial laws, the added complications of the customs, the preposterous stevedore and port regulations were shutting out all trade. Any traders left within Turkey were shutting up shop. The monopolies which Ismet had created and which might have been used for bargaining for capital, he had given as presents to his personal friends.

Ismet was to Turkey, they said, like a tourniquet round

a sound arm, shutting out all the blood until it withered and died. He must go, and at once.

Their attack had much justice in it. Poverty after such wars as they had fought was inevitable, but Mustafa Kemal, the dictator, and Ismet, his assistant, had made it far worse. They were both soldiers. They were without the most rudimentary knowledge of economics or finance. As a young man, Mustafa Kemal had read Rousseau and John Stuart Mill, but he had no aptitude nor liking for finance. The subject wearied him. He gladly left it to Ismet. And Ismet had even less knowledge and aptitude than Mustafa Kemal. He knew less than the average Levantine clerk in a Constantinople bank.

Away up in Angora, in the middle of the Anatolian desert, sat Ismet, divorced from all the economic life of the world, yet quite satisfied with his own ability. He had promised Mustafa Kemal that he would handle the finances. He had his office in the Ministry of Finance. There he sagely discussed finances and economics with subordinates as ignorant as himself; the Greeks and Armenians, who had handled these things, were gone. Except for one or two, such as Javid the Jew of Salonika, who were all political suspects, no Turk was capable of filling the places of the departed Christians. Ismet would call in no foreign experts nor send out Turks abroad to be trained. He talked glibly of a Turkey rich in its factories and industrial endeavor, but he did no constructive work. He passed laws without realizing their effects, and so ill-considered that they blotted out what trade was left. In his profound ignorance, the deaf little staff officer was all-wise. Meanwhile Turkey was dying.

LIV

THE motion of censure on Ismet was narrowly defeated. Ismet raged with annoyance, but Mustafa Kemal sat in Chan Kaya and made no sign. The opposition grew bolder. Under the presidency of Rauf they met in Constantinople in the home of Javid the Jew of Salonika, and formed a new party, "The Republican Progressives." All the opposition which had grouped round the expelled Caliph, together with the remnants of the old Committee of Union and Progress, joined them. Many of Mustafa Kemal's close supporters sided with them. They issued the program of the party; a constitutional government and resistance to all dictatorship. But Mustafa Kemal sat still in Chan Kaya.

The opposing political parties grew bitter. Tempers flared up at the least provocation.

Angora was no more than a ramshackle village in the middle of barren steppes. There were no amusements or relaxations. The life was bleak and as uncomfortable as the country round. While the wars were on, patriotism had kept the deputies and officers buoyed up. The wars over, they felt the discomforts acutely. They were used to the luxuries and amenities of Constantinople. In Angora the only work and the only relaxation was politics. The politicians were cheek by jowl all day. They could not get away from each other. Their nerves were on edge.

Mustafa Kemal's supporters got out of hand. It was a dangerous situation where there was a dictator who could control neither his opponents nor his supporters. There were scuffles and quarrels in the streets, in the worm-eaten hotels and in the decrepit restaurants. The opposition were called traitors, followers of the traitor Sultan. They retaliated by calling the supporters of Mustafa Kemal a gang of bullies bolstering up an autocrat.

In the Assembly there were fierce scenes. Revolvers were drawn. A Colonel Halil denounced Ismet. He was shot in the stomach at close quarters across the floor of the House in front of the Speaker, by one of the "desperadoes," and the police did not dare to arrest the "desperado."

Another deputy, one Ali Shukri, led an attack on Mustafa Kemal. He was a particularly forceful and vindictive speaker. Osman Agha, the head of the Lazz bodyguard, decided to deal with Ali Shukri.

Osman had been a brigand and the mayor of Kerasund, a town on the Black Sea coast. In 1920 he had gained an evil reputation for the brutality of his treatment of Christians. It was said that he had shot five hundred in cold blood as revenge for Greek atrocities on Turks at Smyrna. He had suffered from venereal disease. The disease had touched his brain, so that he delighted in killing. He was a wild, evil brute, and it had long been a scandal in Angora that he was the head of the President's bodyguard.

Whether Mustafa Kemal gave him the order is not clear, but Osman Agha acted. He made friends with Shukri, asked him to dinner in the guard-house at Chan Kaya and then with his Lazz assistants he strangled Ali Shukri and threw his body down the cliff-side.

When the body was found, all Angora was up in arms. The Assembly demanded the arrest of Osman. The Lazz claimed the protection of the Gazi, stating that he had acted under orders. For a short time Mustafa Kemal refused to give him up. Then he gave way.

Osman barricaded himself in the guard-house against the police. His Lazz companions mutinied in a fury, tried to kidnap Mustafa Kemal, who escaped with a few minutes to spare in a car, by a back door, and took refuge with Rauf in his house by the station. They rushed to the help of Osman. Troops were sent up to Chan Kaya; there was a pitched battle: Osman was killed, cursing Mustafa Kemal for having betrayed him, and the Lazz guard was broken up. The news went out to the Black Sea coast, and the Lazzes swore vengeance on Mustafa Kemal. In Angora and in all Turkey, as the story became known, feeling ran high against Mustafa Kemal.

Then Mustafa Kemal tried to compromise. He abolished the tithe tax, hoping to please the country people, but this was soon forgotten in the gnawing poverty which remained. Lastly, he dismissed Ismet and made Fethi Prime Minister.

He had grown very weary of Ismet. The little man had become pompous and irritable. He had made himself very unpopular. He was the martinet in the Assembly, as he had been in the army. He ruled the Assembly, the Government offices and his subordinates with a rod of iron. He had become stiff-necked. He had shown himself ignorant of finance and incompetent in politics, and yet he refused to listen to any advice.

Moreover, he had begun to interfere in Mustafa Kemal's private affairs, shown his disapproval of his friends and his hostility to the "desperadoes." On more than one occasion he had taken sides with Latifa against him.

With all the trouble in the country a change would be good. Fethi, with his shy, pleasing manner and his unfailing good-nature, was popular with every one. He would make Fethi Prime Minister.

The opposition looked on this not as a compromise, but as a victory for themselves. They attacked Mustafa Kemal himself.

They were determined to smash his power and share the ruling of the country between themselves. They brought forward a Bill to reduce the powers of the President drastically. The debate became vehement, and the Bill was defeated only by a small majority.

For Mustafa Kemal it was a critical moment. The whole country was in the post-war reaction, and resentful. The Lazzes were preparing to revolt. The People's Party was losing its discipline. Many of his best supporters, thinking that the tide was turning, had left him and joined Rauf.

Fethi.

"He is finished, he is *foutu,* played out, no more good," said one of his women with a sneer, as she packed her clothes and left him and went back to Constantinople.

He could not count on the army. In the eastern provinces the priests were out preaching a crusade against him; the Nestorians had revolted, and England had sent in an ultimatum on the possession of Mosul which struck at the basis of all his prestige.

221

LV

IN his house in Chan Kaya, tired, ill, debauched and besotted with drink, Mustafa Kemal sprawled inert. With public feeling hostile, his grip of affairs slipping from him, his friends deserting him, and battered by his enemies, it looked as if he was a spent force. His opponents were already sure he was done.

Suddenly the Kurds, the tribes who lived high up in the mountains on the Persian frontier, revolted. Sheik Said, the hereditary chief of the Naksibendi Dervishes, raised the standard of revolt with the battle-cry: "Down with the Infidel Republic of Angora and long live the Sultan and Caliph!"

The Kurds were primitive, wild mountaineers and fanatically religious. With their priests leading them and the green banner of the Prophet unfurled, they marched out to save Islam and destroy the infidel Turks.

Within two months they had swept over the provinces of Kharput and Marmuriet-el-Aziz, wiping out the Turkish garrisons, and were threatening the great city of Diarbekir. All Kurdistan went up in revolt. All the eastern provinces of Turkey were in danger. New Turkey staggered at the blow and rocked to its fall. The State and the Nation were in vital danger.

Mustafa Kemal roused himself with a growl, pushing aside the bottle and his women. Danger and the need for action was like a trumpet-call. There was fighting, and soldiers to be handled. All the latent energy in the man boiled up in him.

He threw off his lethargy. He put out his hands and once more took a grip. He called to the nation: Turkey was in danger: the great foreign enemy, England, was behind the Kurds, supplying money and arms.

Every Turk sprung to arms at the call. The flat reaction, the political opposition, the religious resistance was burnt up in a flame of patriotism. From every part of Turkey, from every class and type of men and women came telegrams with offers of help and declarations of loyalty. Turkey was in danger. The Gazi alone could save it.

Once more Mustafa Kemal dominated: ordering, directing, controlling. He swept his troops forward. Within two months more he had smashed the revolt. He lashed out ruthlessly. Kurdistan was laid waste with fire and sword; the men were tortured and killed, the villages were burnt, the crops destroyed, the women and children raped and murdered. The Turks of Mustafa Kemal, in revenge, massacred the Kurds with the cruelty and ferocity with which the Turks of the Sultan had massacred Greeks, Armenians and Bulgars.

Mustafa Kemal sent special military tribunals—Tribunals of Independence they were called. They hanged, banished and imprisoned thousands with military brevity. Many were tortured. Forty-six chiefs were hanged in the great square of Diarbekir. The last was Shiek Said, the leader. He turned to the President of the Tribunal which had condemned him.

"I have no hatred of you," he said. "You and your master are accursed of God. We shall settle our account before the Judge at the Day of Judgment."

The President of the Tribunal smiled softly. Ali was his name: Bald Ali he was called. He was noted for his gentle smile as he sent men to the gallows. He was a typical supporter of Mustafa Kemal: a man without beliefs, an evil liver, a free thinker and a materialist, but nonetheless a

223

patriot working for Turkey. The Kurd was dying for his country too, but also for religion and faith, great ideals hard to destroy and only tempered to finer steel by the fire. Never yet has the materialist destroyed the things of the spirit.

With a nod the President bade the executioner do his work! "The Day of Judgment?" He shrugged his shoulders as he watched the Kurd twitching to death. Then he went to the telegraph office to wire to Mustafa Kemal that the sheik was dead, and the revolt over.

LVI

THEN Mustafa Kemal turned back to the Turks and his political enemies. All opposition, great or small, official or personal, was to him a private quarrel. He neither forgot nor forgave anything. He would have his revenge.

He summoned the Assembly and addressed the deputies. He was roused now. The dull, prosy diction of his ordinary conversation was gone. His voice, usually muffled, hoarse and indistinct, rang out clear as a trumpet. He knew how to handle these men. He swayed them this way and that at his will. Now he stung them into anger, now he appealed to their patriotism until, like one man, they shouted with him.

He denounced the opposition leaders, especially Rauf and the four military pashas. He had evidence against them all. Here was a letter from Kiazim Kara Bekir to Sheik Said, a simple letter no doubt, but did they know what other letters had passed between the Turkish general and the Kurdish rebel? he asked, holding up the letter; the deputies must not forget that only two weeks before the revolt Kiazim Kara Bekir and Ali Fuad had resigned their commands, the commands of the very troops who would have to fight the Kurds; they had left their posts, come back to the Assembly, and, led by Rauf, with the rest of the opposition, made a big attack on the Government; the Government had been caught unprepared by the Kurds; the opposition were responsible for that.

But what made it worse was that England was behind it all, he continued. England had always used the Kurds to injure Turkey; in the World War she had sent her agents, Lawrence and Noel, to rouse them to stab Turkey in the back; at the Treaty of Sèvres she had promised to make them into a separate state; her agents had been found there again this time, arming and inciting the tribes.

England wanted Mosul and its oil. The Kurds were the key to Mosul and the oil of Irak. She was using this backhanded blow to force Turkey to give up Mosul. Had not Sheik Said gone into battle shouting for the Sultan-Caliph, for Vaheddin the traitor? They all knew the connection between England and that old toad. And the opposition leaders had joined forces with this gang to break the Republic and destroy their Turkey.

They were traitors, and they had been at work throughout the whole country stirring up the people. The Kurds were beaten, but Turkey was still in grave peril. The danger came from within. The country must be purged.

It was thin evidence, much of it fantastic, but enough in the excitement of the minute and under the personality of Mustafa Kemal to rouse the deputies. They went traitor-hunting, broke up the opposition party by force and drove it out. Some of its leaders, Rauf, Rahmi, Adnan, and Halideh Edib, had left the country already.

On Mustafa Kemal's demand the Assembly by a Statute of Law and Order suspended the constitution and gave him full powers, as absolute dictator, to save the country. The personal immunity of the deputies from arrest was abolished. The Press was rigidly censored. Any act or verbal criticism against the Government was made treason. The Tribunals of Independence were to cleanse Turkey, and at once.

Mustafa Kemal decided to impeach the opposition leaders. Fethi, the Prime Minister, the other members of the Cabinet and many of the Gazi's supporters were against this; many of the opposition were their friends; many of them, such as Rauf, Ali Fuad, Kiazim Kara Bekir, were gallant men who had done great service for Turkey; the evidence of prepared treachery was very poor, good enough for a political maneuver, but not good enough for a court of law; it would be very unsound policy to carry matters as far as that, they said.

Mustafa Kemal called a meeting of the Central Committee of the People's Party to discuss the question. The Committee were equally divided. The discussion became a quarrel, and revolvers were drawn and brandished. Fethi was called a flabby traitor and blamed for weakly letting the opposition get out of hand, but many stood with him.

Mustafa Kemal saw that as yet he could not impeach, nor get his fingers on the throats of his real opponents, without splitting up his own supporters. He must wait for a better chance.

But he would have no more shilly-shallying, no more giving way or taking half-measures. He ejected Fethi from being Prime Minister, and called back Ismet—Ismet the rigid staff officer, the merciless, hard little martinet.

The leaders might escape this time, but their followers should suffer. He sent out the Tribunals of Independence. They combed through Turkey, making a reign of terror and a bloody assize. They sent men to the gallows for an ill-timed jest, an implied criticism, or a refusal to carry out some minor regulations.

If the judges slackened, Mustafa Kemal urged them on with threats. He was absolute dictator, and power brought out in him the wild beast and the brute. The Gray Wolf of Angora raged up and down. With prison, torture and the gallows, with blood and terror, he branded his mark on Turkey.

LVII

FORCED to wait his opportunity, Mustafa Kemal was yet as determined as ever to get his big opponents. He was by instinct a conspirator and he knew the mentality of conspirators. His experience with the *Vatan* and the Committee of Union and Progress had taught him the machinery and technique of revolutions and counter-revolutions.

He knew that he had narrowly prevented a counter-revolution, which would have finished him. He believed that if he had been beaten, New Turkey would have been destroyed. Though he despised and distrusted each and every person he met, yet he had a fanatical belief, a great driving faith, in that indefinable personality, the People of Turkey, and in his mission to create out of it a great nation.

He had become a fanatic in his mission and also he had become a fanatic of Ego.

"I am Turkey," he said. "To destroy Me is to destroy Turkey." Almost as if he had dared to say, "I am the Son of God."

He was determined that no counter-revolution should even be possible.

He knew all the factors in the game. In Turkey it was always the same. There was no educated middle class. There were a few capable men and the rest of the Turks were

227

ignorant and simple-minded. However bad the times they would sit placid, suffering without complaint. They were not revolutionary by instinct or impulse as the Spaniards or the Irish, but they were easily worked up by capable and unscrupulous leaders, and then they would follow blindly. He must concentrate on and silence the leaders.

The danger to him came not from the people, but only from his big opponents. If it had not been for the flabbiness of Fethi, he would have impeached and hung them all, however good or bad the evidence. Rauf and two or three more had bolted like curs, but the rest would certainly go on working against him, underground. During the last few months secret societies had been formed in all the big towns, and especially in Constantinople. The Committees of the old Union and Progress Party had been reorganized. The old gangs were at work.

He was sure that the man behind them all was Javid the Jew of Salonika, the friend of Enver and Talat, the old Treasurer of the Committee of Union and Progress. The little fat Jew, with his Orient Freemason friends and his contacts with the international financiers, was the man with whom he had to reckon. He was the big brain behind it all.

They had thought that he was finished. He would teach them their mistake with the hangman's noose. He must get them all, but especially Javid. If he did not, they would finish him. Once they were dead, he would be supreme and secure.

For the minute, however, he must go slow, hold his hand and wait his chance.

Behind the gray mask of his face he hid his anger and his intentions, and went back to Chan Kaya. He appeared to have given up all idea of impeaching the opposition leaders.

228

In reality he was at work. As ever crafty, the master conspirator, able to wait his time, unforgiving, relentless, driven by his persistent hatred, he was laying his plans. A vast system of secret police, spies, plain-clothes men, agents-provocateurs covered Turkey. Mustafa Kemal had inherited it from the Sultan and he had developed and expanded it.

He warned the police to be more alert. He needed evidence against his enemies. They must find it. Like some gray spider, relentless, venomous, sitting watching from the center of its web for its prey, Mustafa Kemal waited for his opponents.

His opportunity came very soon. He was about to make a state visit to Smyrna. Two days before his arrival the police arrested three suspicious characters. They were found with bombs, ready in a window over the street down which he must pass, full plans to kill him and some letters which inculpated one of the opposition deputies of the Assembly, a certain Said Hurshid.

At once Mustafa Kemal struck. By third degree, by torture, bastinado, by any means they liked, the police must get enough evidence to incriminate the opposition leaders, the four military pashas, and any of the old Committee of Union and Progress, especially any of Enver's gang.

The police did their work. All the opposition leaders in the country were arrested, and a Tribunal of Independence was nominated to try them.

"This time there must be no mistake. It must be an end," said Mustafa Kemal to the judges, with his teeth clenched.

The trial was held in two parts: the first in Smyrna for the less important prisoners. Without bothering about procedure or evidence the court sentenced them all to be hanged.

The death-warrants were sent to Mustafa Kemal for his signature in his house at Chan Kaya. He sat at the table from where he could look across the plains to where Angora clustered on a bare hillside. Behind him on the wall was the green cloth covered with cryptic signs, where Fikriye had hung it.

Among the death-warrants was one for Arif. After his quarrel with Mustafa Kemal he had joined the opposition. Arif, his one friend, who had stood loyal beside him throughout all the black days of the War of Independence, at Samsun, at Amassia, at Erzerum, when he had been condemned to death by the Sultan, and at the Sakkaria; Arif with whom he had gambled and drunk in this very room; the only man to whom he had opened his heart and shown himself intimately.

One who was there reported that when he came to this warrant the Gazi's gray mask of a face never changed; he made no remark; he did not hesitate. He was smoking. He laid the cigarette across the edge of an ash-tray, signed the death-warrant of Arif as if it had been some ordinary routine paper and passed on to the next. He would allow no memories or sentiment to soften his will.

LVIII

THE second part of the trial was held in Angora. It was staged as a political demonstration on the approved style as used by the Bolshevics.

In the dock were all the opposition leaders except those, such as Rauf and Rahmi, who had escaped. These were condemned in default.

The President of the Court was Bald Ali, the Hanging Judge. He was in appearance a kindly old gentleman with the benign dignity of a Scotch elder. In point of fact, he was a scandalous and bloodthirsty old ruffian, whose proudest boast was that he had hanged more Turks than any one since Mahmud II had executed seven thousand Janissaries. He was assisted by —— Ali, a rough, swaggering bully, and by a public prosecutor. All three were members of Mustafa Kemal's gang of "desperadoes" and had his orders to hang.

Bald Ali conducted the case with no attempt at justice. The prisoners were allow no counsel for defense; they were bullied unmercifully; long before the defense was started Bald Ali had told the newspapers that the prisoners were guilty and the gallows ready. The prosecution made no attempt to sift the evidence. That the accused had opposed Mustafa Kemal, and in the case of his death would have endeavored to seize power, was clear. It was equally clear that they had no part in the actual murder plot with which they were charged.

The accusation consisted of a description of the history of Turkey for the last twenty years, bringing out how Enver and Talat, with their friends in the dock, and especially Javid, had seized power and misused it, made an alliance with Germany and so dragged Turkey into the World War and so to destruction; how they had all deserted Turkey and bolted to other countries at the Armistice to save their skins, though the Gazi had remained at his post and faced the victorious enemy; and finally how they had all persistently opposed the Gazi in his great work.

Now and again one of the judges, now Bald Ali, now —— Ali, would burst in with a harangue on the virtues of the Gazi—his godlike foresight, his wonderful patriotism, his supreme genius, all his noble actions, his amazing cour-

231

age. Then they would compare them with the infamous evil characters of his opponents in the dock.

The court did its work well, and the newspapers broadcast the proceedings. Mustafa Kemal was lauded to the sky. The prisoners were shown up as dastardly traitors. The four military pashas had their characters torn publicly to pieces, their faces blackened before the world; their influence with the army was destroyed, and they were driven out of public life. Then as an act of grace, to show the noble character and the great heart of the Gazi, they were released.

The rest, Bald Ali, with his benign smile, gently condemned to death.

LIX

BALD ALI took the death-warrants to Chan Kaya himself. Mustafa Kemal was waiting for them. More than ever he was sure that the condemned men were dangerous. Since the trial had begun, from many directions efforts had been made to get their acquittal. Powerful Jewish organizations in New York, Paris and Berlin had sent messages and telegrams asking for clemency. A number of great financial concerns, including the banking houses of the Rothschilds in Vienna and London, had tried to persuade the English and the French Governments and the leading newspapers in both countries to use all their influence to save Javid. Sarraut, the Frenchman, had come to Angora to make a personal appeal for Javid. Sarraut was an outstanding figure in the Orient Lodges of Freemasons. He had appealed to Mustafa Kemal as a brother-mason of the craft. All the forces which Mustafa Kemal feared had shown their hands behind those plotters: the foreign financiers and foreign governments with their greedy claws, the secret societies with foreign gold undermining his power.

The knowledge stiffened his will. The prisoners must hang, and at once. He signed the death-warrants. They must go by hand to Angora and the executions be carried out that very night.

He would do the thing properly. He would give a ball at Chan Kaya that night also. Every one must come—Bald Ali, the judges, the Cabinet, the Ambassadors, the Foreign Ministers, all the notables, all the beautiful ladies. The invitations must go out at top-speed by telephone and hand. Every one must come. All Angora must celebrate the occasion.

. . . . .

The dance began quietly. Many of the guests had arrived. Mustafa Kemal had come in with a tall man with a weak, unhealthy look, Kiazim Pasha, the President of the Assembly. Dressed in immaculate evening-dress cut for him by a London tailor, the Gazi stood talking in a corner to a diplomat.

The guests moved cautiously, watching him. Until the Gazi showed his mood, they must step delicately and talk in subdued tones; very dangerous to be merry, if he happened to be morose. The Gray Wolf was a very unpleasant brute, unless handled properly.

But the Gazi was in the best of spirits. This was to be no staid State function. They must all enjoy themselves. It was to be a night of rollicking fun.

"We must be gay. We must live, be alive," he shouted, as he caught hold of a partner and fox-trotted on to the floor with her.

The guests one and all followed him. They danced—if they did not, the Gazi made them. They grasped each other close, waggled and twisted, gyrated, fox-trotted, bumped each other gallantly—for they were not very expert. They sweated and strained in their unaccustomed evening-clothes,

233

trying to keep time to the negro music and determined to show themselves, as the Gazi had ordered, *tout à fait civilisés*.

As the night went on, the fun increased. There was plenty to drink—rakhi, beer and the sweet champagne that was *de rigueur* in polite Turkish society.

Ismet and the Gazi had a playful quarrel in the middle of the floor over a mountain of flesh of a Turkish lady. The band stopped to listen, and every one shouted with laughter at their rib-tickling jokes on the lady's ponderous protruding proportions.

Bald Ali, who had been playing poker in another room with Kiazim Pasha, looked in benignly, and a couple of the desperadoes swaggered across to talk to him.

The Gazi was at his best, tearing his partners round at a great pace, and giving them drinks between the dances.

Tewfik Rushti, the Minister for Foreign Affairs, had been to the bar. He was trying to smooth his black, oily hair back off his face. Now and again he smacked his thick negro lips, peered dimly through his enormous horn-rimmed spectacles and waved wildly with a cheer to an acquaintance.

"Dance!" shouted the Gazi at him. "Dance! Every one must dance."

Rushti staggered on to the floor, saw Soubhi Bey, tried to kiss him and lurched back again to the bar.

"Dance! Of course he could dance. The Pasha was right. All civilized modern peoples danced. It was the sign of civilized people. Dance! Of course he could dance."

The room was wild with excitement, thick with tobacco smoke, heavy with stench of spilt liquor and drunken breaths.

Four miles away in Angora the great square was lit up with the white light of a dozen arc-lamps. Round it, and into the streets beyond, was collected a vast crowd.

Under the arc-lamps below the stone walls of the prison stood eleven giant triangles of wood. Under each was a man in a white gown like a surplice, his hands pinioned behind him, and a noose round his neck—the political opponents of Mustafa Kemal about to die. The Gray Wolf had shown his teeth.

The heat of the August night was great. There was no wind, and now and again a faint gust brought up the pungent dry smell of the open Anatolia plains. Soon it would be morning. Overhead the Milky Way swung its great arch of luster across the sky. The Sword of Orion hung close over the black edge of the earth. Except for a tree cricket or two up by the old fortress, and a stray dog howling in the distance, there was a great silence.

In the great silence each condemned man in turn spoke to the people. One recited a poem, another said a prayer, another cried out that he was a loyal son of Turkey, and Javid the Jew, who loved life and laughter and women, and who loved power too when he could handle it in secret, made a little grimace. He had refused to be bullied by Bald Ali and the prosecutor at the trial and had made a great speech in his own defense. He was not frightened now that the end was near.

"I must ask you to forgive me, brothers," he said. "I feel that I may have made some mistake in the procedure; got this tie of rope at the wrong angle or something like that. To tell you the truth, I've had no practice. I've never even been in this position before," and with this light jest on his lips he died gallantly.

At Chan Kaya most of the guests had gone. The rooms were stale—stenching. A few women still danced, white-faced and tousled. Here and there in corners a few men sat talking, arms round each other, slobbering, kissing. Tewfik Rushti was gone. A little way up the road he had run his car into a ditch and lay asleep on his back. The Soviet Ambassador had seen him there and ordered his chauffeur to hurry on and forget what he had seen. Dangerous to stop by a man lying in a ditch in this country. "Let sleeping or dead dogs lie," was his sentiment, as he hurried on.

The Commissioner of Police had reported that the executions were finished. The bodies below the triangles had ceased to twitch.

Mustafa Kemal walked across and looked out of a window. His face was set and gray; the pale eyes expressionless; he showed no signs of fatigue; his evening-clothes were as immaculate as ever.

The dawn was coming, red and hot over the brown, burnt-up plains that stretched away below him.

With a sneer he looked round the ball-room, at the white-faced women, at the gibbering, slobbering, evil men.

"Dogs, and tools to be used," he had called them.

At last he was supreme. His enemies were banished, broken or dead.

He called for drinks, cards, shouted for his intimates, the "desperadoes." He played poker, quarreled, haggled, and won until the sun was well up the sky, and it was time that he went to his office and to his work to modernize and make a great nation of his Turkey.

PART ELEVEN

LX

MUSTAFA KEMAL was absolute dictator. His opponents and enemies had all been safely hanged or driven into exile. The Turkish people were placid and obedient.

All power in the State was concentrated in his hands. The People's Party, the party he had created and of which he was president, was both the Government and the whole machinery of government. From the most insignificant official and clerk in the smallest village up to the Prime Minister every man in Turkey who held any power or position must be a member of the party. Its district committees were responsible for local government, for keeping the central committee in touch with everything of importance and carrying out its orders. It was organized and disciplined on military lines and it gave unhesitating and absolute obedience to Mustafa Kemal.

From it Mustafa Kemal chose the Cabinet Ministers; they were more like permanent officials than ministers, for there was no opposition party.

From it also he chose the deputies for the Assembly. Nominally the Assembly was elected by the people by a free vote. In reality no opposition candidates were allowed to stand, so that only those approved by Mustafa Kemal could be elected.

Each deputy was well paid. In addition to his monthly

237

salary he received allowances for acting on commissions of inquiry and special missions. He was allowed certain patronage, and his position helped him, if he was interested in any business. He was given four or five months' leave each year, and in addition he received a substantial allowance from the party funds, which were under the direct control of Mustafa Kemal.

In return he was expected to give absolute obedience and to vote all Mustafa Kemal's wishes into law with the steadiness of a well-oiled machine.

Alternatively, any sign of disobedience by any member great or small, whether he was a deputy or merely a village policeman, was punished by dismissal from the party, which meant loss of employment, ostracism and want, if not starvation.

The party was like an army of occupation, controlling all the administration; the Assembly a central committee of commanding officers, smart, regular, and obedient; the ministers the general staff with Mustafa Kemal as the commander-in-chief, and responsible to himself alone. The people of Turkey had no say in the matter.

Mustafa Kemal retained the forms of popular government, elections and parliamentary procedure, but with such a machine under his hand he ruled absolutely.

He ceased to interfere with details, but ruled through three men. Each night these three reported to him at Chan Kaya and received their orders; Zia Sefet, the Secretary-General of the People's Party, a capable and quick-witted Jew, gave him a précis of the important events of the day and the work of the party; Fevzi reported on the army, and Ismet on the Assembly and the work of the Government offices.

Sefet supplied the information, Ismet controlled the

routine work and Fevzi was responsible for keeping the army contented, loyal and efficient

Towering high over them with his great prestige, his driving energy and his force of character was Mustafa Kemal. He was President of the Republic, President of the Assembly, of the People's Party and of the Council of Ministers, and Commander-in-Chief of the Army.

LXI

WITH success and power Mustafa Kemal had developed from the rebellious boy, the revolutionary cadet, the ambitious, disgruntled officer into a ruthless and strong dictator.

He believed in strength; he was always quoting the Tartar saying, "Only the hand that can wield the sword should hold the scepter." He was ruthless because with the concentration of a fanatic he believed in himself and his mission.

His mission was to make Turkey prosperous, civilized and rich.

"We must make this country," he said, "a place worthy of its name. We must give it what is the best in its own civilization, but also the best we can take from all other civilizations.... Turkey must become a civilized country in all the meanings of the term."

He set to work at once. He must make the people the foundation of the future.

"Every great movement," he used to say, "must find its source in the depths of a people's soul, the original spring of all strength and greatness."

But the soul of the people of Turkey was weighted

239

down with a great weariness and overlaid with the filth of centuries of maladministration.

The Turks did not respond readily. There was no great outburst among them of national spirit released and searching for progress. They had roused themselves in the War of Independence to a supreme effort to save themselves from annihilation. They had succeeded. Utterly weary, ignorant, and dull, they asked now to be left in peace, and to be ruled. They did not wish to be hurried into the effort of education or ruling themselves.

Mustafa Kemal saw that to succeed in his mission he must train and drive the people. He must be the benevolent despot. He must deal with his Turks as a schoolmaster deals with children. They were like children, as simple and foolish. He believed that like children they were soft and malleable material out of which he could fashion something fine and enduring.

He delighted in the part of schoolmaster, the teaching, instructing, explaining. Like a schoolmaster, also, if he could not persuade, he used force, being convinced that what he did would ultimately be the best for his pupils.

LXII

First he set out to finish the destruction he had started. He must cut Turkey away from the corrupting past; he must clear away all the débris. He had already torn up the whole political fabric, changed a monarchy into a republic, reduced an empire down to a country, made a religious State into a lay republic, ejected the Sultan, the Caliph, and repudiated all connection with the Ottoman Empire.

Now he set out to change the whole mentality of the people—their old ideas, their habits, their dress, manners,

240

customs, ways of talking, all the most intimate details of their lives, which linked them with the past and their Oriental upbringing.

This was far harder than rebuilding the political structure. As he had said, "I have conquered the enemy. I have conquered the country. Can I conquer the people?"

The fez must go. It was the hall-mark of the Ottoman and the Moslem.

Mustafa Kemal's line of action was characteristic of him. He knew there would be fierce opposition. He would be striking right at the most deeply ingrained sense of fitness of every Turk.

He moved with caution. He gave peaked caps to his bodyguard. When they did not object, he issued them to the whole army, and sent out instructors to explain their advantages in sun or rain as against the old peakless fez. The soldiers made no protest.

Sure now of the army, he set out to convert the people. He made a tour of the Black Sea coast. At Kustamuni he stopped, called a public meeting and himself appeared in a panama.

The crowd gasped. Had the King of England or the President of the United States of America appeared in public in a convict's uniform with broad arrows, they would have produced the same effect. To the ordinary Turk the hat was the mark of the beast, the sign of the unclean, accursed Christians and of the foreigners.

Mentally, as well as physically, Mustafa Kemal was fearless. To clap on a hat instead of a fez and appear at a public meeting might easily have been taken as a piece of clownish buffoonery. The crowd might have laughed or jeered. He was no more afraid of laughter or jeers than of physical violence.

"If we will be a civilized people," he preached, "we must wear civilized, international clothes. The fez is the sign of ignorance." Everywhere, as he traveled, he wore a hat, and preached the same thing. He met with no success. Public opinion was shocked. The few men who wore hats were so conspicuous and so self-conscious that they went back to the fez.

Having failed to persuade the Turks, Mustafa Kemal decided to use force. If they would not wear hats willingly, they must be forced to do so.

At his orders the Assembly passed a law at once, making the fez illegal and the wearing of it a criminal offence. Two days later in every town and village the police took up positions at principal points and confiscated all fezzes. Any one who resisted or even complained was imprisoned.

A growl of anger went up from all the country. The peasants who came into market resisted, when their fezzes were torn off their heads. They were forced to go home bare-headed, which was a shameful thing for a Moslem—it touched his pride—or they had to buy at fantastic prices the hats they hated.

They refused to obey. They would not have the accursed hats. At Sivas, Erzerum, Marash and a dozen other towns angry crowds stoned the officials. The priests urged them on; this was another attack by the devil-government of Angora on their sacred religion; the Koran and the Prophet forbade the peaked hat. In the Assembly the famous General Nureddin Pasha spoke in protest.

From schoolmaster Mustafa Kemal passed rapidly to ruthless despot.

"Revolutions," he said, "must be founded in blood. A revolution that is not founded in blood will not be permanent."

He ejected General Nureddin Pasha from the Assembly.

242

Into the country he sent out Tribunals of Independence with troops. They hanged, shot, imprisoned and bastinadoed hundreds of Turks.

The resistance ceased. Every Turk hurried to find him a hat. They were not easy to find; only Christians had worn them, and the Christians had all been deported.

In one village behind Smyrna the villagers discovered, in the closed shop of a deported Armenian, a pile of women's summer hats. They wore them, feathers, ribbons and all.

They wore old bowlers, ancient straw-hats, hats made out of a piece of cloth by their wives, with unskilled hands, caps imported in haste from Austria, anything with a brim that the traders could get for them, anything that carried out the orders of Gazi Mustafa Kemal, anything with a peak to save them from the prison, the bastinado, and the hangman's noose.

The fez was gone; the dangerous fez was hidden away. Every man in Turkey wore a hat.

To establish the fact before the world Mustafa Kemal sent his close friend Edib Servet as delegate to the Moslem Conference in Mecca. To this Holy of Holies had come representatives from Central Asia, from Africa, Arabia, India and the Malay States. Many of them were wild fanatics; all of them were devout Moslems, followers of the Prophet, standing by the letter of the Koran.

Edib was small, fat, and red-faced. He appeared at the Conference among the wild men with their flowing native clothes in a lounge suit and a bowler hat. Yet such was the prestige of Mustafa Kemal, the Gazi, that Edib Servet was not murdered nor even insulted.

Then Mustafa Kemal returned to religion. It was still clogging the machinery of the State. Islam was still the

State religion. "All our troubles come from the misuse of religion in the State. . . . It is a weak man who needs religion to bolster up his rule," he said and ordered the State to be secularized.

"Religion is a personal matter," he continued; "each citizen of the Republic may decide his religion for himself."

Nonetheless he sneered openly at religion. He made it clear that for him the religious man, the man who went to the mosque and prayed, must be a knave or a fool, and, in either case, useless.

The opinions of Mustafa Kemal were the faiths of the People's Party, so that it became fashionable to sneer at religion and unwise and even dangerous to practice it. The men went no more to the mosques. Religion went out of fashion.

Further, there were the dervishes and the monastic orders. They must go. All the richest property and land belonged to them. They were like locusts; they were drones and a dead weight in a working community. Moreover, they would be the backbone of any reaction; they had been connected with the Kurdish revolt.

By a Bill passed in a night through the Assembly, Mustafa Kemal closed the monasteries, dissolved their organizations, turned the dervishes into the streets to be ordinary citizens who must work or starve, and confiscated their wealth to the State.

Mustafa Kemal had destroyed the whole religious basis and outlook of the Turkish state and people.

LXIII

WITH the ground partially cleared, Mustafa Kemal set out to reconstruct. He had destroyed the old laws and the social life based on the religion of Islam and the dictates of the Holy Sheri laws.

Now he called in European experts and adopted almost wholesale the German Commercial, the Italian Penal and the Swiss Civil Codes. They changed the whole legal structure. The Swiss Code revolutionized the status of the family and the rights of ownership, forbade polygamy and the harem, and radically adjusted the position of women, who ceased to be chattels owned by their husbands: they became individuals and free citizens.

Then he set out to make Turkey completely Turkish. Since the days that he had talked revolution in Monastir, since the time he had organized the *Vatan* in the Military School in Constantinople, this had been his one consistent aim, the basis of all his ideas, the backbone of his resistance to the foreigner—"Turkey for the Turks."

"Our principle is the same in relation to Asia as to Europe," he said to an inquirer. "We shall take the best from each, but we shall guard our independence. We shall look at everything through Turkish eyes, watching Turkish interests alone."

By a succession of laws and regulations he ordered everything in Turkey to be Turkish.

The language was full of foreign words, Arabic and Persian. They must be eliminated. Tartar was the basis of the language. Tartar words and phrases must be discovered out of old books, documents and songs, revived and used to replace the foreign words.

Ismet and Fevzi were even more furiously Turkish than

245

Mustafa Kemal. Ismet carried the idea to such an extent that in one of his annual reports to the Assembly the deputies, while getting the general drift, could not understand the details of his speech.

The Koran and the New Testament were translated into Turkish, and orders given that all prayers in the mosques must be in Turkish also. The stamps were printed with a picture of the gray wolf of the original Turks.

Foreign schools must be discouraged, especially those run by missionaries. All primary education must be done in Turkish schools. Any foreign school which remained must omit all reference to religion. It must employ a percentage of Turkish teachers and teach Turkish.

So also in business, each firm must contain a high percentage of Turkish capital, directors and staff, use Turkish signs and keep their correspondence and accounts in Turkish.

Many professions and trades such as those of doctors, lawyers, wheelwrights, and toy-makers were closed to all but Turks. Heavy import duties and quotas were imposed to shut out foreign goods and to encourage Turkish manufactures. A campaign was organized to persuade the people to buy Turkish goods, local broadcloth instead of Manchester cloth, and camomile leaves from Brusa instead of foreign tea.

"Turkey exclusively for the Turks" became the policy.

In addition Mustafa Kemal introduced a hundred minor changes to adjust the routine of life, which affected the lives of the individuals even more drastically than the big structural changes. Friday was made the one legal day of rest each week. Previously there had been Fridays for the Moslems, Saturdays for the Jews, and Sundays for the Christians.

The phrases and motions used in conversation, in introducing, in saying good-day and good-by, the saluting of superiors and the acknowledgment of salutes by inferiors were changed. The salaam was forbidden; coffee might not be offered to visitors as a sign of respect in offices; the hat was to be raised so many inches from the head to acknowledge a salute, and so many inches in making one; the handshake was to replace the old triple obeisance.

Mustafa Kemal introduced the metric system and the Gregorian calendar. Previously the hours were counted from the changing hour of dawn; now they would be counted from the fixed hour of midnight.

Having chosen all those things from Europe, he went even farther than the Europeans. He drove all beggars off the streets; made it a punishable offense to laugh at the mad, eccentric or crippled; and forced both parties to a marriage to produce clean bills of health before they could marry. He had no belief in marriage as a religious ceremony or a sacrament, but he believed in its physical sanctity as a duty to the State.

LXIV

By ability Mustafa Kemal was a soldier, by instinct he was a schoolmaster, by inclination a politician. Like many another soldier who has become a successful politician he soon found politics and the routine of ruling excessively dull. The endless talk and the weak compromises annoyed him. The driving enthusiasm and the uplift of fighting for freedom, the struggle for power, had collapsed into the humdrum of success.

Moreover, he was disappointed. He had visualized himself choosing from all the world the best of each civilization, and then with a few of his brisk orders and laws imposing these on an expectant, revived nation which would at once become progressive and prosperous.

He had not realized that laws are not constructed in a study by a few clever men, but must evolve through years of effort out of the soul of a people. He did not know that culture follows commodities, that a people living in Eastern squalor and poverty could not adopt European ideas and methods until they had the wealth and the desire to raise their standards of living.

The Turks had not responded to his bounding enthusiasm. He could not even lead them. He had to drive them every inch along the road of progress that he had chosen.

He had determined to make Angora a capital worthy of Turkey. Against much advice he had chosen the disheveled little country town. The natural facts were against him. In winter it was a quagmire of mud; in the summer a group of hovels, dusty and tired, squatted round a barren rock in a desert of dried-up plains. It was full of fever.

All these things he could conquer. He would conquer the country. He set to with fighting enthusiasm. He sent for experts, Professors Jansen from Berlin and Oerley from Vienna, and bade them plan a great city with wide open streets and majestic houses. He worked over the plans with them. The Assembly voted the money to his orders. He drove the builders and contractors, urging them to speed. He planted millions of trees. He constructed roads, drained the marshes, wiped out the fever. Within a very short time he had spent thirteen million pounds.

But the new city did not grow to plan. The ultra-modern houses of Professor Jansen did not suit the climate. The trees died in the miserly soil. Even if he conquered the country, could he conquer the people? The Turks built with little heart or enthusiasm. In the native quarter and

248

in the country round they lived as before, huddled in their poor hovels.

The city that Mustafa Kemal had planned grew into a cheap lath-and-plaster affair among hovels mixed with a few fine buildings.

A story was told of how when a certain hotel was being built it could not be finished because the builder had ignored the stairs. So here Mustafa Kemal built without the will of the people.

Gradually Mustafa Kemal relaxed his hold on the control of affairs. More and more he retired back to Chan Kaya, shut himself away, became elusive and rarely seen by any one except his intimates, his women, and a few Government officials, leaving Ismet to deal with the routine of government.

And Ismet, the little deaf staff officer, picked up eagerly all the power his hands could grasp. He was the typical office-man, dictatorial, prosy and exacting. He loved routine and red-tape, and he was becoming as jealous of his control and position as any civil servant with long service.

LXV

AT Chan Kaya, Mustafa Kemal kept his court. His outlook was oriental, his life wild and bizarre.

He was now forty-seven and showing some of the signs of middle age. He was growing stout from over-indulgence. His almost colorless hair was thinning and receding back from his forehead. At times his face was haggard, drawn and full of lines. His eyes had always a set, penetrating look. He had cultivated that look until it had become a fixed stare artificially sustained and a menace. On the very few

249

occasions when he relaxed a smile lit up his face with a rare charm. As quickly the smile was gone like a lamp damped suddenly out in a gray dusk, and the man was once more stern, dominating, aloof and menacing.

His health varied rapidly. For nights at a time he suffered from insomnia. He would be attacked by fits of black depression; the old kidney trouble gave him acute pain. As suddenly he became alive and vital. One day he might be seen walking like an old man, and the next hale and hearty.

Nonetheless his immense vitality showed no signs of failing. Sometimes he worked with tremendous energy, calling for reports, interfering with government departments, summoning ministers, attending the Assembly, ordering and driving. On one occasion he delivered a speech reviewing the whole history of the Nationalist Revolution. The speech took seven whole nights to prepare and all the working hours of six continuous days to deliver. It was a weary, acid oration, an apologia for his own career, without one line of humor in it to relieve the tension, and full of criticism of all those who had helped him. Only during the last few hours, when the tired deputies were struggling to keep awake, did his voice grow a little hoarse from the prolonged strain.

Then for days he would stay cloistered in Chan Kaya, inaccessible, drinking, gambling, debauching the whole night through, and much of the day, with his intimates—his "desperadoes" and his women.

After such nights, or when he was white and restless from insomnia, he would take a horse and in the dawn ride out to the model farm he was constructing in a valley.

The farm was the joy of his life. For it he bought the latest machinery, the best prize bulls and pigs, the best fodder and manure. He delighted to play the gentleman-farmer.

But beyond the model farm he saw a fine vision of Turkey prospering with agriculture, a land full of corn and oil. He gave orders for coöperative societies and agricultural banks, for the granting of loans to the peasants, the distribution of seeds. He planned irrigation schemes, new roads, new railways and demonstrations of the latest machinery.

Without doubt, despite his faults and his egoism, the man was a patriot. Much that he said and did was illogical, untrue, even unsound to stupidity, but he believed passionately in his work and its success.

But he was hindered by lack of money, by the immense inertia of his people, by their poverty, which kept them in squalor living only a little above the starvation line.

In his model farm he could plan and create as he wished and as he saw all Turkey would be one day, when he had succeeded.

He changed much. He became more pompous and prosy, and waxed eloquent in truisms.

In 1921 he had prided himself on owning nothing: all he possessed he had given to the nation; he had been open and liberal handed. Now he grew miserly and close-fisted. He became greedy for money. He began to take part in business affairs, many of which were exceedingly unsound and dubious. After his bad nights, when he was irritable, he became peevish, obstinate, and often childish in his ideas.

He had ridden down to the farm one hot summer morning. He was excessively ill-natured that day. There was a shortage of water. He decided that he must have a reservoir, and at once. Where was M. Yencke?—Yencke was the agent for Holtzmann, who did most of the Gazi's work—Yencke was in Constantinople! Send for him at once!

When M. Yencke arrived after thirty-six hours in the train, he was told to make a reservoir at once. What would it cost?

Yencke gave an estimate; that was far too expensive: it must be reduced. Yencke was obstinate. Mustafa Kemal was getting annoyed.

"Have a reservoir made like the Lake of Geneva," said some one who had seen such a thing in Switzerland.

The idea appealed to Mustafa Kemal. His ill-nature vanished. Certainly the idea was excellent, but the reservoir must be not a model of the Lake of Geneva but of the Sea of Marmora, the Turkish sea; and he took the opportunity there under the hot summer sun to give those round him a learned and elevating discourse on the virtues of patriotism.

"A reservoir modeled to scale of the Sea of Marmora," he ordered, "and see that the scale is exactly correct."

M. Yencke carried out the order. It cost a great deal of money. Mustafa Kemal bargained with him. They left out the Gulf of Ismid to reduce the price. Even then it cost twice as much as the first reservoir.

It was made, a perfect model to scale. From it the cows and the sheep and the melon-beds got their water, and for many days the dictator looked at it with pleasure.

LXVI

MUSTAFA KEMAL kept his life in watertight compartments. On one side were Ismet, Fevzi, Abdul Haki, the Minister for Finance, and the workers. On the other the "desperadoes" and his women. The one for work and State affairs, the other for his pleasure and to flatter his vanity.

As long as he kept the two gangs apart there was peace, but very soon they were at daggers drawn.

"When I see the Gazi depressed," said one of the "desperadoes," "not sleeping, drinking duzico until dawn and then riding off to the farm, white-faced and ill-looking, I am afraid. When he speaks of going to Europe or traveling I am afraid also. Without him we should be ruined.

"I watch him when he is asleep, so that I may be sure that he is well, for I know that should he die, I and the rest of us would die also. Ismet and Fevzi would hang us."

But Mustafa Kemal kept them apart. In his ambitions and his visions of a great Turkey his intimates had no share.

They were a rough, coarse gang, an unhealthy mixture of first-class scoundrels and third-class hangers-on. There was Bald Ali, the Hanging Judge, and —— Ali, the swaggering bully; there was a boisterous, lecherous Circassian with an amusing tongue; there was a thorough blackguard of a scurrilous, shifty journalist and a negroid Turk with a business head when sober, but when drunk very foul-mouthed. In addition there was a number of unimportant soldiers, such as Jemal, who had been adjutant to the Chief of the Police in Salonika and who saved Mustafa Kemal from Abdul Hamid's spies the time he had come from Syria; Mufid Lutfi who had been with him in Syria; and Nuri who had served with him in Tripoli.

As for his women, they were poor cheap things, who were there to satisfy him. Since Latifa was gone he had made no attempt to be faithful to any one woman.

Mustafa Kemal loved flattery. His intimates gave it to him heaped up. He delighted in their extravagant praise, in their subservience, in their dependence on him. Their exaggerated hero-worship was a tonic to him when he was depressed. When he was well, he reveled in their ready applause, as they lauded him to the skies.

"He is the Greatest Soldier of the World and of All History," said one.

"He is like a Sun," said another, not to be outdone, "a Sun that fills the world and lights up every facet of our lives."

Mustafa Kemal demanded that they should follow his every mood. If he was irritated, they must be sad. If he smiled, they must be gay. With them his life was wild and unclean. He drank and gambled with them in the smoke-filled rooms, the floors littered with cigarette ends, the tables strewn with cards and money. He was at home in the stench of stale spilt liquor, the foul breaths, the coarse laughter of coarse women, the oaths and the bestialities. Often he watched them creep, staggering away in the dawn, their eyes bloodshot, their faces white and evil; and then he turned to work in his study or called for his horses and rode down in the first morning breeze to the model farm.

The scandal of his private life was known to all, but it only made him the more popular. The Turks were crude orientals and they understood Mustafa Kemal: he was their ideal of a ruler; he might be cruel, vicious, brutal and spiteful but despite this he was strong and decided; he was a soldier-ruler and a conqueror. His chief vice was the national vice. Lechery had been the oldest boast of their ancestors. They preferred his robust, crude virility to the placid domestic virtues.

A dictatorship depending on one man must always mean a large measure of insecurity. In Mustafa Kemal's café-brothel-like private life this was increased, for his intimates were dangerous men; a sudden quarrel between half-drunks, and revolvers were drawn; a chance shot, a shot fired in quick anger, and the ruler would be gone. What then would happen to Turkey no one could foresee.

The danger was vividly illustrated one evening.

It was late. The evening meal was finished. Mustafa Kemal was gambling in the inner room with some of his intimates, when the guard challenged and then let some one into the hall.

The door opened. —— Ali stepped in and took off his hat.

The room was thick with smoke. The electric light, supplied by the German company, jumped and was uncertain. Ali peered across the room. On the farther side sat Mustafa Kemal quite still. He had a cast in one eye which was more pronounced than ever, and it made him look sinister and menacing. He pointed to a chair.

The room was still. Ali was in disgrace. He had been quarreling with Ismet. He wanted a place for himself and a friend in the Government. Ismet had bluntly refused: he would have none of these desperadoes interfering in his work.

Ali had resented Ismet's tone. He hinted that if Mustafa Kemal disappeared, he would see that Ismet followed him quickly.

Ismet was deaf, but he heard that plainly. As he could not himself deal with an intimate friend of Mustafa Kemal, he complained to Mustafa Kemal, who told Ali sharply to behave himself.

—— Ali had been drinking to get his courage. He sat down heavily with his legs apart. Some one gave him a drink. He toasted the room and drank a second. Then he addressed Mustafa Kemal across the table. He complained of Ismet. He blackguarded Ismet. He demanded a place for his friend and himself in the Cabinet.

Mustafa Kemal turned on him savagely, told him to mind his own business and keep out of politics.

Ali was very drunk. His hand went to his hip-pocket, but he was not a quick revolver shot.

Before he could draw, the others were on him. They knocked him backwards, chair and all; they dragged him out into the hall; they kicked and hacked him, shouting, growling, fighting.

In all the uproar, in the din of this low café quarrel in the smoky room Mustafa Kemal sat unmoved. Suddenly he stood in the doorway. His voice rang out:

"Take his revolver. Pick him up. Stand away from him."

He walked down to Ali with his face set and his whole body taut as if to spring, so that Ali crept back terrified to the door and made off for safety.

All that night Mustafa Kemal was in fine fettle. Danger, men to handle, a man to dominate, to be in the center of the stage: that was life.

LXVII

Mustafa Kemal began to weary of the life at Chan Kaya, its humdrum sameness. He wished to travel, to see life and people, to leave behind him, if only for a short time, the yellow, staring plains that stretched into the empty distance below the villa.

He was ill too. Twice he had severe fainting fits with a heart-attack. The heavy drinking was telling on him. His doctor warned him again that he must go slow and that a change of air would do him good.

Moreover, he realized that he was losing grip. He had secluded himself too much in Chan Kaya. He was out of touch with the people; he had loosened his control over State affairs too freely; he had ceased to be continually in the public eye as he had been before.

Many even said that already he was a back number, a mere figurehead; that the Gray Wolf had been muzzled and chained up in Chan Kaya; and that Ismet and his ministers were the real rulers.

He roused and shook himself. He would allow no one to usurp his place. He must be the center, the controlling force, and the head towering above all the others. No one must even venture to stand beside his shoulder. He must be supreme.

He decided to stage a return, a dramatic attention-catching return, into the limelight. He would go to Constantinople. There, from the palace of the Sultan, he would introduce a drastic reform, which he had long projected. He would change the Arabic characters of Turkish into Latin, and so he would revolutionize all Turkish literature, the whole system of written communication between Turk and Turk. He would revolutionize all thought in Turkey.

Not 10 per cent of the nation could read. The complicated Arabic script had made it so difficult that it had become the monopoly of the priests and a few intellectuals; it had shut the Turks off, as with a wall, from the West, bound them up with the complicated Arabic thought and the Persian artificiality; the language had become so intricate that few foreigners were prepared to undertake the immense labor of learning Turkish; very few Turks could learn any Western language.

Mustafa Kemal saw a great vision. With one sweep of his arm he would destroy all this. He would send the whole of his people back to school, educated with uneducated, priests with porters; they should all learn to read and write. He would open wide for them the great gate of knowledge, and he would lead his people through to success.

He began to prepare. He became more restrained and decorous in public and private. He spent less time with the "desperadoes" and the women. He drank and gambled less and slept better. His health improved. He was at work again and happy.

He studied diligently the alphabets of Western languages. At a conference at Baku in 1924 the Soviet republics had adopted the Latin script for all Tartars throughout Central Asia. Mustafa Kemal learnt their system. He called the language professors to him and together they worked out an alphabet in Latin characters to suit the needs of Turkey. For many hours each day Mustafa Kemal practiced until he had become proficient.

He was ready. He ordered that for the summer vacation of 1928 the Government should move from the dust and glare of Angora to Constantinople and the shore of the soft Bosphorus.

The people of Constantinople turned out *en masse* to greet the Gazi, the Saviour of the Country. He had not been in the city since 1919. In great state, with the flags flying, the guns firing salutes, and the crowds cheering, he drove through the streets down to the Bosphorus and took up his residence in the palace of the Sultans at Dolma Baghche.

He carried out his usual routine: careful preparations, a well-chosen opportunity, a dramatic start; then to act the schoolmaster and persuade, but if persuasion failed, to drive forward with relentless force.

He invited all society to a reception at the palace. The ballroom was arranged with chairs and a platform at one end. In the audience were the deputies, the officials, the senior priests, the journalists, writers, schoolmasters, the society ladies and the well-to-do merchants. On the platform were grouped Ismet and the Cabinet Ministers, with Kiazim, the President of the Assembly, in the chair and Mustafa Kemal beside him. On one side of the platform was a black-board and a box of chalks.

Mustafa Kemal rose. He was in his best clothes, morning-clothes with a frock-coat, and he was also in his best mood. He gave his audience a brief explanation why he had invited them all there; he described the difficulties and disadvantages of the Arabic script, the advantages of the Latin. Then on the black-board he traced the pot-hooks, the strokes and dots of the new alphabet and showed its use.

Out of the audience at random he called a couple of men, explained to them how to use this new alphabet and made them write their names on the board.

He was a wonderful schoolmaster, clear, exact, so conscious of his own superiority over his pupils that he could afford to be humorous and sarcastic at their clumsy efforts.

The audience responded to him. Throughout all that drowsy, hot afternoon, when each would have been enjoying his siesta, no one nodded or let his attention wander— there would have been trouble for any one who did. They were absorbed in the Gazi's instructions; they laughed uproariously at his sarcasms and his jokes.

All Constantinople set to work to learn the new script. Mustafa Kemal sat out on a tour round the country with his black-board and box of chalks, going from town to town, stopping in the villages on the way, calling the townsmen and the yokels to him, giving lessons in the open market-places, making men who had never written anything before write their own names.

The whole country, as well as Constantinople, responded. The idea caught the fancy of the nation: here was the key to golden success, to wealth and prosperity. All work became subordinate to learning the new script. With a whoop of excitement the country went back to school. All started on the same footing—villagers, shepherds, porters, shopmen, journalists, politicians. Young men and old sat in the corners of the mosques, in the cafés, in the squares, with slate and pencil or a bit of chalk on a slab of stone, scrawling out great As and Bs, mouthing out the sounds, and discussing the details with immense gravity.

Mustafa Kemal was the "Professor in Chief," as Ismet called him with half a sneer. He both encouraged and drove. He gave prizes for the best results. He promised work to the proficients. He preached the splendid future for those who succeeded. He lost no chance to test any one who came near him—his dancing partners, a deputy with a petition, a village official making a complaint, any chance acquaintance. Once he stopped dancing in the middle of a ball, called for a blackboard and chalk and gave a lecture. He fixed a day after which there would be a penalty for failures, loss of appointment, even loss of nationality and expulsion from the country. Prisoners would not be released from prison at the end of their sentence, unless they could read and write the Latin script.

Touring up and down the country, all day and most of each night, he worked with his astounding energy, teaching his people. He was once more the center. Every eye was concentrated on him. He held the stage.

LXVIII

An ordinary man would have worn out by the continuous effort, but Mustafa Kemal never slackened. As soon as work was over, he called for his intimates and drank and gambled, though not so wildly as before.

It was the night of the reception at the palace. Three hours of lecturing had been enough for his audience, but Mustafa Kemal was full of life. He had invited a couple of diplomats to dinner and cards.

He was with them, playing at a table. The "desperadoes" sat round drinking and smoking. Now and again one of the women came in. Mustafa Kemal took no notice of them. He was absorbed in the game.

As usual he was winning. The stakes were high; his pile of winnings was rapidly increasing. Still they played, and still Mustafa Kemal won, while the black night died in the dawn.

The diplomats, white-faced and weary, got up to go. Mustafa Kemal opened his shoulders. He had been so concentrated on the game that he had not noticed even the passing of the night.

He walked across to the mullioned window beyond the rooms where had been the old harem of the Sultan. His face showed no signs of weariness. His eyes stared out with their usual set expression.

Below him the Bosphorus was a gleam of dark water, powdered with a few pale stars. Opposite, the Asiatic shore stood black against the gray light of the false dawn. The fisher-fleet was going by on its way up to the Black Sea. He could hear the thud of the oars in the rowlocks and the men talking in the silence across the black water. Somewhere chanting and grunting together he could hear men heaving on a rope.

He came back to the table. For a little he looked at his winnings. With a gesture he piled them all together and pushed them into the center.

"Sort out what was yours," he said, "and take it."

It was the gesture of the Oriental Potentate in the Palace of the Sultan on the Bosphorus.

He wished the diplomats good-by and went to his study. He had arranged to start out, early, on a tour of instruction, and he had much work to finish before that.

LXIX

HALF back in the saddle, Mustafa Kemal drove on with more and more reforms. All the arts must be modernized. For four hundred years the priests had forbidden all delineation of the human form. He ordered statues of himself to be set up. He opened a mixed school in Angora to study the nude.

He called in Western music. The high nasal caterwaul that the Turks had learned from the Arabs must go. He sent for the latest Viennese waltzes, the last negro jazzes and fox-trots.

To these he made every one dance—the ministers, the deputies and Government officials. Dancing was the criterion of the civilized. He gave balls and dances. If the young men stood sheepishly aside, he found them partners and started the dance himself. He opened schools of dancing, where young men of good family were taught how to be good gigolos; and good-looking girls, provided they had a sense of rhythm and did not stutter, were taught to be partners and conversationalists.

He had chosen a number of orphan girls as his "adopted daughters." Some sneered, and made evil suggestions, but others who had seen them and realized that they were plain beyond all redemption, decided that it was a real patriotic gesture on his part. These girls had to become proficient dancers as their first duty as good Turks.

He decided that the Turkish dances should be modernized as well. The *Zeybek* should be adapted to the ballroom; but as the *Zeybek* was a murderous affair in which wild highlanders leapt round a camp fire with knives in their mouths it was not such a success in a ball-room as it was after a drinking party.

Once only did the Gazi hesitate. He found a renowned diplomatist from a great western civilized State, who could not dance even when offered an exquisite partner. The Gazi was profoundly shocked. Was Western civilization going to fail him?

He had long set his heart not only on the complete emancipation of women but their active coöperation in all the life of the State.

He encouraged them to shed their veils and come out into the open. He gave them votes in the municipal elections and promised them votes for the Assembly. He made them members of the People's Party on an equal footing with men. He helped them to become lawyers and doctors. Two women were made judges in Angora. Four women were elected to the municipal council of Stambul.

His sister, Makboula, and his favorite "adopted daughter," Afet, helped him. With them he opened schools for social service. They produced the Children's Bill, regulating the employment of children, forbidding them to be taken to bars, cafés-chantants and uncontrolled cinemas. They instituted the Children's Week during which for one week in each year each Government official was nominally replaced by a child and the whole State administered by children.

Once more Mustafa Kemal became the active President of the People's Party and of the State. He called for reports on all subjects; he summoned ministers, deputies, heads of departments to him; he demanded that all decisions be placed before him—that all control should be his.

He met with opposition. During the months he had secluded himself in Chan Kaya, Ismet had become more and more the executive head of the State. He refused to give way to Mustafa Kemal.

Ismet had neither the brain nor the genius of Mustafa Kemal. In many ways he was extremely stupid and ignorant. He made mistakes into which no man with brains and experience would have fallen, but he would listen to no advice. Advice meant to him opposition; he crushed it at once. Power had given him a pompous belief in his own ability. From the stern, placid little general in the trenches before Eski Shehir he had grown into an irritable and dogmatic martinet. His health had deteriorated and with it his temper. He had become rigid in his views, an extreme nationalist and a hater of foreigners. But he was absolutely honest and he was also as persistent, obstinate and strong-willed as Mustafa Kemal. He did not hesitate to speak his mind. He would accept Mustafa Kemal as chief of the State, but he would not hand back executive control. His principles were summed up in:

"Though the Gazi represents, it is the Government governs the State."

To which the Gazi replied shortly:

"*I* govern."

Between the two men there were constant disagreements, and at times quarrels, when Fevzi would come in to

264

make peace between them. Mustafa Kemal ordered the Government to move to Constantinople for the summer of 1930; Ismet ordered all ministers to remain at their posts in Angora. Mustafa Kemal ordered all representatives coming from abroad to report direct to him; Ismet ordered them to report to their own departments. Mustafa Kemal wanted one man as Minister of Education; Ismet insisted on another though he was uneducated and boorish. Mustafa Kemal called for reports direct; Ismet insisted that they come through him.

The "desperadoes" and Mustafa Kemal's intimates increased the tension, for they began to interfere in political and state affairs. Ismet hotly resented their interference.

Mustafa Kemal was not used to opposition. He could not do without Ismet, but Ismet's obstinacy, his pompous self-assurance, his rigidity and his deafness irritated Mustafa Kemal to distraction.

LXX

IN the summer of 1930 these disagreements came to a head. Fethi, who was ambassador in Paris, had written a letter of protest to Mustafa Kemal expressing his view that under Ismet's direction Turkey was on the road to disaster. The Treasury was empty; the army had not been paid for some weeks; the Government was very unpopular. He had followed it up by a visit to the Gazi.

That summer Mustafa Kemal was taking his holidays in Yalova, a village a few miles out of Constantinople, on the shore of the Gulf of Ismid. To make Yalova a first-class watering-place was his hobby that year. He had built new roads, improved the train service, constructed an hotel and repaired the Roman baths.

To encourage the élite of Constantinople to come to

Yalova he gave a ball. It had been exceedingly gay: plenty of sweet champagne and duzico had enlivened it; every one had danced. After the guests had gone Mustafa Kemal called Ismet, Fethi and a few friends and politicians to join him in an ante-room.

He was in his best mood. He was expounding his favorite theory that all civilized nations were originally of Turanian or Turkish stock. With fine sarcasm he had demolished the latest discoveries of the savants that the Turks were akin to the Japanese or to some obscure Chinese tribes. With grave, compelling accents, occasionally raising two fingers to a temple like some learned pundit before his disciples, he explained that the English were of Turkish extraction: Kent came from the same root as Tash—Kent; that the many rivers in England called Ouse had got this name from the Turkish tribe of Uz on the Black Sea coast; that the French, the Germans, and even the Americans were of Turkish origin.

Like disciples, his audience sat listening. Many believed in him implicitly. Some believed that he had the power of divination. It was long since any one had contradicted Mustafa Kemal. Isolated on his pedestal with a grateful and admiring nation burning the incense of extravagant flattery round him, it was natural that at times he forgot that his feet were fixed to earth. He had become the Oracle—and like many Oracles he often propounded the most devastating platitudes—and occasionally, as on that night, the most profound nonsense. The Oracle was talking nonsense.

The talk became general. It turned to politics and certain acts of the Government. The air became tense, the discussion bitter; harsh things were said in criticism.

"Why not bring these matters before the Assembly?" asked the Gazi.

266

"The Government allows no discussion either inside or outside the Assembly," was the reply.

The Gazi turned to Ismet, but the little man would make no answer.

"This is not the place for politics," he said abruptly. "I will answer criticism or questions in the proper place, the Assembly. Let Fethi or any one else who wishes to do so, organize a constitutional opposition and oppose me." And he stumped off in annoyance.

After he had gone Mustafa Kemal stayed talking. It was clear that much was wrong in the country and that there was much discontent. An opposition party would act as a safety valve. It would also teach Ismet a lesson; he had become altogether too big for his boots.

Moreover, it would be one step forward in his great work of educating his people. He would form an opposition party. He would call it the "Republican Liberal."

An opposition in the Assembly would turn the rigid autocracy of a one party rule into a constitutional parliamentary government.

He would himself supervise the experiment.

LXXI

MUSTAFA KEMAL prepared his experiment with care. It was his first big testing-out of the political sense of the Turks, his first big trial of his belief in his people.

Many, especially foreigners, had laughed at the elections of the last six years because the people had been able to vote only for his nominees.

He had meant those elections to be lessons for the voters in the routine of voting: as a preparation for the time when

267

they should take on their own responsibilities, elect their own representatives and rule themselves.

He created the Republican Liberal Party out of a dozen well-known deputies in the Assembly, with Fethi as their leader. He let it be known that he wished the public to join. His sister Makboula and three of his intimates were the first members.

He had studied and approved of the English system. He lectured Fethi and Ismet and their immediate supporters on the details; in the Assembly and in stumping the country both parties must attack each other; out of office hours they must be the best of friends; in the Assembly Fethi might blackguard Ismet as he liked, and Ismet reply as hotly; outside they should dine together in all friendliness; both were working for the good of Turkey.

Ready at last, he ordered the experiment to be opened at Smyrna. Fethi went down to speak.

The routine did not work. The local officials dispersed the crowds that had collected, arrested Fethi's supporters and refused to let him go into the street.

Next day arrived Ismet primed with his reply, and with him the Gazi to supervise. He promptly gave orders that Fethi should be given all facilities, an audience collected for him and even a claque provided to applaud when required.

The townsmen and the officials were at a loss. This was altogether outside their experience: no government allowed an opposition; it certainly never encouraged it; it was the duty of officials to silence opposition, and if any one disagreed, he kept quiet; this could only mean that the Government was finished.

There were ugly riots. The newspaper office was stoned and burned. Many rioters were beaten, numbers were imprisoned, one was shot. The police and the officials were expected to protect both sides. This was not at all their idea of politics.

The next step was in the Assembly in Angora. Again the stage was carefully set. It should be a demonstration of how parliamentary government should be run. In the President's box, supervising as the "Professor in Chief," sat Mustafa Kemal.

Led by Fethi, the Liberals made a fierce attack on the Government. For six years the People's Party had ruled: the result, they said, was disastrous, with economic and financial ruin ahead; they had been spending beyond the income of the country on useless roads, unnecessary railways and such expensive toys as municipal gardens; they had created state monopolies for their own personal financial advantages; exports were down to bed rock; the Turkish money was falling out of the market; they needed capital, but they could get none because no one would trust them; Ismet with his anti-foreign views was the cause: Ismet with rigid policy, his repeated mistakes, was the cause of the acute depression and the discontent that was general throughout the country; the self-sufficient infallibility and incompetent ignorance of Ismet and his government had led the country into this morass.

Ismet replied equally warmly. The temper of the house grew hot. The People's Party had not been criticized for years. They resented it. Insults were shouted. Threats were used. Bald Ali leapt to his feet.

"Shall we listen to this traitor talk?" he shouted. "There is the man who signed the Armistice at Mudros, pointing to Fethi, "and there is the man who signed the Treaty of Lausanne," pointing to Ismet. "Can there be any choice between the weak traitor and the patriot? When Fethi was

Prime Minister, the Kurds revolted. Ismet settled that revolt."

Under the eye of Mustafa Kemal both Fethi and Ismet played their parts admirably. They walked out of the Assembly arm in arm, talking and laughing.

But their followers, forgetting all their instructions, all the Gazi's careful explanations, oblivious that he was in the

Ismet Pasha.

box above them watching them, they came to blows. Revolvers were drawn; a dozen fights began; deputies had to be separated by friends and attendants; until, still angry, shouting and arguing, they overflowed out into the cafés and restaurants to carry on their quarrels.

Looking down from his presidential box on the angry uproar below him, unable to control or influence it, Mustafa Kemal realized that this was neither what he had wanted nor expected.

LXXII

THE uproar in the Assembly was an indication of what was coming outside.

The municipal elections were just about to be held. For ten years the Government had kept an iron censorship of the Press and a veto on all freedom of speech. To inaugurate the new party Mustafa Kemal lifted both, and gave orders that the voters were to be left free to vote for whom they wished in these elections.

It was as if he had lifted the top from a boiling cauldron. First he heard a few mutterings; a newspaper or two risked a bold article; a speaker or two dared a criticism. When the police took no action, the mutterings grew into growls, the growls swelled up into a great roar of complaints.

From every part of the country and from every class it came, staggering Mustafa Kemal with its volume and bitterness. Gagged for ten years, the Turkish people had sat silent and submissive. Now they spoke out. It was the roar of the nation at last voicing its discontent. Here and there it burst out in uncontrolled fury.

The traders and shopmen complained bitterly: there was no money and no credit—as long as Ismet with his obstructive policy was in power, there would be none; the monopolies injured trade and helped no one; new taxes suddenly imposed without consideration of their results made business precarious and ate into their profits; the junior officials were as dishonest as ever; before it had been possible to know whom to bribe—now a whole chain of officials had to be squared; how could they compete against ill-considered, stupid legislation and even more stupid and vexatious official interference in everything?—they were being ruined.

271

The shipowners, exporters, lightermen and stevedores had the same complaints. Ill-planned regulations for the ports and harbors were bankrupting them; the customs and passport officials were obstructive and dishonest; with the wholesale thieving, the uncertainties, the difficulties and the changes of confiscation no ships would put into Turkish ports—all the ships went to Athens; Constantinople, Smyrna, Trebizond, all the ports that once flourished, were empty; business was at a standstill.

The banks and the big business houses sent out a warning: the attitude of the Government was leading to ruin; it was over-spending; the national income was falling; more than one-third of it was spent on defense, and the much-needed internal reorganization was neglected; capital was a vital necessity—it could only come from outside; as long as Ismet sat his face against all foreign loans there was no chance of a trade revival; as long as he showed his anti-foreign sentiments and refused to meet the Turkish debts on old loans no outside capitalist would trust Turkey.

Among the Government officials there was deep discontent: their pay was small and irregularly paid to them; the cost of living was up 100 per cent; they were expected to be honest, to live up to and dress up to European standards, yet they were forbidden to supplement their meager pay by outside work; it was unreasonable.

The farmers and the peasants were even more bitter; they had been promised loans, seeds, roads, machinery and irrigations—they had received none of them; they had suffered from three years of drought—the Government had not helped them; in fact the taxes were heavier than ever, the tax-collectors more dishonest and rough-handed than before; what was the use of these new ideas—a republic, new clothes, new ways of counting time, new ways of talking and writing—if they were still struggling on the edge of starvation, with no reserve against misfortune, living little better than their own beasts? Their fields were empty; their land was desolate; they wanted food not new ideas.

The women of all classes joined in: food, clothing, fuel, rent were all more expensive and there was less money; the Republic had given them liberty; what was the use if liberty meant the liberty to starve? They were worse off than under the Sultan.

Behind Fethi, the mild, good-tempered, easygoing Fethi, carrying out Mustafa Kemal's experiment, began to mass all the disgruntled elements, the thousands who were suffering from the stagnation of trade and the ruin of agriculture; the thousands who resented and were shocked at Mustafa Kemal's reforms. They were joined by the priests and the dervishes, all who looked back with regret to the old régime and the Sultan, the remains of the Committee of Union and Progress, and the survivors of the opposition which Mustafa Kemal had stamped on in 1926.

There was a new and dangerous spirit throughout the country. Hitherto, despite all complaining, there had been a general belief, a quiet blind faith, that, as long as the Gazi was at the head, everything would in the end come right.

The roar of complaint and criticism was affecting the massed psychology of the nation. That belief, that blind faith, in the Gazi was going. If it went, with it would go the stability of the Turkish Republic. It was the rock on which the future was built.

The papers began to fill with personal invective against Ismet and his men. Mustafa Kemal's name was bandied about; he was no more sacrosanct. Tnere were several plots to kill him made not by ambitious politicians or revolutionaries, but by disgruntled individuals.

Serious trouble showed in many places. There was a

strike of the fig-packers in Smyrna organized by communists; it was followed by general rioting. In the south on the French frontier there was a rising in which Armenian revolutionaries had a hand and Kurdish raiders helped. All along the Persian frontier the Kurds were in revolt again, murdering and burning. Fifteen thousand Turkish troops under General Salib Pasha were finding it difficult to corner and defeat them.

In many places the Turkish villagers had refused to pay their taxes, fought the tax-gatherers and had driven them away. The Committees of Union and Progress and the old opposition were forming again underground. The priests and the religious orders were working for a return to the old régime. Among the police, the soldiers, gendarmes and the civil services there was discontent and disloyalty.

Finally there came as a warning a serious revolt round the town of Menemen.

Menemen stands in the rich country behind Smyrna. Late in December 1930 a certain dervish, Sheik Mehmed, declared himself to be the Mahdi, come to save Turkey from the black impiety of Mustafa Kemal and his Republic.

He preached in the market-place of Menemen and crowds flocked in to hear him. An officer, Kublay by name, was passing. He endeavored to interfere. The Sheik told him to go about his business. He tried to drag the Sheik off his platform. With the help of his disciples, the Sheik seized Kublay, held him down and slowly sawed his head off with a broken scythe, while the whole town sat round applauding.

The governor called on the police to act: the crowd chased them away. He summoned the gendarmerie: they were too weak. He ordered up troops, the 43rd Infantry Regiment: the soldiers refused to fire on the crowd.

Like flame in summer grass the revolt spread. For months the dervishes had been preparing, and making converts. Led by the priests and the dervishes throughout a wide area from Konia to Adalia up to Smyrna and Brusa, the villagers drove out the Government officials. The women cheered them on. From Erzerum and Sivas came news that trouble was likely to break out there also.

The Kurds were fighting fiercely; they had invented the "Blind Man's Court Martial": before it every Turk captured was summarily tried and brutally mutilated.

Turkey and the Republic were in danger.

LXXIII

LOOKING down on the country, as he had looked down from the President's box over the turmoil in the Assembly, Mustafa Kemal saw that the time was not yet ripe for his experiment. The people were not ready.

The schoolmaster, the "Professor-in-Chief," the Oracle talking nonsense, the man fiddling with his expensive hobbies in Angora and Yalova, the man drinking and card-playing with his cheap companions and his loose women on the Bosphorus, disappeared.

The Dictator put out his strong hands and once more took a grip. The Gray Wolf showed his teeth. He was the ruler of a brutal, primitive people in a brutal, hard land. He must be strong and brutal.

He declared martial law, reimposed the censorship of the Press and shut the door on all freedom of speech. He punished severely all the newspaper editors who had criticized the Government.

He made up his quarrels with Ismet. He needed the merciless, hard, little man, the rigid staff officer, the martinet.

He sent orders to the Turkish troops to retaliate cruelly on the Kurds; he would hang and imprison the leaders, and

275

those who remained he would deport. He crushed the revolt in the south and ejected every Armenian on whom he could lay hands. He wiped up the Communists and punished the Smyrna rioters. On Galata Bridge, across the Golden Horn, he hanged those who had plotted to kill him. From Constantinople he dragged out the eighty-year-old leading Sheik of the Dervishes, and hanged him with his followers.

*Mustafa Kemal
(Commander-in-Chief of
the Turkish Army).*

To Menemen he sent troops. They arrested, bastinadoed, and imprisoned a thousand Turks by drum-head court martial and hung twenty-eight of the leaders with a brutal savagery which equaled that of Sheik Mehmed in his murder of Kublay.

The frontiers were cleared, the revolts crushed. The roar of complaints silenced suddenly. The people, the army, the police, the gendarmes, the civil servants—every class, every man and woman—felt and knew the master's hand. There was once more quiet and security, and once more the old blind faith in the strong man who had taken control.

LXXIV

Now Mustafa Kemal decided that he would himself rule. First he must get the real facts: they had been concealed from him by those round him.

He set off on a tour of the country. He would get into personal touch with his people, reëstablish his personal prestige, study the grievances of all classes and find their remedies.

He found conditions worse than he had expected, and he came back with clear plans.

His dictatorship—a benevolent, educating, guiding dictatorship—was the only form of government possible at the moment.

An opposition party was out of the question. He shut it down. Fethi, poor, genial, weak Fethi, hurried away out of public life as quietly as possible, before he suffered for the storm he had unwittingly raised.

Then Mustafa Kemal turned to the People's Party. It must be, not only the instrument of government, but the means of educating the people to their responsibilities. It needed to be drastically purged. Many of the deputies were too old. Many of the local organizations were flabby and inefficient.

Mustafa Kemal ejected Sefet, the secretary-general of the party. He ordered elections and arranged that in the new Assembly there should be ninety fresh members who were laborers, artisans and shop-men, and a dozen independents who, under his orders, would have the right to criticize the Government.

His faith, his driving faith, in the Nation was as strong as ever. He would educate the People until they were ready. He would lead his People to success.

"But," he said in the spring of 1932, "let the people leave politics alone for the present. Let them interest themselves in agriculture and commerce. For ten or fifteen years more I must rule. After that perhaps I may be able to let them speak openly."

PART TWELVE

—

FINAL

LXXV

MUSTAFA KEMAL, alive and vibrating with vitality, is the Dictator of Turkey.

He is a man born out of due season, an anachronism, a throwback to the Tartars of the Steppes, a fierce elemental force of a man.

Had he been born in the centuries when all Central Asia was on the move he would have ridden out with Sulyman Shah under the banner of the Gray Wolf, and with the heart and instincts of a Gray Wolf.

With his military genius, and his ruthless determination unweakened by sentiments, loyalties or moralities, he might well have been a Tamerlane or a Jenghis Khan riding at the head of great hordes of wild horsemen, conquering countries, devouring and destroying cities, and filling in the intervals of peace between campaigns with wild and hideous orgies of wine and women.

Whereas he was born heir to a dead empire, which he has pruned down to a country, a little poverty-stricken peasant country.

He is caught up in the meshes of petty politics, in small reforms, in the routine of teaching a dull and laggard people.

With the mind of an Emperor he lives in brutal royalty in a suburban villa in the poor village of Chan Kaya: a primitive chieftain in a morning-coat with a piece of chalk and a black-board for his weapons.

.   .   .   .   .

His greatness has lain in his knowledge and his acceptance of the narrow limits of his opportunities.

Above all he is great in a great Faith—Faith in the splendid future of this people.

"I have known all nations," he said, "I have studied them on the battle-field, under fire, in the face of death, when the character of a people is laid naked. I swear to you, my people, that the spiritual strength of our nation transcends that of all the world....

"I will lead my people by the hand along the road until their feet are sure and they know the way. Then they may choose for themselves, and rule themselves. Then my work will be done."

Perhaps that is the voice of one crying in the wilderness. Perhaps it is the voice of one inspired by the Great Architect of the Universe to build fine and true.

He is Dictator. The future lies in his strong hands. If they fail, grow flabby, tremble, if though strong to destroy they cannot build, then Turkey dies.

A lone man without family, without friends, he has made the people of Turkey the heirs to his private possessions and to his power.

He is Dictator in order that it may be impossible ever again that there should be in Turkey a Dictator.

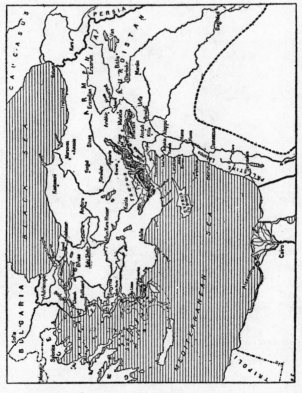

General Map of Turkey (and the Ottoman Empire in 1910)

EPILOGUE

I

The scene was the Turkish community center—*halko-dasi*—in a highland village, its mud dwellings glued to the boulderstrewn foot of the hill, wary of impinging on the productive land of the valley. The male villagers were eager to meet the western guest, and questions were bandied about in the amber light of the dusk. Turkey's foreign policy was being discussed.

Most vocal member of the group was an oldster, a "typical" Turk seeking to enlighten the benighted visitor about his martial deeds. In countless wars the oldster had fought the "Muscovite"—the Turks' name for the Russian. He had faced the abominable snowman of the North in the searing sand of North Africa's Tripolitania early this century. The baffled visitor broke in to remark that Turkey's foes in those days were the Italians, not the Muscovites. Heatedly, the oldster interjected that in that war, too, he had been fighting the Russian.

Then he started listing the wars in which he faced the hated neighbor in the North. He fought him, the Turk said, in the Balkan wars early this century. The Ottoman empire was then at war with Serbians, Bulgarians, Greeks— history books relate—but to the Turkish oldster and his kith the enemy was the Muscovite. It was really the Russian whom he fought during the Great War in the mountains and valleys of the Caucasus.

Having reached this point of his narrative, the oldster raised his voice to a high pitch. He said that he had fought the Russians in the great war of liberation under the command of Kemal the Conqueror. In that war his "Muscovite" was, of course, the Greek. However, to him and his unlettered countrymen all the Italians, English, Greeks and other enemies were the Muscovites.

This is, then, the Turkish tradition, deeply imbedded in the nation's soul. The Muscovites had acquired a continental country, one-sixth of the globe's land surface, and yet they felt thwarted because they lacked outlets to important maritime and trade routes—to southern warm waters. Their only outlet was via the Straits, in Turkish hands. Many times the Muscovites had attempted to wrest this vital waterway from the Ottomans' faltering hands. Russia's was a nightmare mansion of thousand windows but no gate.

"Never shall a foreign policy become an article of faith," Mustafa Kemal declared. Yet, Turkey's attitude toward the Russian was just such an article of faith, illustrated by the village oldster's belligerent stand.

The Turk was still "unspeakable" in western eyes after the Great War. Mustafa Kemal had to draw upon all of Turkey's energies to remove the debris of the dead empire and to establish the republic. For this he needed foreign capital and technical aid. In western eyes, Russia, too, was unspeakable, confined to her icy vastness by a *cordon sanitaire* of hostile countries along her western marches. She, too, had to remove the rubbish of the past and create a new civilization, while a peasant country was turned into an industrialized land. The two "outcasts" were thus thrown into each other's arms. Russia was the only country in those days to extend financial aid and technical assistance to Kemal's Turkey. It was the Soviet's Five Year Plan which, later, provided Ataturk with a model. While he had no use for communism and treated Turkey's own embryonic left wing roughly, he changed Turkey's foreign policy. While he was alive, the Muscovite was not Turkey's foe. After Ataturk's death, however, Turkey reverted to her traditional policy. By then, however, Russia was no longer weak and in need of Turkey's friendship.

During Kemal's regime other basic policy changes were also introduced. For many centuries the Ottoman empire had lorded it over the "accursed peninsula," the Balkans, drowned in blood and tears. The Turks were detested and bloody tyrants, but a small minority. The pariahs, on the other hand—Serbs, Bulgars, Greeks and many others— formed the downtrodden majority. The Ottoman Empire employed the age-old device of divide and rule in order to maintain itself, setting the Balkan people at one anothers' throats. This accounted for the perennial bloodshed and the evil name the Balkans acquired.

Particularly bitter was the hatred of the two close neighbors, Turks and Greeks. It was the Osmanli Turks who had smashed the old Eastern Roman empire centering around Constantinople, with its heritage of Greek culture, the Second Rome, the sacred shrines of which were the seat of the Greek Orthodox Church on the Golden Horn. Kemal himself had inflicted smarting wounds on the Greeks.

Now, however, Kemal realized that all of this must be discarded, with the other rubbish. No longer can the Balkan peninsula afford to remain a byword for war and hatred. Turkey needed peace and so did the Balkan neighbors. The dead warriors in the Balkan's Valhalla must have been rubbing their ghostly eyes at the unspeakable Turk's next deed. On February 9, 1934, Kemal's delegate signed a Balkan Pact with Yugoslavia, Rumania and Greece. "United in the desire," it said, "to contribute toward the permanence of peace in the Balkans, animated by the spirit of mutual understanding and conciliation. . . ." the signatories mutually guaranteed their Balkans frontiers. This was the beginning of the Balkan Entente. Kemal decided that the Balkans were to be a by-word for peace.

Turkey's relations had also been troubled by frontier disputes with Asian nations. Kemal's delegate signed the Saadabad Pact on July 7, 1937, with Afghanistan, Iraq and Iran. "The high contracting parties agree to follow a policy of absolute abstention from interference with the internal affairs of the others." They agreed to respect the inviolability of their common frontiers and agreed to mutual consultation in all cases of international conflicts having a bearing on their common interests.

Kemal's greatest work was the revolutionary change he effected in the status of the Turkish Straits. That waterway had been wrested from Turkish hands in the wake of the Ottoman defeat, and had been entrusted to an international commission.

The time was ripe for change in the middle thirties. Kemal saw the emergence of untamed forces of belligerence. Extreme chauvinism appeared now in a new shape—fascism—which glorified war as demanding the noblest expression of man, the sacrifice of his life for his country. In the most sensitive areas of the globe aggressive nations precipitated conflicts. In defiance of their covenanted obligations, the Japanese had invaded the Chinese mainland. Their aim was the control of East Asia. Then, in 1935, Italy invaded Ethiopia, the last independent country in East Africa. The following year civil war erupted in Spain, which was turned into the proving ground of the physical and ideological arms of two contending forces of the right and left. It turned out to be the dress-rehearsal for the Second World War.

Kemal realized that at the rate things were moving Turkey might be sucked into the whirlpool, if she were weak. This was then the time for her to regain control of her own lifeline, the Straits. The custom in those days for the nations was to snatch what they wanted first and then to talk. Kemal decided to talk first.

He asked that a conference should be convoked to settle the affairs of the Straits. It met in the Swiss city of Montreux in 1936 and drew up a new basic agreement, which is still in force. The control of the waterway was transferred to Kemal's government which also acquired the right to fortify the Straits. The new pact regulated the movement of ships in that waterway in peace and war. This was a telling illustration of the old and new in Turkey.

Few countries appeared to be content with what they had in those days and even fewer would have resigned themselves to Turkey's enormous losses. Kemal, however, wanted to have only Turkish territory—no more, no less. "Father of the Turks" he was called, not "Father of the Middle East."

Of course, sometimes it was a matter of interpretation what was Turkish and what was not. Kemal maintained, for instance, that the so-called Sanjak of Alexandretta, also known as Hatay, a semi-tropical protuberance from Anatolia into the Levant, was Turkish. That region, and everything else around it for many hundreds of miles, had belonged to the Ottomans. After the demise of the empire this region had been incorporated into Syria, a newly created Arab country, which was placed under French tutelage. Kemal held that most of the people in the area were Turks, not Arabs, and that it should be added to his nation. Conversely, the Arabs and French contended that this should not happen. Who was right; who was wrong? Eventually, the problem was solved to Ataturk's satisfaction. The Second World War was approaching and the French wanted to secure the Turks' friendship. Turkey appeared to them part of *l'espace fatal* of western Asia, the possession of which might help to decide the outcome of a war. Kemal got

Hatay with its important harbor of Alexandretta.

Kemal's behavior was sensible in territorial questions, but he had his blind spots. While he wanted to have only Turks in his country, they were not everybody's Turks. He held, for instance, that the Kurds, a breed of tough mountaineers in Anatolia's eastern marches, who speak a dialect of Persian, were Turks. He called them "mountain Turks" and when they rose against his strong-handed policy, he treated them roughly. He even claimed a slice of land of the adjacent Kingdom of Iraq because of these "mountain Turks," but there he did not have his way. Yet Turkey would have benefited from that particular tongue of land in Iraq's Mosul region, which contains some of the richest oil fields in the Middle East.

Kemal's policies were something new, indeed, under the Middle Eastern sun, used to viewing a stagnant world. Did he have a larger concept, too, a global policy? He did, indeed, and in that period and, particularly, in that portion of the world it was original. "The whole world," Kemal said toward the end of his life, "should be considered one body and the nations should be its organs. We should never say: 'I don't care about troubles in remote corners of the globe.' On the contrary, such troubles should be our concern. . . . International measures should be taken to insure eternal peace. In all parts of the globe, prosperity should replace misery. The citizens of such a world should be free of envy, hate and greed."

Long before that term "one world" gained currency, Mustafa Kemal Ataturk defined its essence.

II

"Turkish villagers in remote corners of western Anatolia, sitting on the ashes of their homes which contained the corpses of their kith and kin," wrote Madame Halidé Edib, a noted writer and follower of Kemal, "hardly knew whether Europe was a country or a man." But they knew that it was the cause of countless bloody misery in Turkey and they said over and over again: "What has the poor villager done to that *man* Europe that he persecutes us so?"

This was the type of ignorance Mustafa Kemal encountered in his country. When he assumed command only 350,000 pupils attended school in Turkey's 40,000 villages. The standard school in Ottoman days was the *medrese,* attached to the mosque. Furrowed into the mud-covered hills were carved the caves that served as "schools," and the children were sprawling on the naked floor. The equipment was simple and, above all, cheap. It was a greasy Koran, a famished teacher, and his cane. In a flat voice the teacher recited a *sura,* a sentence from the Holy Script, which the children had to repeat in unison. Those who failed to bellow loud enough got the cane. The pupils were Turks and the reading was in Arabic, a language they did not understand.

Ismet Inönu, republican Turkey's second man in command, called Ataturk *profesör,* while other Turks called him their Great Teacher. "Public instruction," Kemal said, "is the most productive and important duty of the state." Then he added, significantly: "We must view truth with penetrating eyes and come to grips with it in the world of experience."

Ignorance, he said, entailed disease and poverty, while knowledge provided the gateway not only to health and affluence but also to national greatness. Even his much-publicized interest in the Turks' headgear was a manifestation of his deep concern with public instruction. Forcing the Turks to remove their fez was part of his educational shock treatment. But he was far more interested in what was in a man's head than what was on it.

Many handicaps encumbered the road to education in Kemal's Turkey. His had been a nation of rulers and warriors, not of teachers and scholars. As always, he was in a hurry and he outlined an educational crash program which could be implemented only after he was gone. His program was unique, centering around the *Köy Enstitüt*—Village Institute. At first there were a score of them, but soon there were many more. These institutes taught bright older children to teach the younger ones, and they were established in strategic areas all over the country.

This is how the system worked. After five years of instruction groups of bright children were selected for teacher training. They were then transferred to the Village Institutes where they were provided with additional instruction for five years. They were taught the best methods of teaching, the elements of sanitation and farming, and the regular academic subjects.

After their graduation they returned to their villages where they performed multi-purpose functions. Primarily, they were to teach young children. Also the adults were to learn from them what "Europe" was, if not a man, and other useful knowledge. They were also to spread information about hygiene and improved farm methods.

Schools were built, too, through the cooperative efforts of the people and the state. They represented the new age —many of them white, even attractive, in contrast with the drab and dreary mud-dwellings. They were the tools of modernization and symbols of a great national effort. Schools were built usually for several villages; to enable the students to reach them roads had to be improved. Some 10,000 schools were built in fifteen years, manned by 3,000 graduates of the Institutes. This, indeed, was a crash program.

Both higher and adult education invited Kemal's attention. The importance of the intellectual élite was known to him. Educated persons were to serve as powerhouses in the process of national modernization. His opportunity was provided by the inter-bellum authoritarian trend in Central Europe, especially the return to the dark ages in Hitler's Germany. The Third Reich in Germany was the age of the superman—of the brawn, not of the brain. On the contrary, no sooner had Hitler reached power in 1933 when he proclaimed: "The German fatherland has too much knowledge, and that inhibits the springs of deeds. What we need is Will, Will, Will!" When the exodus of German learning set in, Kemal opened his country to refugee teachers. With the aid of foreign professors he established a medical faculty in Istanbul, installed a school of Politics and Social Sciences in Ankara, and launched other schools for the study of engineering, farming and trade. He also drew upon the creative teaching talents of other nations.

Nor did he overlook the educational problems of those who were too old to sit on school benches. He did not want the western Anatolian peasants to think that Europe was a man. With these considerations in mind he established *halkevis,* the "People's Houses," all over the country, and the *halkodasi,* village rooms, in smaller places. These community centers served the aims of varied activities. Facilities were made available in some of them to teach the three R's to the adults. Newspapers and books were on hand in these houses and rooms of the people. The radios of these centers opened up a wider world to the country folk. The larger *halkevis* were provided with clinics and swimming pools. Through them Kemal also hoped to counteract the stultifying influence of the cafes. He hoped that, eventually, the satisfaction derived from the excitement of learning, reading, sports, might erode the people's traditional fatalism and apathy.

In the realm of the instruction of the younger generation, Kemal had good reason to be content. A new generation began to emerge, a young, inquisitive generation, interested not only in the affairs of Turkey but also of the rest of the world. Some of them could be employed in government services and others would start teaching. Still others would fill the gaps left by the disappearance of the Greek and Armenian minorities, and become traders, financiers and "intellectuals." Well-trained Turkish professional workers began to change the intellectual horizon of the nation.

The older generation, however, was not easily led into the new Promised Land of Turkey, infused with a western glow. Many of the old-timers kept on patronizing the cafes, peering into the intoxicating emptiness of the blue yonder and losing themselves in the contemplation of nothing of consequence. Was Kemal disappointed with the result of his efforts to educate the elder people? He was, since he was always in a hurry; he was an impatient man. Had he been less impatient, he would have been heartened by the stirring within the younger generation. It was the best hope of resurrected Turkey and the great achievement of Mustafa Kemal Ataturk.

III

To Kemal a symbol of the West was factory smoke. Not until Turkey had turned her own cotton into garments and her iron ore into steel would she shake off colonial thraldom. The Ottoman Empire had been weak because it was a peasant empire, and only the machine could make a nation rich.

When Kemal took the helm Turkey already had 65,246 "industrial establishments," according to the official census. However, only three such establishments in the entire realm had a labor force of more than a hundred employees. The Turk would never demean himself to serve the machine. There were few Turkish financiers and traders—hardly any. Such lowly occupations were left for the Armenians, the Greeks and the Jews. Even educated Turks studying abroad took little interest in what appeared to them a particularly dismal science, economics.

This was so because tradition was deeply rooted in the Oriental mind. The old had been sanctified by revered forebears and therefore it was good. What was the use of stirring abroad, when sitting in the sun was so pleasant? The serenity of fatalism ran deeply in Oriental ways. Also, work was unprofitable because it attracted the special attention of the ubiquitous tax-collector. New-fangled ideas were the handiwork of *Seytan,* the evil one. Electric light was the devil's work, but the tallow candle was heaven's gift.

Kemal, however, wanted electricity, not only for light but also for power. In that respect, too, he was in a frenzied hurry. But where was Turkey to obtain the capital, technical know-how and the impulse to pioneer on this new path? The funds for the "industries," transportation and public works had come mainly from foreign sources under the Ottoman rule. The rates were, of course, usurious and the gainers were the alien masters. Kemal was familiar with the work of the Ottoman Debt Administration. Foreign loans had been the entering wedges of intervention, and instruments of foreign control. It was thus that Egypt had become a British colony. Kemal did not want to have this historic process start all over again. In any event, western foreign capital would not have been available to the bankrupt Turk.

Since foreign capital was not available to get Turkey's industries started, would it be possible to obtain native capital? There were some wealthy people in Turkey, but wealth had its own ways of investment. The Turkish nabob invested his money in land or gold or hoarded it in stockings but more likely he transferred it to safe foreign marts in the West. Risk capital for industries was simply not available. Besides, none of the ancestors had ever invested in steel mills and chemical plants, and whatever was not good for the father was not good for the son. Where then was the Father of the Turks to obtain the funds to get the machines started?

There appeared to be one way and one way only—the government. No matter how poor a country is, its resources are more abundant than those of the individuals. There is taxation in even the poorest countries. Let, then, Turkey start producing—producing more, consuming less, and plowing the surplus back into production. This was the way for a poor country to get industrialized.

The government had to get things started. Also, it had to run and own many of the new industries. However, Kemal, though not an economist and not particularly interested in economics, knew enough of that dismal science to realize that there was no more powerful lever of getting things started than the private profit motive. The West—Kemal's point of orientation—had become opulent through *laissez-faire*, free enterprise.

Kemal's Turkey—short of funds but long on ambition—introduced a new sort of hybrid economy, a combination of private and public enterprise. Ataturk coined a work for this system, *étatisme,* and it was incorporated in his country's Constitution.

Turkey would have to eliminate waste and duplication, and concentrate on the most essential projects. This called for the establishment of priorities and a measure of planning. For the last several years, Kemal had observed Soviet Russia's bold experiment, its Operation Bootstrap, *Piatiletka,* the Five Year Plan.

Certain features of the Soviet Five Year Plan did not appeal to him. Russia concentrated on heavy industries. Kemal had no time to wait until the machines would produce other machines which, in turn, would produce the goods that people would wear. He was in a hurry to clothe his tattered people and to fill their stomachs with more food. He gave precedence to production of consumer goods and to light industries that would produce textiles, hemp products, rayon, paper, chemicals, fertilizers, and cement for dwellings and factory plants. He also wanted to develop electric power stations, iron foundries, and plants for the refining of minerals.

Mustafa Kemal set down his thoughts on Turkey's economic development, and this is what he wrote: "Turkey should have industries to serve as the supports of higher living standards." At the same time, he wished to avoid the blemishes of the highly industrialized countries. His nation should not contain super-privileged and under-privileged regions and therefore the industries must be dispersed. Nor did he want to witness the emergence of large combinations, cartels and trusts. Labor conflicts must be resolved through mediation and arbitration, not by lockouts and strikes. "The entire country must be run as one economic unit."

He obtained his first loan from the Soviets, a mere $18 million. This was also the Russians' first venture into the international economic field. Years later they were to offer billions in loans and technical assistance to foreign countries. Kemal, too, got Russian technical assistance and that was also for the first time in the Soviets' history. He launched his nation's first Five Year Plan in 1934. Turkey was the first country to employ a device introduced by the Russians. It should be recalled, however, that Kemal was not a communist or even a socialist; he was a very outspoken anti-communist, but he was not dogmatic and not afraid of words. The system of *étatisme* appeared to him best suited to Turkey's special conditions.

Three years after his first Soviet loan he initiated Turkey's Four Year Agricultural plan, under which large-scale irrigation projects were undertaken. His government also acquired sizable tracts of uncultivated land which it turned into state farms and small peasant holdings. Turkey's land reform was on the move.

After Kemal's death, his successors inaugurated another Five Year Plan and established an industrial bank. With the aid of the United States and the United Nations, Turkey embarked on an ambitious program of economic development.

IV

"And Moses went up from the plains of Moab unto the mountain of Nebo, to the top of Pisgah, that is over against Jericho. And the Lord shewed him all the land of Gilead, unto Dan."

The Moses of the Turks was Mustafa Kemal. In December 1934 a law was passed to make the Turks assume family names, in addition to their given names. His people asked Kemal to be known to them and to posterity as the Father of the Turks, *Ataturk,* because he had led his people to Moab, unto the mountain of Nebo, to the top of Pisgah. And this is what Ataturk said: "I shall lead my people by the hand along the road until their feet are sure and they know the way. Then they may choose for themselves, and rule themselves. Then my work will be done."

His people chose him again as their president and leader on March 2, 1935, and that was the last time they had the opportunity thus to elect him. Nor did they have any other choice because he, and he alone, was their *Büyük Önder*—Great Leader. His people knew this and he knew it, too.

Mustafa Kemal Ataturk was working rhapsodically and it was given to him to have a tempestuous will-power and flashes of profound insight. It was also given to him to perceive things that others failed to see and to stimulate people to work. But it was not given to him to perform miracles, even though people in his country thought that he was possessed of the power of magic.

He could not, for instance, transform the dismal little hamlets of Turkey into places that looked like the picture-book towns of Normandy. Nor could he turn the Anatolian highlands into highly organized industrial centers like Germany's Wupperthal. Nor could he teach all of his countrymen that Europe was a continent, not a man. He was impatient with his people, and also with the slow pace of time, but could do nothing about that. He did start, though, the process of raising Turkey's living standards, which began to rise, not as quickly as he wanted, but it was a good beginning just the same. He put the torch to pilot lights so that today there are new quarters in some of the new Turkish republic's old towns and also there are some industries. But, above all, there is now a new generation of Turks, whose brains are clear of the cobwebs of the past.

"I have conquered the enemy," he said. "I have conquered the country, but can I conquer the people?" He had his doubts. He expected millions of Turks to be impelled by his own torrential energy. When they were not, he was disappointed. Turkey was not the land of millions of Kemals.

So, he was disappointed and he all but withdrew from public life for years. He emerged from his privacy periodically and then he spoke *ex cathedra* to the Turkish National Assembly, his sounding board. He spoke on several subjects but his most famous message was the one in which he called upon the youth of Turkey to continue his work. In that address he appointed the youth of his country the trustee of his reforms. And thus he surveyed the land from the top of the hill and he realized that he could do no more.

Kemal lived in semi-retirement in the vicinity of Ankara during the summer, and near Bursa and Istanbul during the winter months. His country home at Chankaya was some four kilometers from the capital, a place of exotic charm in the wooded hills of an untamed country, away from the metropolitan crowds in those days. And when the Anatolian highland was gripped by the icy winds from the North he descended to the lowlands, to Yalova, famed for its thermal baths, near Bursa. Also he withdrew to the

Dolma-Bahçe Saray of the former Sultans in Istanbul, north of the Pera quarter, on the Bosporus. That palace had been installed with imperial luxury in the 1850's and was famed for its throne room, reputedly the largest in all Europe.

In his private life this iron man, Kemal, was a weak man, unable to resist his savage impulses. His love-life was violent and he was a compulsive drinker. He was surrounded by his boon-companions whom he called the "desperadoes." Few alcoholic beverages did not rank high in his favor. He liked the national drink *rakhi,* which the Turks distill from grapes. He also liked the exotic Turkish liqueurs made from strawberries, bananas, tangerines and cherries, although he did not at all reject western drinks.

He observed his own code of ethics in his relations with women. He used them and then threw them away. His international fame, virility, good looks, piercing eyes attracted women to him from far and wide. They flew to him, as moths to the flame. Only once did he contract a marriage. We have encountered the name of his wife in a previous chapter. His wife had been Latifa Hanum, exciting, westernized and rich. She had tempted him coyly and then refused herself to him. This was a unique experience to the great conqueror. Latifa exacted the highest price. Impulsively, he married her.

However, he was not the marrying type. Under the Koranic law which Kemal had abolished, nothing could be simpler than divorcing a wife. All the man had to do was to utter the words "I divorce thee," three times, in the presence of witnesses. And he, Mustafa Kemal, the great westernizer of Turkey, divorced Latifa in accordance with the ancient law of the Orient. When he expressed regret years later, it was already too late.

He lived recklessly, with utter abandon. This unbridled zest for life and the irresistible urge to tempt the fates explain his suicidal ways. To him the question was to live dangerously, or not to live at all. This kind of life, obviously, could not last for long.

Republic Day of 1938—on October 29—was celebrated with fireworks in Istanbul. Neither the people of the former capital of the Ottoman empire nor the population of republican Turkey suspected how sick was the Father of the Turks. He was abed in that magnificent palace on the Bosporus, the Dolma-Bahçe. He looked emaciated, a skeleton, unable to digest his food. He had jaundice; the dread telltale symptoms of an incurable disease broke out on his body. Doctors call these symptoms "vascular spiders"—greatly dilated blood-vessels; they are due to alcoholism. Kemal had cirrhosis of the liver.

The final and fatal symptom heralded the end—mental torpor. Mercifully, he lapsed into unconsciousness. It was at five minutes after nine in the morning of November 10 that Mustafa Kemal Atatürk passed away.

When news of this tragic event broke upon the Turkish people, millions of them began to stream into the streets, crying out to heaven, prostrating themselves in dust and mud. Kemal's body lay in state in the vast throne-room of Dolma-Bahçe palace, where four army generals were standing guard at the catafalque. From all parts of the imperial city of Istanbul people were headed toward that throne-room, past the gilt grille of the saray, into the funeral chamber. So great was the crush and so irresistible, that several mourners were trampled to death. Now that the Father of the Turks was no more the entire nation felt orphaned.

Later, the body was transferred to Ankara, the capital Kemal created, and the funeral cortege was accompanied by the representatives of many nations. He was called the greatest contemporary statesman of the world. "The nation lost its teacher," the Turkish governmental proclamation wailed, "its great chief, and humanity one of its great sons."

A vast mausoleum was built for the body of Kemal Ataturk a few years later on a hill overlooking the capital of republican Turkey. Turks view it not only as the tomb of the greatest son of their country but also as the symbol of the resurrection of their nation, the work of Ataturk.

V

Then came the age of the successors. Ataturk's closest collaborator had been Ismet Inönu, his junior by three years. Both as a soldier and a statesman Ismet had a proud record. He distinguished himself in the early twentieth-century Balkan wars under the Ottoman regime. It was no fault of Ismet Pasha—his name then—nor of other distinguished soldiers that the badly wounded empire of the Sultans was bleeding to death.

It was on the vital Syrian front that Ismet fought the British during the Great War. Later he received an even more important assignment as the commander of an entire army corps. Ismet was among the first to join Mustafa Kemal when the "Gray Wolf" struck out for himself against the pack of sycophants in the Sultan's palace on the Golden Horn. The capital of the empire was then under the control of the victorious Allies who kept the gates closed to Turks that might start a nationalist revolution against the Allied dismemberment of Turkey.

Ismet managed to elude Allied vigilance and reached Kemal's headquarters in an adventurous way. He had sneaked out of Constantinople in the uniform of a private soldier. Eventually, he found his way to the revolutionary headquarters of Mustafa Kemal in Angora, the name of which was to be changed to Ankara. It was evident that Ismet Pasha was to play a notable role in Turkey's resurrection.

301

He did play a highly important part, indeed, in the military operations against the Greeks. He was the commander-in-chief on the crucial western front. One of the most crushing defeats he inflicted on the foe was at the town of Inönu, and when Turks came to adopt family names he became General Ismet Inönu.

Kemal the President named Ismet Pasha his Prime Minister. He represented Turkey at important international conferences where he gained the reputation of an able bargainer. Little was known about Ismet's part in domestic affairs because the giant shadow of Kemal eclipsed him, yet those who knew him intimately, spoke very highly of him. Kemal had his quarrels with him, as with everybody else, and Ismet Inönu was not the Prime Minister in the last year of Ataturk. When the question of succession was broached Inönu was deemed to be the worthiest candidate. The Grand National Assembly of Turkey elected him the second president of the country.

The second World War broke out the year after Inönu's election. By that time the German Third Reich had penetrated into the Balkans and its influence extended all the way to Turkey's frontiers.

The role of Turkey in the war has been the subject of controversy. The Allied powers were not of one mind on this subject. It seems that the British wanted the Turks in the war on the Allied side while the American government was not so sure. During much of the war the Germans had a way of overruning countries presumably much stronger than Turkey in a matter of days. What would happen if they steamrollered Turkey into submission? In that case the Middle East, with all its tremendous output of oil would fall into their hands. If there was one vital raw material the Nazis needed it was oil. Was it therefore not better to let

Turkey remain neutral and thus keep the Germans from the oil wells of the Middle East?

Ismet Inönu had to consider Turkey's interests primarily. His country had been in the first World War much longer than any other nation. For Turkey it began with the first Balkan war in 1912 and ended more than a decade later with the final triumph of Mustafa Kemal's war against the Greeks. Then came the painful period of reconstruction and development, the transformation of an Oriental despotism into an Occidental republic. Was Turkey strong enough to hold her own against the seemingly invincible Third Reich? Would it be in her interest to become a battlefield? Was this not Turkey's best chance to profit immensely by selling strategic raw materials to both sides?

Turkey did not participate in the war. However, she declared war on Germany just before the wounded giant was brought to bay. Thus Inönu's country qualified to join the United Nations as a charter member.

Russia was one of the victors of the second World War. Riding high on the tidal wave of victory would not Russia make an attempt to satisfy her perennial warm-water thirst and force the gates open via the Straits? The Soviet Union did precisely that. The cold war was on between the giants of East and West. Skillfully, President Ismet Inönu manoeuvered his country into the western camp.

On March 12, 1947, President Harry S. Truman announced a revolutionary American policy: "Totalitarian regimes imposed on free peoples undermine the foundations of international peace and hence the security of the United States." Turkey and Greece were the outposts of democracy against the greedy Soviets. The United States offered assistance against the Russians to these countries. The "Truman Doctrine" was born.

Ataturk, we have seen, was on good terms with the

Soviets. Had he been alive at this time, would he have continued the good neighbor policy with the "Muscovites"? Or had a basic change taken place in Turkey's relations with Russia and in the power parallelogram of the world?

While Turkey was now a bulwark of the free world was she herself free? Kemal's own creation, the Republican People's Party was a monopoly. "Power corrupts, absolute power corrupts absolutely," Lord Acton said. The Republican People's Party wielded power and, indeed, wielded absolute power. It was carried away by its own importance. It was in the name of Kemal that some of the leaders of Turkish public opinion in parliament and in the press began to urge a change in the political system. A group of members of parliament established the Democratic Party. Turkey had now two major political parties.

The Democratic Party now made a claim to represent the real Kemalist policies. However, its opponent, the Republican People's party, was firmly entrenched. Finally, in 1950 the election for the Grand National Assembly was free. The Turkish voters spoke with unmistakable conviction. The Democratic Party scored against the Republicans in a landslide victory. Thus ended twelve years of the age of Inönu who had taken the Turks by the hand after Kemal's death and helped them continue the great nation builder's work. In retrospect, it seems that Ismet Inönu was a seasoned diplomat and an able political leader, but he lacked the spark of the late Ataturk, the spark of the creative man.

Again it was in the name of Ataturk that the Turkish leaders spoke. This time they were at the head of the victorious Democratic Party. "We are the true heirs of the Kemalist tradition," they said, "and the spirit of the Eternal Chief will guide our steps." The third president of Turkey was Celal Bayar, former banker, the man whom Kemal had placed in charge of his Five Year Plan. The Prime Minister was Adnan Menderes, a landowner, a strongly western-oriented man. Both of them were known as brilliant pupils in Kemal's training school.

Now it was the turn of the Democratic Party to strengthen its hand at the helm. Claiming to follow in the footsteps of the Eternal Chief it considered opposition to itself disloyalty to Kemal's legacy. Stringent measures were taken against the Republican People's Party and the press. Some of the basic principles of Kemalism, however, were revised. In economic matters, free enterprise gained the upper hand. Numerous industries were denationalized. Kemal's *étatisme* was under a cloud.

During all this time, Turkey cooperated with the United States in strengthening the defenses of the country. In a dozen years America was pouring some three billion dollars into Turkey. The government claimed to follow the guidance of the Eternal Chief in speeding up the process of industrialization. Evidently, however, the country was not prepared for the accelerated tempo. Prices were rising, inflation set in, the value of the currency declined. "The road to Turkey's bankruptcy," commented an American economist, "is paved with dollar bills."

Dissatisfaction swept the country in the major urban centers. It was particularly the youth of Turkey, to which the late Kemal had entrusted his legacy, that manifested strong opposition to the high-handed Democratic regime. The university students in Ankara and Istanbul staged spectacular demonstrations against the regime, speaking in the name of the legacy of Ataturk.

Then, suddenly, the blow fell. On May 27, 1960, a military junta ousted the Democratic Party, arrested many of its leading members, including the president and prime minister, and established itself as the new government. Head of the junta was General Celal Gursel, former commander of the Turkish land forces. He arraigned the deposed politicians on the ground that they had betrayed the Kemalist tradition. "We are animated," he declared, "by the spirit and the deeds of Mustafa Kemal."

Thus all political factions in Turkey continue to claim Ataturk as their inspiration. This was as true of the Republican People's Party as of the Democratic Party, of all the other political parties, liberal, conservative or reactionary, whether calling themselves the "Association of Nationalists," a chauvinist group, or the "Divine Light," which claimed religious inspiration.

Increasingly, it became evident that Turkey was in great need of standing up to the tasks entrusted to her by the founder of the republic. The country faced the question: Where was it to find a worthy successor of the Father of the Turks?

VI

How had Kemal evaluated his own record? And how does the contemporary world evaluate Ataturk's historic rôle?

This seemingly most successful man of the Middle East did not consider himself a success. The reckless life that led to his untimely death was perhaps an expression of his personal discontent. Was he aware of his historic rôle and of the fact that his name was famed throughout the globe? He was fully aware of these facts—he was not a modest man. But he was also aware of the fact that republican Turkey was a small country and that his was not the age of the giants. He would not have felt frustrated in the epoch of the world empires of Alexander the Great, Julius Caesar and Napoleon. While it is true that he had created modern Turkey and that no other man has cast a more abiding spell on the Middle East, he did feel that his real mission would have been to build great empires and to transform the world. It was by his own sky-storming standards that he was not a success.

And what was the world's opinion about him? History knows that he released Turkey's latent potentialities. It knows, too, that he was a blend of the divine and diabolic, a man with hypnotic power and without fear, an unusual and very great man. When he appeared on the world scene there was only a dynasty in the Middle East, and he needed a nation—Turkey. He surveyed the Orient and disliked what he saw: countries mired in the past, pipe-dreaming about it, a sick and slothful world, corroded by ailments of the body and the mind.

Then he viewed the Occident and did not like it much either. Yet it was preferable to the East because people in the West had more food, schools and medicine, so that they lived longer and grew stronger. Mustafa Kemal knew that there could be no strong nation of weak individuals and that a nation could never be strong as long as it was ridden by disease, ignorance and poverty.

There was one aspect of the West that Mustafa Kemal particularly disliked and that was the spirit of savage competition among the nations, constantly scoring points at others' cost, driving to the limits of the feasible, sometimes beyond it, and having no balance, no balance whatever. He wanted his Turkey to be the creator, not the destroyer. He saw that even the greatest nations of the West were frequently destructive, always for noble causes, as they saw it, because they deemed themselves superior to other nations —always much superior.

He did not want Turkey to be better, just good within her own sphere, but not beyond it; no Manifest Destiny for him. The Ottoman Empire had pursued the chimera of world power, always pushing onward, hitching its own security to the most recently acquired anchor and then driving onward again to secure security. He saw what had happened to the Sultan's realm, and he wanted nothing more than the safety and prosperity of Turkey, inhabited by Turks.

APPENDIX

OUTLINE HISTORY OF PERIOD

YEAR	DATE	ITEM
1288	—	Coming of the Osmanli Turks out of the Plains of Sungaria and the Great Desert of Gobi.
1453	May 20th	Capture of Constantinople by the Turks.
1517	—	Sultan Selim becomes Caliph.
1520	—	Sulyman the Magnificent: the Peak Period of the Ottoman Empire.
1528	—	Sulyman attacks Vienna.
1700–1800	—	Rise of Russia.
1821	—	Greeks revolt.
1876–1909	—	ABDUL HAMID II.
1876	—	Bulgarians revolt.
1877	—	Russia declared war on Turkey. Siege and capture of Adrianople. Russians advance as far as San Stephano.
1878	—	CONGRESS OF BERLIN.
1881	—	MUSTAFA KEMAL BORN IN SALONIKA.
1882	—	British troops landed in Egypt.
1889	—	First Armenian massacres, followed by others in 1894, 1896, 1915 and 1920, ending in the complete disappearance of all Armenians in Turkey.

YEAR	DATE	ITEM
1889	—	Entry of Germany as protector of Turkey. Visit of Kaiser to Sultan Abdul Hamid.
1897	—	Revolt of Crete. Turks defeat the Greeks under Prince Constantine.
1903	—	Mustafa Kemal at Monastir Military School.
1905	—	Mustafa Kemal at Staff College, Constantinople.
1906	—	Committee of Union and Progress in Salonika.
1908	—	Mustafa Kemal on Staff of 3rd Army Corps, Salonika.
1908	—	Revolution of the Committee of Union and Progress.
1908	—	Bulgaria declared herself independent.
1909	—	Counter-revolution in Constantinople against the Committee of Union and Progress. Counter-revolution crushed. Abdul Hamid deposed and imprisoned.
1910	—	Mustafa Kemal with mission to French maneuvers.
1911	—	War in Tripoli between Italians and Turks.
1912	October	First Balkan War: Montenegro, Servia, Greece and Bulgaria against Turkey.
1913	October	Second Balkan War: Bulgarians against the Greeks, Servians and Rumanians. Turks re-take Adrianople.
1913	—	Mustafa Kemal as Military Attaché in Sofia.
1914	—	The World War.
1915	February	British naval attack on Dardanelles.

YEAR	DATE	ITEM
1915	April	Mustafa Kemal to the 19th Division in the Dardanelles.
1915	August 8th	Mustafa Kemal given command of Anafarta front.
1916	——	Mustafa Kemal to the Caucasus Army. Transferred to the 7th Army of the Yildirim, but resigned his command.
1917	——	Mustafa Kemal with Prince Vaheddin to Germany.
1918	——	Mustafa Kemal to the 7th Army of the Syrian Army.
1918	October 30th	Armistice between Turkey and the Allies.
1918	November	Mustafa Kemal returns to Constantinople.
1919	May 15th	Greeks land in Smyrna.
1919	May 19th	Mustafa Kemal lands in Samsun, as Inspector-General of the Northern Army Zone.
1919	July 23rd	Congress at Erzerum.
1919	September 13th	Congress at Sivas.
1919	December	French take over Syria from the English.
1920	January 28th	Turkish Parliament opens in Constantinople, and publishes the National Pact.
1920	March 16th	Allies occupy Constantinople and arrest principal Nationalists and deport them to Malta.
1920	April 23rd	Grand National Assembly meets in Angora.
1920	June 22nd	Greek Army attacks.
1920	July	Greeks clear Nationalists out of the Constantinople area.
1920	Autumn	Kiazim Kara Bekir smashes the Armenians.

YEAR	DATE	ITEM
1920	November	Bolshevics defeat Wrangel's White Russian Army.
1920	November	Venizelos expelled from, and King Constantine recalled to, Greece.
1920	December	Troubles with the Irregulars. Mustafa Kemal orders that they be smashed.
1921	January 11th	Battle of In Eunu.
1921	July 10th	Big Greek offensive.
	July 19th	Greeks take Eski Shehir.
	July 25th	Turks retire east of the Sakkaria River.
1921	August 5th	Mustafa Kemal made Commander-in-Chief, with powers of Dictator.
	August 14th	Battle of Sakkaria.
1921	October 20th	French made secret Treaty of Angora with the Turks.
1922	August 26th	Mustafa Kemal attacks Greeks and completely defeats them.
	September 9th	Turks reoccupy Smyrna.
1922	September	Turks and English face each other at Chanak.
	September 29th	Mudania Conference.
1922	November 1st	Abolition of the Sultanate.
1922	November 17th	Sultan left Constantinople. Abdul Mejid made Caliph.
	November 21st	Lausanne Conference.
1923	July 24th	Treaty of Lausanne.
1923	October 2nd	Final evacuation of Turkey by foreign troops.
	October 13th	Angora made the capital of Turkey.
	October 28th	Declaration of the Turkish Republic. Mustafa Kemal as President.
1924	March 3rd	Caliphate abolished. Turkey secularized.
1925	March	Kurdish revolt.

YEAR	DATE	ITEM
1926	July	Smyrna plot to kill Mustafa Kemal. Mustafa Kemal smashes the opposition.
1926	Summer	Hats for fezzes. Introduction of German, Italian and Swiss Legal Codes.
1928	November 3rd	The Latin alphabet.
1929	——	Second Kurdish revolt.
1930	August	Experiment of a Liberal Opposition under Fethi. Menemen riots.
1931	——	Mustafa Kemal rules again as Dictator.
1932	——	Mustafa Kemal's new policy.

(See Epilogue for subsequent developments)

WORKS CONSULTED AND GENERAL
REFERENCES

ABELOUS, FRÉDÉRIC: *L'Evolution de la Turquie dans ses rapports avec les étrangers.*

AGÂH, M.: *Gázinin Vecizeleri.*

ARIF (MEHMET): *The Anatolian Revolution.*

ARMSTRONG, HAROLD: *Turkey in Travail.*

Ditto: *Turkey and Syria Re-born.*

ASPINALL-OGLANDER, Brig-Gen. C. F.: *Military Operations in Gallipoli. Australian Official History, The.*

BARCLAY, Sir THOMAS: *The Turco-Italian War and its Problem.*

BÉRAUD, HENRI: *Men of the Aftermath.*

CHURCHILL, WINSTON: *The World War.*

Ditto: *The Aftermath.*

Ditto: *The World Crisis. The Eastern Front.*

DENY, J.: *Souvenirs de Mustafa Kemal.*

ELLISON, GRACE: *An Englishwoman in Angora.*

EMIN BEY: *Turkey in the World War.*

ENGLISH NEWSPAPERS AND PERIODICALS:

> The Times.
> Manchester Guardian.
> Daily Telegraph.
> The Near East and India.
> The Spectator.
> The Sunday Times.

ESREF (RUSEN): *Anafartalar Kumandarin Mustafa Kemal ile Mülâkat.*

EVERSLEY, Lord: *The Turkish Empire.*

FALKENHAYN, General Von: *General Headquarters, 1914–1916.*

FERRIÈRE, A.: *La Turquie nouvelle et ses écoles.*

GAULIS, Mme B. G.: *La Question turque.*

Ditto: *Angora, Constantinople, Londres (Mustafa Kémal et la politique anglaise en Orient).*

Ditto: *La Nouvelle Turquie.*

Ditto: *Le Nationalisme turc.*

GENERAL STAFF WAR OFFICE: *Notes on the Balkan Wars*, 1912–1913.

GENTIZON, PAUL: *Mustafa Kemal, ou l'Orient en marche.*

GRAVES, PHILIP: *The Question of the Straits.*

GRAEVNITZ, G. V.: *Geschichte des italienisch-türkische Krieges*, Berlin, 1912.

HALIDEH, EDIB: *The Turkish Ordeal.*

HAMILTON, General Sir IAN: *Gallipoli Diary.*

HEATHCOTE, D.: *Fortnightly Review*, January, 1927: "Mustafa Kemal and New Turkey."

HERBERT, AUBREY: *Mons, Anzac and Kut.*

HOWELL, Major P.: *The Campaign in Thrace*, 1912.

IZZET PASHA, Marschall: *Denkwürdig Küten.*

JEMAL PASHA: *Memoirs of a Turkish Statesman.*

KANNENGIESER, HANS: *The Gallipoli Campaign.*

KEMAL, MUSTAFA: *Le Discours du Ghazi Mustafa Kemal.*

KIAZIM PASHA: *Yéni Ses.*

KIRKWOOD, K. P. *See* TOYNBEE, A. J.

KNIGHT, E. F.: *The Awakening of Turkey.*

KORGANOFF, General: *La Participation des Arméniens à la Guerre Mondiale.*

LAWRENCE, T. E. (*alias* SHAW): *The Seven Pillars of Wisdom.*
  Ditto: *The Revolt in the Desert.*

MACCULLUM, FRANCIS: *The Fall of Abdul Hamid.*

MARRIOTT, J. A. R.: *The Eastern Question.*

MARZIO, CORNELIO DI: *La Turchia di Kemal.*

MEARS, E. G.: *Modern Turkey.*

MELIA, JEAN: *Mustafa Kemal, ou la Renovation de la Turquie.*

MIKUSCH, DOGBERT VON: *Mustafa Kemal, Betwix Europe and Asia.*

MORGENTHAU: *An International Drama.*
  Ditto: *Secrets of the Bosphorus.*

NOGALIS, G. R. DU: *Memoirs of a Soldier of Fortune.*

PECH, EDGAR: *Les Alliés et la Turquie.*

PRICE, CLAIRE: *The Re-birth of Turkey.*

PRIGGE: *Der Kampf um die Dardanelles.*

REVOL, J.: *La Guerro Italo-Turque*, 1911–1912.

Revue des Etudes Islamiques, 1927. Cahiers I and III.

Revue du Monde Musselman. Volume LXIII.

ROSSI, E.: *Il Ghazi Mustafa Kemal Pascia.*

SAMSON, Air-Commodore C. R.: *Fights and Flights.*

SANDERS, LIMAN VON: *Five Years in Turkey.*

SFORZA, Count C.: *Makers of Modern Europe*.
   Ditto: *Dictators*.
SHERIDAN, CLARE: *East and West*.
TITTONI, First Lieut. RENATO: *The Italo-Turkish War, 1911–1912*.
TOYNBEE, A. J., and KIRKWOOD, K. P.: *Turkey*.
TOYNBEE, ROSALIND: *The Turkish Woman of To-day*.
TURKISH NEWSPAPERS:
   Le Vaquit.
   Le Milliet.
WAUGH, A.: *Turkey To-day*.
WAVELL, Colonel A. P.: *The Palestine Campaign*.
WOODS, H. C.: *Fortnightly Review*, November, 1927: "Ghazi Mustafa Kemal Pasha."
WORTHAM, H. E.: *Mustafa Kemal of Turkey*.

INDEX

321

CAPRICORN TITLES

1. *Dewey*, ART AS EXPERIENCE. $1.35 (Hardcover $2.50).
2. *Rilke*, NOTEBOOKS OF MALTE LAURIDS BRIGGE. $1.25.
3. *Adler*, WHAT LIFE SHOULD MEAN TO YOU. $1.25.
4. *Bell*, ART. $1.25.
5. *Whitehead*, MODES OF THOUGHT. $1.15.
6. *Adams*, DEMOCRATIC DOGMA. $1.25.
7. *Olmsted*, SLAVE STATES. $1.25 (Hardcover $2.50).
8. *Jefferson*, AUTO. OF THOS. JEFFERSON. $.95 (Hardcover $2.50).
9. *Matthews*, THE FUGGER NEWSLETTERS. $1.25 (Hardcover $2.50).
10. *Hough*, DARK SUN. $1.25.
11. *Hawkes*, COLERIDGE'S WRITINGS ON SHAKESPEARE. $1.35 (Hardcover $2.50).
12. *Shaw*, ADVENTURES OF THE BLACK GIRL. $.95 (Hardcover $2.50).
13. *Whitehead*, SYMBOLISM. $.95.
14. *Golding*, LORD OF THE FLIES. $1.25.
15. *Chekhov*, ST. PETER'S DAY. $1.25 (Hardcover $2.50).
16. *Nashe*, THE UNFORTUNATE TRAVELLER. $1.15 (Hardcover $2.50).
17. *Weil*, WAITING FOR GOD. $1.25.
18. *Coates*, EATER OF DARKNESS. $1.15.
19a. *Bryce*, THE AMERICAN COMMONWEALTH—Vol. I. $1.35.
19b. *Bryce*, THE AMERICAN COMMONWEALTH—Vol. II. $1.35 (Hardcover 1-vol. ed. $5.00).
20. *Moore*, CONFESSIONS OF A YOUNG MAN. $1.25.
21. *Tolstoy*, LAST DIARIES. $1.35 (Hardcover $2.50).
22. *Wain*, LIVING IN THE PRESENT. $1.25.
23. *diPrima*, VARIOUS FABLES FROM VARIOUS PLACES. $1.15 (Hardcover $2.50).
24. *Lovejoy*, ESSAYS IN THE HISTORY OF IDEAS. $1.45.
25. *Symonds*, THE REVIVAL OF LEARNING. $1.45.
26. *White*, THE BESTIARY. $1.45.
27. *Chesterton*, THE MAN WHO WAS THURSDAY. $1.15.
28. *Dewey*, QUEST FOR CERTAINTY. $1.25.
29. *Wood & Edmunds*, MILITARY HISTORY OF THE CIVIL WAR. $1.35.
30. *Pasternak*, POETRY OF BORIS PASTERNAK. $1.25.
31. *Wish*, ANTE-BELLUM: THREE CLASSIC WRITINGS ON SLAVERY IN THE OLD SOUTH. $1.35 (Hardcover $2.50).
32. *Valency & Levtow*, THE PALACE OF PLEASURE: AN ANTHOLOGY OF THE NOVELLA. $1.45 (Hardcover $2.50).
33. *Adler*, THE PROBLEM CHILD. $1.25 (Hardcover $2.50).

34. *Walter Lord, ed.,* THE FREMANTLE DIARY (THE SOUTH AT WAR). $1.25.
35. *Fowlie,* FOUR MODERN FRENCH COMEDIES. $1.25. (Hardcover $2.50).
36. *Torrey,* LES PHILOSOPHES. $1.65.
    Torrey, LES PHILOSOPHES (Cloth) $3.00.
37. *Ault,* ELIZABETHAN LYRICS. $1.75.
38. *Symonds,* AGE OF THE DESPOTS. $1.65.
39. *White,* MISTRESS MASHAM'S REPOSE. $1.35.
40. *Gilbert,* THE LETTERS OF MACHIAVELLI. $1.65.
41. *Still,* THE WEST. $1.65.
    Still, THE WEST. (Cloth) $2.50.
42. *Myers,* HISTORY OF BIGOTRY IN THE UNITED STATES. $1.65.
43. *Armstrong,* GRAY WOLF. $1.45.
44. *Auerbach,* INTRODUCTION TO ROMANCE LANGUAGES & LITERATURE. $1.65.
    Auerbach, INTRODUCTION TO ROMANCE LANGUAGES & LITERATURE. (Cloth) $2.50.
45. *Viereck,* METAPOLITICS. $1.75.
48. *Symonds,* FINE ARTS. $1.65.
49. *Bemelmans,* SMALL BEER. $.95.
50. *Dangerfield,* STRANGE DEATH. $1.75.
52. *Jaspers,* QUESTION OF GERMAN GUILT. $.95.
53. *Tawney,* EQUALITY. $1.35.
54. *La Guardia,* MAKING OF AN INSURGENT. $1.25.
55. *Cooper,* HOME AS FOUND. $1.35.
56. *Quiller Couch,* ART OF WRITING. $1.35.
57. NEWGATE CALENDAR. $1.45.
58. *Symonds,* LIFE OF MICHELANGELO. $1.75.
59. *Disraeli,* CONINGSBY. $1.75.

CAPRICORN GIANTS

201. *Hauser,* DIET DOES IT. $1.25.
202. *Moscati,* ANCIENT SEMITIC CIVILIZATIONS. $1.65.
203. *Chin P'ing Mei,* HSI MEN AND HIS 6 WIVES. $2.45.
204. *Brockelmann,* ISLAMIC PEOPLE. $1.95.
205. *Salter,* CONDITIONED REFLEX THERAPY. $1.75.
206. *Lissner,* LIVING PAST. $1.95.
207. *Davis,* CORPORATIONS. $2.45.
208. *Rodman,* CONVERSATION WITH ARTISTS. $1.45.
209. *Falls,* GREAT WAR 1914-1918. $1.95.
210. MEMOIRS OF A RENAISSANCE POPE. $1.85.
211. *Schachner,* FOUNDING FATHERS, $2.45.

G. P. PUTNAM'S SONS

210 Madison Avenue ● New York 16, N. Y